MW01097002

Utah
Real Estate Law
Principles
And
Practices

3rd Edition

Paul Naylor
Daniel Naylor

With Excerpts from Utah Law
And
Utah Administrative Rules

This publication is designed to provide accurate and authoritative information about the subject matter covered. It is sold with the understanding that the publisher and authors are not engaged in rendering legal, accounting or other professional service. If legal advice or other expert assistance is required, the reader should seek the counsel of a competent professional.

© 2017 by Daniel R Naylor

ISBN: 978-1-365-40226-5

Published by OurClasses.com, LLC / Bountiful
380 North 200 West Suite 208
Bountiful, UT 84010
801.797.9870

All rights reserved. The text of this publication or any part thereof, may not be reproduced in any manner whatsoever without written permission from the publisher.

Printed in the United States of America

02/2018

Table of Contents

Preface

When I decided to open a real estate pre-licensing school I began searching for suitable texts. I found several texts that teach general real estate topics. I did not find any publications that deal with Utah real estate law. I have found the format and readability of the "law" to be confusing and hard to understand for many novices. I believe teaching from the law in its original format introduces difficulty not necessary for the new student. I determined that the student would be better served by a text such as this.

This text is primarily the literal law of the state of Utah governing real estate. I have clarified the language in places and added explanation where needed. The text is grouped into what I feel are logical divisions. To aid the student I have supplemented the "law" with review questions and sample tests to strengthen the students understanding of the "law."

Real estate is one of the greatest professions. We who participate in the industry find great opportunity. We, for the most part, are self-employed entrepreneurs. We treasure our independence. We all thrive or fail because of our initiative or lack thereof. We associate together for strength, networking, and ideas. I cannot think of a greater way to spend our lives. I hope you find the profession as rewarding as I have.

Paul Naylor

Introduction

This book is broken into chapters with sample questions at the end of each chapter.

We recommend that you should:

First, read the chapter. Use a highlighter to mark the material that seems to summarize main points so that you can scan through the chapter and remind yourself of the main points and concepts.

Second, attend and participate in the class. The background you have acquired from reading the chapter will make the lecture and discussion much more meaningful. The concepts of the chapter will become part of you.

Third, complete the review questions. Do the questions without referring back to the chapter text. See what you have learned and what you need to review. Then go back to the chapter and review the areas that were difficult. The review questions will focus your review and clarify the material in your mind. If you can complete the review questions, you are prepared for the sample final exam.

Fourth, after you have completed reading all of the chapters and completed the review questions successfully you are ready for the sample final exam. This exam is an example of the type of exam questions you may encounter when you sit for the state real estate qualification exam. If you have trouble on a question, you will know what you need to review.

1. License Law

Learning Objectives:

Upon completion of this chapter, the student should be able to:
- Name the three different licenses available
- Explain the qualifications for licensure
- Explain the relationship between the principle broker and the sales agent.
- Describe the required process to change broker affiliation.
- Understand the effect of the broker's death, incapacity, bankruptcy, etc., on the sales agent licensee.
- Define the process of renewing a license.
- Describe the continuing education requirement.
- Explain the difference between an active and an inactive license and articulate the process for bringing a license off inactive status.

Definitions

Active Licensee is one who:
(a) Has paid all applicable license fees; and
(b) Is affiliated with a principal brokerage

Branch Broker: An associate broker who manages a branch office under the supervision of the principal broker.

Branch Office: A real estate office affiliated with and operating under the same name as a Principal Brokerage but located at an address different from the main office.

Business Opportunity: The sale, lease, or exchange of any business, which includes an interest in real estate.

Brokerage: A real estate sales brokerage or a property management company.

Certification: The authorization issued by the Division to:
- Provide courses approved for licensing requirements,

- Provide courses approved for renewal requirements, or

- Function as a real estate instructor.

Company Registration: A Registration issued to a corporation, partnership, Limited Liability Company, association or other legal entity of a real estate brokerage A Company Registration is also issued to an individual or an individual's professional corporation.

Continuing Education: Professional education required as a condition of renewal of license.

Credit Hour: Fifty minutes of instruction in a sixty-minute period.

DBA (Doing Business As) Authority issued by the Division of Corporations and Commercial Code to transact business under an assumed name

Distance Education:Education in which instruction does not take place in a traditional classroom setting.
- Instruction delivered with interactive setting and instructional methods.
- The student and instructor are separated by distance and sometimes time.
- Examples: computer conferencing, video conferencing, interactive audio, interactive computer software, internet based instruction and other interactive online courses.

Expired License: A license is "expired" when the licensee fails to pay the fees due by the close of business on the expiration date. If the expiration date falls on a Saturday, Sunday or holiday the effective date of expiration shall be the next business day.

Inactivation: The placing of a license on an inactive status, either voluntarily or involuntarily.

- Voluntary inactivation initiated by an active licensee terminating affiliation with a principal brokerage.

- Involuntary inactivation
    a. Inactivation of a sales agent or associate broker license resulting from the suspension, revocation, or non-renewal of the license of the licensee's principal broker, or death of the licensee's principal broker, or

    b. Inactivation of a sales agent or associate broker license by a principal broker when the licensee is unavailable to execute the transfer forms

Inactive Licensee:
- One who has paid all applicable license fees
- One who is not affiliated with a principal brokerage

Net listing: A listing wherein the amount of real estate commission is the difference between the selling price of the property and a minimum price set by the seller

Non-resident Licensee: A person who holds a Utah real estate principal broker, associate broker, or sales agent license whose primary residence is in a jurisdiction other than Utah

Property Management: The business of providing services relating to the rental or leasing of real property, including: advertising procuring prospective tenants, negotiating lease or rental terms, executing lease or rental agreements, supervising repairs and maintenance, collecting and disbursing rents.

Provider: Any entity, person or professional organization approved to provide continuing education courses by the Division of Real Estate.

Reinstatement: To restore to active or inactive status, a license which has expired or been suspended.

Re-issuance: The process by which a licensee may obtain a license following revocation.

Renewal: To extend an active or inactive license for an additional licensing period

Real Estate Sales Agent: Any person employed or engaged as an independent contractor by or on behalf of a licensed Principal Broker to list properties, represent buyer, lease properties, represent tenants etc.

School: The Division of Real Estate for the purpose of licensee education will consider the following as schools:
- Any accredited college or university that received its accreditation by any agency recognized by the United States Department of Education.
- Any community college, vocational school, state or federal agency.
- Any nationally recognized Utah or local real estate organization that has been approved by the Real Estate Commission.
- Any proprietary real estate school.

Traditional education:Education in which the instruction takes place between and instructor and students all physically present in the same classroom.

Who needs a real estate license?

Anyone who performs even one of the following acts in exchange for payment needs a real estate license to act within the law:

- Buying, selling, leasing, managing, or exchanging real estate for another person,

> You need a license if you are someone's agent in a real estate transaction and they are paying you for your services

- Offering for another to buy, sell, lease, manage, or exchange real estate

Exceptions:

- Any person who, as **owner or lessor** buys, sells, leases, exchanges or manages their own property or property they lease.
- **A regular salaried employee of the owner** or lessor of real estate buys, sells, leases, exchanges their owner / employer's property

> Owners and their employees generally do not need a real estate license

- A regular salaried employee of the owner of real estate who performs property management services to real estate **owned by the employer**, except that the employee may only manage property for one employer;
- A person who performs property management services for the **apartments** at which that person resides in exchange for free or reduced rent on that person's apartment;
- A regular salaried employee of a **condominium homeowners' association** who manages real property subject to the declaration of

> Many property management tasks do not require a license so long as salaried employees perform them.

condominium that established the homeowners' association, except that the employee may only manage property for one condominium homeowners' association; and

- Regular salaried employee of a **licensed property management company** who performs support services, such as:
    1. Accounting,
    2. Maintenance,
    3. Sign installation,
    4. Secretarial duties,
    5. Placing advertisements, written and approved by a licensee,
    6. Showing available space to prospective tenants so long as prices are only quoted not negotiated,

Some actions by an owner or an employee of an owner are not exempt:

- Employees engaged in the sale of properties regulated under, Utah Uniform Land Sales Practices Act and, Timeshare and Camp Resort Act. Both of these Acts are discussed later in this book.
- Employees engaged in the sale of cooperative interests (Co-op) regulated under Real Estate Cooperative Marketing Act (Title 57, Chapter 23); or
- Any person whose interest as an owner or lessor was obtained by him or transferred to him for the purpose of evading the application of this chapter, and not for any other legitimate business reason.

Some professions are exempt from licensing as real estate licensee's because they are licensed or regulated in some other way. These are:

- Isolated transactions by persons holding a duly executed **power of attorney** from the owner;
- Services rendered by an **attorney at law** in performing his duties as an attorney at law;
- A **receiver, trustee** in bankruptcy,

> Under most circumstances:
> - Attorneys
> - Trustees in bankruptcy or foreclosure authority
> - Executors under court order
> - Public Utility employees doing utility business
>
>   **Are Exempt**

administrator, **executor**, or any person acting under **order of any court**;

- A trustee or its employees under a deed of trust or a will; or
- Any **public utility**, its officers, or regular salaried employees, unless performance of any of the acts is in connection with the sale, purchase, lease, or other disposition of real estate or investment in real estate unrelated to the principal business activity of that public utility.

Review Questions

1. Indicate who needs a license and who does not in the following list.

    _____ A. Owner selling own property

    _____ B. Owner managing own property

    _____ C. Employee managing multiple owners' property

    _____ D. Tenant selling owner's house

    _____ E. Employee doing maintenance on owner's office building

    _____ F. Employee representing owner in purchase of new warehouse building

    _____ G. Trustee selling property under foreclosure

    _____ H. Resident apartment manager in exchange for rent

    _____ I. Employee collecting rent on owner's rental property.

    _____ J. Broker's employee showing property for sale

    _____ K. Friend selling house for owner who lives out of state

2. A real estate license is not required for
    a. An attorney that sells real estate for a living
    b. Someone acting as agent in a single transaction for a commission
    c. A trustee selling real estate under a trustee's deed
    d. A salaried property manager who receives a leasing commission

3. A real estate license is required in Utah for anyone who is;
    a. A receiver selling property under court order
    b. An executor selling property under court order
    c. A buyer's agent employed under salary by a utility company who negotiates for right of way property
    d. A seller's agent paid a commission each time a property sells

4. When acting for another, a real estate license is required for all the following except:
    a. Advertise real estate for sale.
    b. Represent buyers in the purchase of real estate.
    c. Title insurance agents
    d. Manage property owned by another.

5. W needs to be a licensed real estate agent to;
    a. Help his girlfriend sell her house in exchange for a commission.
    b. Work in a property manager's office placing newspaper ads.
    c. Act as a principal when buying property
    d. Manage a motel

6. W needs a real estate license if she is to;
    a. Sell her own property
    b. Work as a resident apartment manager paid by reduced or free rent
    c. Work as a salaried employee of the owner of a large office complex with primary duties to collect rents
    d. Obtain her law degree and specialize in assisting sellers find buyers

7. A real estate license is required if you
   are;
   a. A salaried condominium manager
      employed by the association
   b. Regular salaried employee of the
      owner who manages property for
      multiple clients
   c. A registered timeshare sales person
      showing property on site
   d. Regular salaried employee of a
      property management company with
      primary responsibility to manage
      accounts payable

2. Licensing Requirements

Learning Objectives:

Upon completion of this chapter, the student should be able to:
- Recite license criteria
- Explain measure of moral character
- Name licenses available
- List timeframes for the licensing process
- Explain Broker Experience Requirements
- List Broker/brokerage requirements

Exam and License Application Requirements

Exam Application

Any person 18 years of age or older and who has graduated from high school or received their GED may become a licensed broker or sales agent. A candidate with education that they feel is equivalent may request a hearing and present their case to the Commission. Candidates must submit an application for examination together with the applicable examination fee to the testing service designated by the Division. The testing service is currently PearsonVue. This testing service is an independent contractor providing services to Utah under contract. The fees paid are for their services only. If an exam is scheduled with PearsonVue and the scheduled examination is not taken, the fee is forfeited.

Sales Agent Qualifications:
- 18 Years old or older
- High school diploma, GED, or equivalent
- High Moral Character
- Completed 120 hour Course
- Successful Licensure Exam
- Application for License
- Submit Fingerprints
- Pay License Fee

The first set of questions presented on the licensing exam, are background questions. These questions are intended to alert the Division to any matters that require special attention in the licensing process. These questions are listed on the next page. A "yes" answer to questions two through nine may impair the applicant's ability to become licensed in the state of Utah. After completing pre-licensing requirements, the Utah Division of Real Estate will review the information provided and make a decision about qualifications.

Pre License Qualifying Questions

Carefully and accurately, answer the following questions. False or inaccurate answers to the exam questions may result in license denial, revocation, or other disciplinary action.

I. Do you now hold or have you **ever** held a real estate registration, license or certification in any jurisdiction other than Utah?

2. Have you **ever** had a license or registration of any kind in appraisal, mortgage, real estate, or any other occupation or profession denied, restricted, suspended, or revoked?

3. Have you **ever** resigned, surrendered or allowed a professional registration to expire while you were under investigation, or while action was pending against you by any government agency?

4. Is any investigation or disciplinary action **currently** pending against you by any government agency?

5. Are you **currently** charged with, or under investigation for a felony or misdemeanor in any jurisdiction?

6. Have you **ever** been convicted of, or pled guilty, or no contest to, or entered a plea in abeyance or diversion agreement to, a felony or misdemeanor in any jurisdiction? Consult court records to determine the nature of any offenses, including traffic offenses, which may be felonies or misdemeanors.

7. Have you **ever** been on probation or ordered to pay a fine or restitution or complete community service, in connection with any criminal offense or a licensing action? (If you answer "yes" to this question, you will be asked at the time of application for licensure to provide proof of completion of your probation and payment of all fines.)

8. Have you **ever** had a civil judgment entered against you based on fraud, misrepresentation, or deceit?

9. Have you read and do you consent to the fingerprint notice of waiver?

10. Are you **under** 18 years of age?

11. Do you certify that you have a High School diploma or GED?

Candidates are **not** eligible for licensure if they have been convicted or entered a plea in abeyance or completed a sentence of confinement for a:

- Felony within the past 5 years
- Misdemeanor involving fraud, misrepresentation, theft or dishonesty within 3 years.

WARNING

The penalty for false answers to qualifying questions is revocation of the newly issued real estate license. New Applications after revocations will only be accepted after five years.

The candidate will be asked to certify the truthfulness of these same questions at the time of examination.

The exam is in three parts. The first part is the pre-qualifying questions already discussed. The second part of the exam is the

Passing Exam Score
Sales Agents 70%
Broker Candidates 75%

"General" portion. This part of the exam contains questions on general real estate topics that would be appropriate in any state or locale. The last portion of the exam contains questions on Utah topics such as Utah Law and licensing rules. The candidate must receive a passing score on the national portion and a separate passing score on the state portion. The testing center will provide test results as soon as the exam is completed. A sales agent must answer 70% of the question correctly to pass each part of the exam. Broker and Associate Broker candidates must pass both portions of the exam with a score of 75%. The candidate will be fingerprinted upon completion of the exam to assist in the criminal background check that the Division performs on all license candidates.

After a candidate has completed pre-licensing education and passed the examination the candidate must submit to the Division of Real Estate information on answers to qualifying questions such as judgments or any court documents which define convictions, sentencing, and whether all conditions of probation have, been satisfied. The Division and Real Estate Commission will then review the application, make a decision, and then mail a denial or license 7 to 10 business days after they receive the required forms.

Applicants previously licensed out-of-state

a) If an applicant is now or has been actively licensed for the preceding two years in another state, which has equivalent licensing requirements and is either a new resident or a non-resident of this state, the Division will waive part of the national portion of the exam.
b) If an applicant has been on an inactive status for any portion of the past two years, he may be required to take both the national and Utah State portions of the exam.

Licensing Procedure

Within **90 days** after successful completion of the exam, the applicant must return to the Division each of the following:

a) **Exam**: A report of the examination indicating that both portions of the exam have been **passed within a six-month period**
b) **Application:** Candidates must complete an application form obtained from the Division of Real Estate.
c) **Fees**: The license fee is paid at the time of application. This fee includes a mandatory contribution to the Real Estate Recovery Fund.
d) **Education**: A candidate must submit with their application, documentation indicating successful completion of the required education taken **within the year prior to licensing**. If the candidate has been previously licensed in another state, which has equivalent licensing requirements, he may apply to the Division for a waiver of all or part of the educational requirement.
   1. **Sales Agent**: Candidates for the license of sales agent must successfully complete 120 classroom hours of approved study in principles and practices of real estate. Experience will not satisfy the education requirement. *Membership in the Utah State Bar will waive this requirement.*

Three Licenses Available
1. Sales Agent
2. Associate Broker
3. Broker

2. **Broker:** Candidates for the license of *associate broker* or *principal broker* must successfully complete 120 classroom hours of approved study. The licensing course must consist of at least 24 classroom hours in brokerage management, 24 classroom hours in advanced appraisal, 24 classroom hours in advanced finance, 24 hours in advanced property management and 24 classroom hours in advanced real estate law. Experience will not satisfy the education requirement. The Division may waive all or part of the educational requirement by virtue of equivalent education.

e) **Experience Points**: The principal broker and associate broker applicant must submit the forms required by the Division documenting a minimum of three years licensed real estate experience and a total of at least 60 points accumulated within the five years prior to licensing. A minimum of two years (24 months) and at least 45 points must be accumulated from Tables I and/or II, for activities which require a real estate license. The remaining 15 points may be from Table I, II or III.

1. When calculating experience points for Table I, transactions with exclusive brokerage agreements will receive the credit listed. Any other brokerage agreement will earn one-quarter of the experience listed.

2. A minimum of one-half of the points in Tables I and II must derive from transactions of properties located in the state of Utah.

3. When calculating experience points from Table II, the total combined monthly experience credit claimed for "All other property management" combined, both residential and commercial, *may not exceed 25 points in any application to practice as a real estate broker.

Table I

Real Estate Sales Transactions

RESIDENTIAL – points can be accumulated from either the selling or the listing side of a real estate closing

■ One Unit Dwelling	2.5 Points
■ Two to four unit dwelling	5 Points
■ Apartments, 5 units or over	10 Points
■ Improved Lot	2 Points
■ Vacant land / subdivision	10 Points

COMMERCIAL

■ Hotel or motel	10 Points
■ Industrial or warehouse	10 Points
■ Office building	10 Points
■ Retail building	10 Points

TABLE II

Leasing Transactions and Property Management

RESIDENTIAL

■ Each property management agreement	1 point per unit up to 5 Points
■ Each unit leased	1.25 Points per unit
■ All other property management*	.25 pt / month

COMMERCIAL - Hotel / motel, industrial / warehouse, office, or retail building

■ Each property management agreement	1 point per unit up to 5 Points
■ Each unit leased	1.25 Points per unit
■ All other property management*	1 pt / month

The Principal Broker may accumulate additional experience points by having participated in real estate related activities such as the following:

TABLE III

Optional

■ Real Estate Attorney	1 pt / month
■ CPA-Certified Public Accountant	1 pt / month
■ Mortgage Loan Officer	1 pt / month
■ Licensed Escrow Officer	1 pt / month
■ Licensed Title Agent	1 pt / month
■ Designated Appraiser	1 pt / month
■ Licensed General Contractor	1 pt / month
■ Bank Officer in Real Estate Loans	1 pt / month
■ Certified Real Estate Prelicensing Instructor	.5 pt / month

The Division of Real Estate will review each application to determine if the experience requirements have been met. The applicant may petition the Real Estate Commission for reevaluation by making a written request within 30 days after the denial stating specific grounds upon which relief is requested. The Commission shall thereafter consider the request and issue a written decision.

> **Broker License Requirements:**
> - 3 Years Experience (3 of last 5)
> - 120 Hour Broker Course
> - Experience Points from Tables
> - Trust Account
> - Registered Business Name
> - Application
> - Fee

f). **Trust Account:** Broker Candidates must provide proof of properly established Real Estate Trust Account. Such account shall be identified by the name "(*Brokerage Name)* Real Estate Trust Account."

g) **Business Name:** Broker Candidates must provide evidence of approved business name and business entity. The Division of Corporations must approve this entity. Brokerages may be sole proprietorships, corporations, partnerships, limited liability companies, etc.

h) **License History:** An applicant *previously licensed in another state* must   provide a written record of his license history from that state and documentation of disciplinary action, if any, against his license.

Determining fitness for licensure:

The Commission and the Division will consider information necessary to determine whether an applicant meets the requirements of honesty, integrity, truthfulness, reputation and competency, which shall include the following:

- Whether an applicant has been denied a license to practice real estate, property management, or any regulated profession, business, or vocation, or whether any license has been suspended or revoked or subjected to any other disciplinary sanction by this or another jurisdiction;

- Whether an applicant has been guilty of conduct or practices which would have been grounds for revocation or suspension of license under Utah law had the applicant then been licensed;

> **Fitness for License Requires:**
> - Honesty
> - Integrity
> - Truthfulness
> - Reputation
> - Competency

- Whether a civil judgment has been entered against the applicant based on a real estate transaction, and whether the judgment has been fully satisfied;

- Whether a civil judgment has been entered against the applicant based on fraud, misrepresentation or deceit, and whether the judgment has been fully satisfied

- Whether restitution ordered by a court in a criminal conviction has been fully satisfied;

- Whether the probation in a criminal conviction or a licensing action has been completed and fully served;

- Whether there has been subsequent good conduct on the part of the applicant. The Commission and the Division may approve the applicant relating to honesty, integrity, truthfulness, reputation and competency if, because of lapse of time and subsequent good conduct and reputation or other reason deemed sufficient, it appears to the Commission and the Division that the interest of the public will not likely be in danger by the granting of a license,

Applicants for license renewal must also meet fitness requirements. Renewal will be denied if the applicant:

- Has been convicted of or entered a plea in abeyance to a felony during the term of the last license period through the time of application for renewal or reinstatement

- Had a finding of fraud, misrepresentation or deceit entered against the applicant do to activities requiring a real estate license by a court or government agency

Company Registration

A Principal Broker shall register with the Division the name under which his real estate brokerage or property management company will operate. Registration will require payment of applicable non-refundable fees and evidence that the Division of Corporations has approved the name of the new company.

The real estate brokerage must continuously have affiliated with it a principal broker. The Principal Broker must be authorized to use the company name.

The Division will not accept a proposed business name that could mislead into thinking that they are not dealing with a licensed real estate brokerage or property management company.

Individuals associated with the licensed real estate brokerage may only engage in activity, which requires a real estate license, if they are also a licensee.

Changing in Principals in a Brokerage:

If a company changes it's Principal Broker it is required to immediately notify the Division of the change on the official "change card" form. If the outgoing principal broker is not available to properly execute the form, the change may still be made, provided a letter advising of the change is mailed by the Brokerage by certified mail to the last known address of the outgoing principal broker. A verified copy of the letter and proof of mailing by certified mail must be attached to the form when it is submitted to the Division

If the change of members in a partnership either by the addition or withdrawal of a partner creates a new legal entity, the new entity cannot operate under the authority of the registration of the previous partnership. The dissolution of a corporation, partnership, Limited Liability Company, association or other entity, which has been registered, terminates the registration.

The Division must be notified of any change in a partnership or dissolution of a corporation, which has registered prior to the effective date of the change.

Licensing Non-Residents

Persons living outside the State of Utah may apply for a nonresident License. To qualify they need to meet all of the requirements a resident agent must meet except that if the agent is currently licensed in another state the national portion of the licensing exam may be waived. The applicant must also meet each of the following requirements:

a) If the applicant is an associate broker or sales agent, the principal broker with whom he will be affiliated shall hold an active license in Utah.

b) If the applicant is a principal broker, he shall establish a real estate trust account in this state. He shall also maintain all office records in this state at a principle business location.

c) The application for licensure in Utah shall be accompanied by an irrevocable written consent allowing service of process on the Commission or the Division

d) The applicant shall provide a written record of his license history, if any, and documentation of disciplinary action, if any, against his license.

Reciprocity

The Division, with the concurrence of the Commission, may enter into specific reciprocity agreements with other states on the same basis as Utah licensees are granted licenses by those states.

Review Questions

1. The three types of real estate licenses available in Utah are:
   a. _____
   b. _____
   c. _____

2. All sales agents and associate brokers must license under a _____ _____.

3. Sales Agent license candidates must complete a _____ hour education course approved by the State of Utah.

4. The Licensing Exam first asks the _____ questions. These questions ask such things as _____ history, judgments, and licenses in other _____.

5. The candidate must pass the State licensing exam with a _____% score or better for Licensee candidates and a _____% score or better for Broker candidates.

6. The Finger_____ card is submitted to help the State perform a _____ check of licensee candidates

7. Broker candidates need to document their _____ by providing proof they have earned at least _____ points.

8. Broker candidates must have been active licensees _____ of the last five years.

9. Broker candidates must register their _____ name and provide documentation to the Division of such registration before they may be licensed as a Principal Broker.

10. Broker candidates may substitute experience points from table _____ for non-real-estate brokerage experience.

3. License Status Change

Learning Objectives:

At the conclusion of this class the student will be able to:
- List 10 day notice changes
- List advance notice changes
- Use the RELMS system
- Explain voluntary & involuntary activation
- Describe the renewal process
- Differentiate between core and elective classes

License Status Change

A licensee must notify the Division within ***ten business days*** of any status change. Status changes are effective on the date that the properly executed forms and appropriate non-refundable fees are received by the Division. Notice must be on the forms required by the Division.

a) Change of name requires submission of official documentation such as a marriage or divorce certificate, or driver's license.

b) Change of business, home address or mailing address requires written notification. A post office box without a street address is unacceptable as a business or home

---

Notify the Division:

Within 10 days
- Name change
- Address change
- Business location change
- Brokerage name change

Prior to change
- Change of broker

address. The licensee may designate any address to be used as a mailing address. Change of name of a brokerage must be accompanied by evidence that the Division of Corporations has approved of the new name.

c) Change of Principal Broker in a real estate brokerage, which is a sole proprietorship, requires closure of the registered entity. The new principal broker must activate the Registered Company and provide proof from the Division of Corporations of the authorization to use the DBA. Change cards will be required for the terminating Principal Broker, new Principal Broker and all licensees affiliated with the brokerage.

d) Change of a Principal Broker within an entity, which is not a sole proprietorship, requires written notice from the entity signed by both the terminating Principal Broker and the new Principal Broker.

Unavailability of Licensee

If a licensee is not available to properly execute the form required for a status change, the status change may still be made. The broker must notify the licensee of the change, which they can do by email, or by certified letter. If they are notified by email, then the change will take effect 10 days after the email is sent. If a certified letter is used, it must be sent to the last known address of the unavailable licensee. A verified copy of the letter and proof of mailing by certified mail must be attached to the form when it is submitted to the Division.

Transfers

Prior to transferring from one principal broker to another principal broker, the licensee must submit a change form through the Real Estate License Management System (RELMS) and get confirmation from each broker though the same system.

Inactivation

To voluntarily inactivate a license, the licensee must deliver or mail to the Division a written request for the change signed by both the licensee and principal broker.
a) Prior to placing his license on an inactive status, a principal broker must provide written notice to each licensee affiliated with him of that licensing status

change. Evidence of that written notice must be provided to the Division. The inactivation of the license of a principal broker will also cause the licenses of *all affiliated licensees to be immediately inactivated*, if they do not transfer their licenses in accordance with the *Transfer* provisions above, prior to the effective date of the principal broker's status change.

b) The non-renewal, suspension, or revocation of the license of a principal broker will cause the *licenses of all affiliated licensees to be immediately inactivated* if they do not transfer their licenses in accordance with the *Transfer* provisions listed above, prior to the effective date of the principal broker's status change.

When a principal broker is notified that his license will be suspended or revoked, he must, prior to the effective date of the suspension or revocation, provide written notice to each licensee affiliated with him of that status change. The Division will send written notice to each sales agent, associate broker, or branch broker of the effective date of inactivation and the process for transfer.

c) The principal broker may involuntarily inactivate the license of the sales agent or associate broker by giving notice as described in *Unavailability of Licensee* above.

Application to change to active status

All licensees changing to active status must submit to the Division the applicable non-refundable activation fee and a written request for activation on the form required by the

> **Inactive → Active**
> Requires:
> - Application
> - Documentation of required 18 hrs. C.E. education
> - Pay fee

Division in RELMS. If the license was on an "inactive" status at the time of the last renewal, the licensee must provide proof of completion of the licensing exam within 6 months of activation or proof of completing the 18 hours of continuing education required for most recent license renewal. Activation continuing education must be completed within one year prior to activation.

Renewal

Licenses are valid for a period of two years. A license may be renewed by submitting all forms and fees required by the Division prior to the expiration date of the current license. Licenses not properly renewed shall expire on the expiration date.

a) **A license may be reinstated within thirty days** after expiration by complying with all requirements for a timely renewal and paying a non-refundable late fee.

b) **A license may be reinstated after thirty days** and within six months after expiration by complying with all requirements for a timely renewal, along with a few additional requirements. They must pay a non-refundable reinstatement fee and submit proof of having completed 6 hours of continuing education in addition to the regular 18 hours of continuing education required to renew a license on active status, for a total of 24 hours.

c) **After the six-month period and until one year** after the expiration date, the license may be reinstated by paying a renewal fee and a late fee providing to the division proof of satisfactory completion of 24 hours of continuing education, in addition to the regular 18 hours of continuing education required, for a total of 42 hours.

d) A license that has been expired **for more than 12 months** may not be reinstated and an applicant must apply for a new license following the same procedure as an original license.

e) The commission with concurrence of the division may exempt a licensee from all or a part of the continuing education requirement for a reasonable period upon a finding of reasonable cause, including:
- military service;
- if an individual is elected or appointed to government service which the individual spends a substantial time addressing real estate issues;

Renewal Requirements

a) Continuing Education: To renew a license on active status an applicant must submit to the division proof of having completed, during the previous license period and by the 15th day of the month of expiration, 18 hours of continuing education from courses certified by the division.

b) During the first license period, a licensee must take the 12-hour "New Sales Agent Course" certified by the division plus six additional hours of CE courses including elective courses.

c) During subsequent license periods, a licensee must take at least 9 hours of continuing education from courses certified by the division as "core." A licensee must take any remaining hours of continuing education from courses certified by the division as "elective."

1) Core: Courses in the following subjects may be certified as "core":

- state approved and other industry forms/contracts
- ethics, fair housing
- agency
- prevention of real estate and mortgage fraud
- federal and state real estate laws
- brokers' trust accounts
- property management
- short sales, REO sales
- environmental hazards including meth, asbestos and radon
- water law, rights and transfer

2) Elective: Courses in the following subjects may be certified as elective courses.

- Real estate financing, including mortgages and other financing techniques
- real estate investments
- real estate market measures and evaluation
- real estate appraising
- accounting and taxation as applied to real property
- estate building and portfolio management for clients
- settlement statements
- real estate mathematics
- real estate law; contract law
- real estate securities and syndications
- regulation and management of timeshares, condominiums and cooperatives; resort and recreational properties
- farm and ranch properties
- real property exchanging
- legislative issues that influence real estate practice

- land development; land use, planning and zoning
- construction
- real estate inspections
- accounting procedures
- landlord/tenant relationships
- Americans with Disabilities Act, affirmative marketing
- commercial real estate
- tenants-in-common

d) Licensees must retain original course completion certificates for three years following renewal and introduce those certificates when audited by the division.

e) Principal Broker. To renew a principal broker license on active status an applicant must certify that the business name under which the licensee is operating is current and in good standing with the Division of Corporations and that all real estate trust accounts are current and in compliance with Division trust account rules.

f) Agents renewing their license may not have:

- been convicted of or entered a plea in abeyance to a felony during the term of the last license or during the period between license expiration and application to reinstate an expired license;
- had a finding of fraud, misrepresentation or deceit entered against the applicant, related to activities requiring a real estate license, by any court of competent jurisdiction or any government agency, unless the finding was explicitly considered by the Division in approving the applicant's initial license or previous license renewals.

g) Any misrepresentation in an application for renewal will be considered a separate violation of these rules and separate grounds for disciplinary action against the licensee.

h) A principal broker's failure to renew his license when due, which causes the licenses of those affiliated with him to be placed on an inactive status, shall be separate grounds for disciplinary action.

i) If the Division has received a licensee's renewal documents in a timely manner but the information is incomplete, the licensee shall be extended a 15-day grace period to complete the application. Education credit may be given for a course taken in another state provided the course has been certified for continuing education purposes in another state. These courses shall meet the Utah requirement of protection of the public, except that credit may not be given for education where the subject matter pertains to another state's license laws.

Prior approval must be obtained from the division before credit will be granted. Evidence must be provided to the Division that the course was certified by another licensing jurisdiction at the time the course was taken.

Review Questions

1. A license may be renewed on _____ status by simply paying the renewal fee.

2. T's Broker died this morning in a car accident. Her real estate license is now considered _____ until she affiliates with a new broker by submitting a change in _____.

3. To renew a license the licensee must:
   a. Provide proof of 18_____ Continuing _____ and pay the _____ fee.
   b. Inactive agents who have been inactive through a license renewal period must complete all _____ education requirements before they are eligible to apply to activate their license.

4. Your license expired today before you submitted your renewal application. You may reinstate your license by paying the renewal fee plus a late fee during the next __ days. After that, the requirements change.

5. Which of the following courses would not qualify in Utah as a core course?
   a. State approved forms
   b. Industry forms
   c. Ethics
   d. Tenants in common

6. Which of the following classes is a core class?
   a. Settlement Statements
   b. Property Management
   c. Real Estate Math
   d. Real Estate Investment

7. Which of the following is not a core course?
   a. Real Estate Inspection principles
   b. Short Sales
   c. REO Sales
   d. Federal Law

8. Which of the following is a core class?
   a. Broker Trust Account Procedures
   b. Accounting Procedures
   c. Landlord Tenant Relations
   d. Sales Agents and the Appraisal Process

9. If a candidate has submitted their application but in reviewing the application the Division determines that the candidate must submit additional documentation, then the application period is extended by:
   a. 5 days
   b. 15 days
   c. 10 days
   d. 30 days

10. If a license is not renewed for more than 6 months but less than one year after expiration, which of the following number of hours of additional continuing education is required to reinstate the license?
    a. 12 hours
    b. 18 hours
    c. 20 hours
    d. 24 hours

11. B a principal broker failed to pay his renewal fee on time. The sales agents licensed with him are;
    a. Automatically notified that they have 5 days to find another broker
    b. Given 10 business days to close all of their transactions
    c. Automatically changed to inactive status, unable to act as agents
    d. Able to sell but not close until the broker renews his license

12. To renew a real estate license an associate broker must do all of the following except;
    a. Complete of 9 hours of core courses
    b. Provide evidence of adequate points earned
    c. Complete 9 additional hours of continuing education
    d. Pay a fee

13. An agent is going to be terminated, and they are not available to be notified in person. If the broker sends an email to notify them, when is their termination effective?
    a. 10 days after the email is sent
    b. 30 days after the email is sent
    c. Immediately
    d. When the agent confirms the change

4. Office Procedures

Learning Objectives:

Upon completion of this chapter, the student should be able to:

- Explain the sales agent's responsibility to the principle broker and the broker's responsibility to the sales agent.
- Explain the sales agent's responsibility to follow brokerage policies.
- Explain the laws relevant to all real estate licensees regarding trust accounts.
- Explain the laws regarding referral fees.
- Differentiate between those duties that require a real estate license and those that do not.
- Explain how personal assistants should be paid.

Involuntary inactivation:

a) Inactivation of a sales agent or associate broker license resulting from the suspension, revocation, or non-renewal of the license of the licensee's principal broker, or death of the licensee's principal broker, or

b) Inactivation of a sales agent or associate broker license by a principal broker when the licensee is unavailable to execute the transfer forms

Definitions

Principal Brokerage: The main real estate or property management office of a principal broker.

Property Management: The business of providing services relating to the rental or leasing of real property, including: advertising, procuring prospective tenants or lessees, negotiating lease or rental terms, executing lease or rental agreements, supervising repairs and maintenance, collecting and disbursing rents.

Regular Salaried Employees: For the purposes of Utah Real Estate Law, "regular salaried employee" shall mean an individual employed other than on a contract basis, who has withholding taxes taken out by the employer.

Records and Copies of Documents

The principal broker must maintain and safeguard all records pertaining to a real estate transaction for a period of at least three calendar years following the year in which an offer was rejected or the transaction either closed or failed. These records must be made available for inspection and copying by the Division.

Location of Records

Unless otherwise authorized by the Division in writing, the business records of the principal broker shall be maintained at his principal business location or, where applicable, at the branch office. If a brokerage closes its operation the principal broker must, within ten days after the closure, notify the Division in writing of where the records will be maintained. If a brokerage files for bankruptcy, the principal broker must, upon filing, notify the Division in writing of the filing and the current location of brokerage records

Transaction Identification

All transactions, whether pending, closed or failed, must be numbered consecutively and identifiable in a manner that, in the opinion of the representative of the Division the transaction can be readily followed in all pertinent documents. A sequential transaction number is to be assigned to every offer, and a separate transaction file is to be maintained for every offer, including rejected offers involving funds deposited to the brokerage trust account. A sequential transaction number need not be assigned to rejected offers, which do not involve funds deposited to trust. The principal broker may, at his option, maintain a separate transaction file for each rejected offer which does not involve funds deposited in a trust account or keep such rejected offers with accepted offers.

Statement of Account

At the expiration of 30 days after an offer has been made by a buyer and accepted by a seller, *both party may demand, and the principal broker must furnish, a detailed statement* showing the status of the transaction. On demand by either party, the principal broker must furnish an updated statement at 30-day intervals thereafter until the transaction is closed.

Closing Statements

A principal broker charged with closing a sale shall cause to be prepared and delivered to the buyer and seller, upon completion of a transaction, a detailed closing statement of all their respective accounts showing receipts and disbursement.

Closing statements for all real estate transactions in which a real estate principal broker participates must show the date of closing; total purchase price of the property; an itemization of all adjustments, money, or things of value received or paid, and to whom each item is credited or debited. The dates of the adjustments must be shown if they are not the same as the date of the closing. Also shown must be the balances due from the respective parties to the transaction, and the names of the payees, makers, and assignees of all notes paid, made, or assumed. The statements furnished to each party must contain an itemization of credits and debits.

The principal broker or his authorized representative must attend all closings. The principal broker is responsible for the content and accuracy of all closing statements regardless of who closes the transaction.

The principal broker closing the transaction must show proof of delivery of the closing statement to the buyer and seller. Signatures of the buyer and seller on the file copy of the closing statement or a copy of a transmittal letter sent by certified mail, 'return receipt requested' when signatures are not attainable, will satisfy this requirement.

Death or Disability of Principal Broker

Upon the death or inability of a principal broker to act as a principal broker, legal entities such as corporations and limited partnerships shall immediately notify the Division of the circumstances and a written appointment of a succeeding broker to act as a principal broker for the firm. In the interim between the release of the former broker and the appointment of the succeeding broker, no real estate activity may take place that would otherwise require a licensed principal broker to supervise. Thus all agents must remain inactive and not perform any real estate activity until the new broker is appointed and in place.

In the case of a sole proprietor, all brokerage activity must cease and a family attorney or representative shall:
- Notify the Division and all licensees affiliated with the principal broker in writing of the date of death or disability. **Licensees immediately become *"inactive"* until they affiliate with a new broker**;
- Advise the Division as to the location where records will be stored;
- Notify each listing and management client in writing to the effect that the principal broker is no longer in business and that the client may enter a new listing or management agreement with the firm of his choice;
- Notify each party and cooperating broker to any existing contracts;
- Retain trust account monies under the control of the administrator, executor or co-signer on the account until all parties to each transaction agree in writing to disposition or until a court of competent jurisdiction issues an order relative to disposition.

Trust Accounts

All monies received in a real estate transaction must be deposited in a separate non-interest bearing "Real Estate Trust Account." If the broker and the parties to the transaction agree in writing, then the money may alternatively be placed into an "Interest Bearing Real Estate Trust Account," in a Utah bank, credit union, or other approved escrow depository in this state.

The principal broker will be held personally responsible for deposits at all times. The principal broker must notify the Division in writing of the location and account numbers of all real estate trust accounts, which he maintains. The "Real Estate Trust Account" and the "Interest Bearing Real Estate Trust Account" must be used exclusively for real estate transactions. Funds received in connection with rental of tourist accommodations for any period of less than 30 consecutive days shall not be deposited in the "Real Estate Trust Account" or the "Interest Bearing Real Estate Trust Account."

Deposits

All monies received by a licensee in a real estate transaction, whether it is cash or check, must be delivered to the principal broker and deposited within three banking days after receipt of the funds by the licensee. This rule does not apply when:

- The Real Estate Purchase Contract or other agreement states that the earnest money or other funds are to be held for a specific length of time or are to be deposited upon acceptance by the seller; or
- The Real Estate Purchase Contract or other agreement states that the earnest money or other funds are to be made out and paid to the seller, or to the person or company named as the escrow closing agent; or
- A promissory note is given as the earnest money deposit or otherwise credited to the transaction. The promissory note must name the seller as payee and be retained in the principal broker's file until closing. If a promissory note is used in a real estate transaction, the Real Estate Purchase Contract or other agreement must disclose that the consideration is in the form of a promissory note.

Commingling

Not more than $500 of the principal broker's own funds can remain in the "Real Estate Trust Account" or the "Property Management Trust Account," or the Division will consider the account to be commingled.

Builder Deposits

If a principal broker, who is also a builder or developer, receives deposit money under a Real Estate Purchase Contract, construction contract, or other agreement which provides for the construction of a dwelling:

- the deposit money must be placed in the "Real Estate Trust Account"
- if the broker and the parties to the transaction agree in writing, the "Interest Bearing Real Estate Trust Account"
- Deposited monies may not be used for construction purposes unless specifically provided in the document or by separate written consent of the purchaser.

Interest Bearing Account

An interest bearing account may only be used when all parties to the transaction request in writing that an interest bearing account be used. The written request must designate to whom the interest will be paid upon completion or failure of the sale. The parties may also elect to direct the interest earned from the account to an affordable housing program that is non-profit and qualifies under IRS rules. The Division of Real Estate must be notified of any payments made to any such organization.

A principal broker may elect to maintain an interest-bearing "Real Estate Trust Account" only if the interest earned on the account is paid to a non-profit organization that has qualified, and remains qualified at the time of the payment, under IRS rules. Such non-profit organization must have as its exclusive purpose the providing of grants to affordable housing programs in the State of Utah. The affordable housing program that is the recipient of the grant must also be qualified, at the time of the grant, as a non-profit organization under IRS rules. If a principal broker makes this election, the Division must be notified in writing of the location and account number of the interest-bearing "Real Estate Trust Account" at the time the account is opened.

The Utah Association of Realtors Housing Opportunity Fund (UARHOF) has been approved as a beneficiary of an interest bearing trust account. Most banks and credit unions have already set up UARHOF as a beneficiary and can provide the federal tax id number to be used when setting up the interest bearing account.

Liability for Receipt

The licensee is required to have physically received all amounts shown on the receipt. A licensee must not rely on a buyer's or a lessee's promise to deliver the consideration at a future date.

The signature of the agent on the receipt indicates that the amount listed on the receipt has been received. If the money indicated on the receipt is required to meet contract obligations

---

EARNEST MONEY RECEIPT

Buyer _John J. Buyer_ offers to purchase the Property described below and hereby delivers to the Brokerage, as Earnest Money, the amount of $_5,000.00_ in the form of ___personal check___ which, upon Acceptance of this offer by all parties (as defined in Section 23), shall be deposited in accordance with state law.

Received by: _William Z. Agent_ on _15 March 2001_

Brokerage: _Woodland Brokerage_ Phone Number _801-555-1000_

---

and the agent in fact had never received it, the agent and brokerage could be held financially accountable for the monies. Failing to collect monies receipted constitutes a breach of the fiduciary duty of 'accounting'. The agent and broker could be subject to disciplinary action by the Division if this occurred.

Property Management Trust Account

Each principal broker engaged in property management shall establish a separate "Property Management Trust Account." A principal broker who collects rents for others only occasionally or who does so as a convenience for his clients, and manages no more than six accounts, may use the "Real Estate Trust Account" for this purpose and need not maintain a "Property Management Trust Account".

Disbursements

All disbursements from the Real Estate Trust Account must comply

> If the brokerage manages property for more than 6 clients the brokerage **must** maintain a separate property management trust account

with the real estate purchase contract instructions for disbursement, or be the result of a written authorization signed by the parties to the transaction or by court order. *If there is no written authorization by the parties then funds must remain in the account.*

The withdrawal of any portion of the principal broker's sales commission must not take place without written authorization from the seller and buyer.

When closing statements have been delivered to the buyer and seller and the buyer or seller has been paid for the amount due as determined by the closing statement then the broker must remove any balance relating to the transaction and apply it to commissions earned. This amount should match entries on the closing documents indicating the money be credited to the broker's commission. *Failure to remove funds after a transaction is fully executed could place the broker in a position of commingling*, mixing the broker's money with trust funds.

Commissions due the principal broker, other licensees associated with the principal broker or other principal brokers may be paid directly from the trust account only after the transaction is closed or otherwise terminated. If commissions are so disbursed, a record of each disbursement is to be recorded on the trust account ledger sheet for the transaction.

When it becomes apparent to the principal broker that a transaction has failed, or if a party to the failed transaction requests disbursement of the earnest money or other trust funds, those funds may only be disbursed by the principal broker following the terms of the real estate purchase contract, by written agreement of the parties or by court order.

Disputes

In the event of dispute over the return or forfeiture of the earnest money or other trust funds, and no party has filed a civil suit arising out of the transaction, the principal broker shall, within 15 days of notice of the dispute:
1) Provide the parties written notice of the dispute.
2) Request them to meet to mediate the matter.

If the parties have contractually agreed to submit disputes arising out of their contract to **mediation**, the principal broker shall notify the parties of their obligation to submit the dispute over funds to an independent mediator agreed upon by the parties. If the parties have not contractually agreed to independent mediation, the principal broker holding the earnest money or trust funds shall use good faith best efforts to mediate.

In the event the dispute is not resolved in either a broker or independent mediation attempt, the principal broker shall maintain the disputed funds in a non-interest bearing real estate trust account. If the parties authorize, or if they previously authorized, deposit into a separate interest bearing trust account, the disputed funds may be maintained in a separate interest bearing trust account for disputed funds.

The principal broker may chose to interplead (deposit) the funds with the court. An interpleader action asks the court to accept the money and distribute it to the rightful claimant. If the broker exercises this option, the total cost of the interpleader action frequently exceeds the earnest money amount. The earnest money funds are used to offset court costs.

The principal broker shall <u>only</u> disburse the funds:
1) Upon written authorization of the parties who will not receive the funds
2) Pursuant to the **order of a court**

If the principal broker has not received written notice of a claim to the funds, including interest if any, within five years after the failure of the transaction, the principal broker may remit the funds to the State Treasurer's Office as "abandoned" property.

Mediation

Disputes involving money held in the Broker's trust account must be resolved by:
- interpleaded the funds,
- the parties file a civil suit
- mediation

The Broker must, within 15 days of receiving written notice of the disputed funds, provide the parties written notice of the dispute and request them to meet to mediate the matter.
- If the parties have contractually agreed to first submit to mediation, the principal broker shall notify the parties of their obligation to submit the dispute to an independent mediator agreed upon by the parties.
- If the parties have not contractually agreed to independent mediation, the principal broker holding the earnest money or trust funds shall use good faith best efforts to mediate.

Unsuccessful mediation: In the event the dispute over funds is not resolved in either a broker or independent mediation attempt,

1. The principal broker shall maintain the disputed funds in a non-interest bearing real estate trust account. If the parties authorize the disputed funds may be maintained in a separate interest bearing trust account for disputed funds.

2. The funds shall only be disbursed by the principal broker:

   a) Upon written authorization of the parties who will not receive the funds;

   b) Pursuant to the order of a court of competent jurisdiction; or

   c) If the principal broker has not received written notice of a claim to the funds, including interest if any, within five years after the failure of the transaction, the principal broker may remit the funds to the State Treasurer's Office as "abandoned" property.

Records

A principal broker must maintain at his principal business location a complete record of all consideration (payments) received or escrowed for real estate transactions in the following manner:

- **Duplicate Deposit Slips:** A duplicate deposit slip must show the amount of money received, the transaction number, and the date and place of deposit.

- **Preprinted Checks and Deposit Slips:** All checks and deposit slips must be preprinted with the brokerages name and the words "Real Estate Trust Account" or "Property Management Trust Account," with the checks numbered consecutively.

- **Transaction Identification:** Checks drawn on this account are to be identified to the specific transaction. Deposits to this account are to be identified to the specific transaction. Voided trust checks are to be marked "Void" and the original check retained in the principal broker's file.

- **Number of accounts needed:** A principal broker may establish, as many trust accounts as desired. However, each trust account must be identified with the type of activity for which the account is to be used and the Division must be notified in writing when each account is established.

- **Check Register:** A check register or check stubs must be maintained which itemize deposits and disbursements in consecutive order showing the date, payee or payor, the transaction information,

> Records must be kept for a minimum of **3 years** plus the year in which the transaction took place

check number, amount of disbursement or deposit, and the current balance remaining in the account.
- **Separate Ledger Sheet:** An individual trust ledger sheet must be established upon deposit of any consideration and assigned a sequential transaction number for each transaction—be it rental, sale, or other. The ledger sheet must show the names of the parties, location of the property, the date and amount of each deposit or disbursement, the name of the payee and payor, the current balance remaining, and any other relevant transaction information. Each ledger sheet, after the transaction is closed, must:
- Show the final disposition of the consideration and
- **Is retained in the principal broker's file for a minimum of *three years* following the year in which the transaction was closed.**
- **Bank Reconciliation:** The trust account is to be reconciled with the bank statement at least monthly. The trust liability, which is the total of ledger cards, and similar books, records, and accounts, must be kept up to date.

Branch Office

A brokerage may open as many branch offices as desired. A branch office **must be registered** with the Division prior to operation.

Exemptions

A branch office does not include a model home, a project sales office, or a facility established for twelve months or less as a temporary site for marketing activity, such as an exhibit booth. Temporary offices may be considered permanent offices if they remain open for one year or more. In this event, the office must be registered as a branch office or closed.

Branch Office Name

A branch office must operate under the same business name as the principal brokerage

Trust Account

The principal broker or branch broker must notify the Division in writing of the location and account number of all real estate trust accounts in which the funds received at each branch office will be deposited.

Branch Broker

The principal broker can supervise the main office, and up to 2 branch offices, for a total of 3 offices. If they have more than 3 total offices, then they must have a branch broker supervise the additional offices. Each branch broker can supervise up to 3 branch offices. The branch broker must be an ***associate broker***. The principal broker must actively supervise the branch broker.

Registration

To register a branch office, the principal broker must submit to the Division, on the forms required by the Division, the location of the branch, the name of the branch broker and the names of all associate brokers and sales agents assigned to the branch, accompanied by the applicable fee.

The principal broker must notify the Division in writing on the forms required by the Division at the time of a change of branch broker.

Review Questions

1. Record of transactions must be kept for _____ calendar years. These records must be available for inspection at the _____ office unless approval has been obtained from the Division to store them elsewhere.

2. Buyers and sellers who have money in the broker's trust account should be provided with a statement every _____ days upon request.

3. The Closing Statement is a record of money received and paid because of the transaction between the
    B_____ and the
    S_____ .

4. The _____ is responsible for the content of the closing statement.

5. The _____ must attend the closing or send a representative.

6. The Broker furnishes the buyer and the seller copies of the closing statement. Which of the following descriptive phrases most accurately describes the process?
    a. Willingly assures that both have copies
    b. Provides copies upon request
    c. The closing agent is the only entity with the obligation to provide copies

7. If the broker dies the agent automatically has an _____ license.

8. M a sales agent obtains an offer Friday before the Monday Labor Day holiday. The offer is accepted Saturday morning. The last day to deposit the earnest money check is _____ .

9. The Real Estate Purchase Contract contains a provision, added by the buyers, which states that the earnest money will be deposited 10 calendar days after acceptance. If the offer were accepted on Wednesday the 11th, the day before Lincoln's birthday, the earnest money would be deposited not later than the _____ .

10. M was asked who the earnest money check should be made out to. She is an agent for ABC Realty. The name on the pay to line of the check should be _____ Real Estate _____ Account.

11. Q wants to make an offer on a new house. He wants to pay his earnest money in the form of a promissory note. The Promissory note should be made payable in favor of
    _____ .

12. J is a Broker opening a Real Estate Trust Account. How much money may he deposit in the account from his own funds to keep the account open and cover account service charges?
    _____

14. Which of the following conditions must be present in order for the broker to use of an interest bearing real estate trust account?
a. Buyer and seller agree
b. The beneficiary of the interest is defined and agreeable to both parties
c. The transaction is for over $500,000
    d. The transaction involves a long due diligence period

14. R a real estate Principal Broker had one of his agents bring in a property management agreement to manage an apartment complex. This is the 7th contract for property management his brokerage has entered into. He must _____ another _____ account to manage this property.

15. A dispute has arisen between the buyer and seller on the distribution of the earnest money in the broker's trust account. Neither side will agree to allow the other to receive the money. The broker must have both parties _____ before he can distribute the funds to anyone. After _____ years, if no agreement has been reached, the money may be turned over to the _____ _____ _____ as abandoned property.

16. The earliest T may receive his commission from the house he just helped sell is:
a. Right after Closing
b. Once the sale is recorded
c. As soon as the wire transfer to Title Company arrives
d. After the seller has been paid.

17. P wants to manage a Branch Office for her broker. She needs a _____ _____ license to be a Branch Broker.

18. K a principal broker just received an accepted offer from his sales agent dated Friday before the Labor Day Monday holiday stating the earnest money was to be deposited upon acceptance. The money must go into the bank no later than;
a. Thursday following acceptance
b. Tuesday following acceptance
c. Monday following acceptance
d. Friday following acceptance

19. B a principal broker has managed six buildings for six of his best customers for the past several years. This year he has agreed to manage an additional building for a new client. B must;
a. Open a property management trust account separate from the brokerage account
b. Notify his other clients that he is now a property management company
c. Hire only licensed property managers as sales agents
d. Disclose to all future customers that his brokerage is now a nonconforming brokerage

20. When establishing a 4th branch office a principal broker must
a. Set up a separate trust account
b. Provide a distinctive name to differentiate the branch office from primary office
c. Appoint an associate broker as the branch broker
d. Remember that all agents' licenses must be assigned to the branch broker instead of the broker.

21. Commingling means
    a. Combining seller's money with buyers money in one account
    b. Combining sales agent money with broker's money in one account
    c. Combining earnest money with down payment in one offer
    d. Combining broker money with trust funds

22. How many branch offices can each branch broker supervise?
    a. Only 1
    b. Up to 5
    c. Up to 7
    d. Up to 3

5. Property Management

Learning Objectives:

At the conclusion of this class the student will be able to:

- Define which property management activities require a real estate license.
- Identify operation requirements for a property management company that differ from a brokerage.
- Explain which support services can be performed by unlicensed personnel.

Property Management

Definition

Property management requiring a real estate license includes; advertising real estate for lease or rent, procuring prospective tenants or lessees, negotiating lease or rental terms, executing lease or rental agreements, collecting rent and accounting for and disbursing the money collected, arranging for repairs to be made to the real estate. It does not include the leasing or management of surface or subsurface minerals, or oil and gas interests, which is separate from a sale or lease of the surface estate.

Dual Broker: A Principle Broker who obtains a Dual Broker License to be the Principle Broker of a property management company in addition to their primary sales brokerage.

Property Management Sales Agent: Sales agent working under a property management brokerage under a Dual Broker, who is designated by the broker to do sales activity under the broker's sales brokerage.

Exemptions

The following individuals are not required to hold active real estate licenses to engage in property management:

a) An owner of real estate who manages his own property;

b) Employees: A regular salaried employee of an owner of real estate who manages property owned by his employer;

c) Apartment Managers: An individual who manages the apartments at which he resides in exchange for free or reduced rent on his apartment.

d) Homeowners Association Employees: A full time salaried employee of a homeowner's association who manages units subject to the declaration of condominium, which established the homeowner's association.

Property Management by a Brokerage

All property management performed by a licensed or unlicensed assistant affiliated with a real estate brokerage must be done under the name of the brokerage and not under a separate business name.

The principal broker shall actively supervise all property management activities of licensees affiliated with the brokerage. In the case of a branch office, the branch broker must also actively supervise the licensees and unlicensed assistants affiliated with that branch.

> A brokerage may perform **property management** within the brokerage operation

Property Management by Separate Property Management Company

A brokerage company may elect to open a separate property management company. The principal broker of the brokerage also acts as the principal broker of the property management company.

A separate property management company registration must be obtained in order to conduct property management business under a name different from that of the real estate brokerage.

> A broker may select to operate a **property management company** separate from the brokerage operation

A

The business of a separate property management company must be exclusively property management. **A property management company may conduct no real estate sales activity**.

A license to operate a property management company in addition to the main brokerage, called a Dual Broker license, will be granted upon compliance with the following conditions:

- **Application**: Submission of the *Property Management Company Application Form* required by the division, signed by an actively licensed principal broker, together with the proper application fees.

- **Business Name Approval**: A property management company must register its business name with the Division of Corporations and provide evidence of the registration to the Division before a license will be issued for the new entity.

- **Property management by unlicensed principals or owners prohibited**. Owners of the brokerage business entity shall not engage in activity, which requires a license unless they are licensed with the division and properly affiliated with the management broker for the brokerage.

Assignment of licensees

All licensees who will be affiliated with the property management company must be formally assigned to the company. The principal broker must sign and submit the forms required by the division to affiliate with the property management company for each associate broker, branch broker and sales agent who will perform property management services for the property management company.

Support Services Personnel

Sales agents whose licenses are affiliated with the property management company under a Dual Broker can only perform property management duties. They cannot perform any real estate sales activity.

If a sales agent affiliated with the property management company wishes to do real estate sales activity, they can, at their broker's option, apply for a Property Management Sales Agent designation. This will allow them to do property management under the property management company, and real estate sales activity under the broker's main sales brokerage.

Individuals who are employees of a property management company may perform the following services under the supervision of the principal broker without holding active real estate licenses: providing a prospective tenant with access to a vacant apartment; providing secretarial, bookkeeping, maintenance, or rent collection services; quoting predetermined rent and lease terms; and filling out pre-printed lease or rental agreements.

> **Non-licensed personnel may not negotiate leases**

All property management activities by an associate broker or sales agent affiliated with the property management company and all activities on behalf of the company by support services personnel shall be actively supervised by the principal broker of the company. In the case of a branch office, the branch broker shall also actively supervise the licensees and support services personnel affiliated with that branch.

Review Questions

1. Which of the following may manage a specific property without being licensed under a broker? (Indicate all correct answers)
   a. Owner
   b. Live in apartment manager
   c. Sales Agent
   d. Employee managing property owned by employer

2. B owns ABC Brokerage. His brokerage has grown to include several contracts to manage property for others. He may open a separate property management company and be the broker of that company by _____ with the _____ of _____ Estate.

3. W has been hired by a property manager to change locks, put up signs, and deliver documents to various offices. W (does / does not) need a license.

4. J really enjoys his workday. He spends most of his time talking to prospective tenants for a large office complex owned by Q Corp. the only tough part of the job is that from time to time he must try to collect late rent from a delinquent tenant. J is probably:
   a. An independent contractor and a licensed real estate agent working as a property manager
   b. A salaried employee and a licensed real estate agent working as a property manager
   c. A salaried employee working as a property manager for one employer on one office property
   d. All of the above could be correct

5. K lives in apartment #1. K shows apartments for rent and collects rent. K also mows the lawn and shovels snow. K receives credit toward his apartment rental costs as payment.
   a. K is in violation of the Utah property management laws because he is not licensed.
   b. K is in violation of the Utah real estate licensing laws because he is not licensed.
   c. K must maintain a trust account for all rental moneys collected.
   d. K is within the law.

6. In a property management company a real estate sales agent license is required to perform the following duties
   a. Accounting ledgers showing rents received and maintenance costs paid
   b. Showing space available to prospective tenants and quoting predetermined rents
   c. Filling out pre-printed lease forms
   d. Acquiring new clients

7. T, a principal broker, owns and manages S Brokerage Company. Many of his clients have asked if his company would manage their investment properties. T has become persuaded to expand into property management.
    a. T may only manage property for others if he has registered his brokerage as a property management company.
    b. T may choose to set up a separate property management company and remain the broker of both enterprises.
    c. T must set up a separate property management division of his company and appoint an associate broker as the property manager
    d. T cannot be the broker of a brokerage and a property management company at the same time.

8. C, a sales agent working under a dual broker in their property management company, can perform real estate sales activity, if they apply, and their broker designates them as a/an:
    a. Associate Broker
    b. Property Management Sales Agent
    c. Branch Broker
    d. Property Manager Supervisor

6. Licensee Conduct

Learning Objectives:

Upon completion of this chapter, the student should be able to:

- Define the difference between the Utah Code and the Administrative Rules.
- Describe each of the following illegal and unprofessional actions:
    1. False Devises. Licensee shall not propose, prepare or cause to prepare any falsified document.
    2. Undisclosed Licensee interest in a transaction
    3. Double Commissions
    4. Misrepresentation
    5. False Promises
    6. Dual Agency without consent
    7. Acting as Sales Agent or associate broker without a formal broker relationship
    8. Failing to account for or remit monies timely or commingling.
    9. Paying or offering valuable consideration outside the Broker Sales Agent relationship
    10. Failing to voluntarily furnish copies
    11. Breaching a fiduciary duty

Improper Practices

Improper practices are also considered unprofessional conduct. Improper practices harm the public and harm the real estate profession. Those who engage in these practices cast a negative shadow on the activities of good, caring professional agents. Utah law specifically prohibits unprofessional conduct. The following are all examples of unprofessional conduct and improper practices.

False devices

A licensee shall not propose, prepare, or cause to be prepared any document, agreement, closing statement, or any other device or scheme, which does not reflect the true terms of the transaction, nor shall a licensee knowingly participate in any transaction in which a similar device is used.

    a. Loan Fraud: A licensee shall not participate in a transaction in which a buyer enters into any agreement that is not disclosed to the lender, which, if disclosed, may have a material effect on the terms or the granting of the loan.

    b. Double Contracts: A licensee shall not use or propose the use of two or more purchase agreements, one of which is not made known to the prospective lender or loan guarantor.

Signs

It is prohibited for any licensee to have a sign on real property without the written consent of the property owner

Licensee's Interest in a Transaction

A licensee shall not buy, sell, or lease or rent any real property as a principal, directly or indirectly, without first disclosing in writing on the purchase agreement or the lease or rental agreement his true position as principal in the transaction. A licensee will be considered to be a principal for the purposes of this rule if:

- Is the buyer or lessee in the transaction
- Has an ownership interest in the property

- Has an ownership interest in the entity that will be the buyer, seller, lessor or lessee
- Is an officer, director, partner, member, or employee of an entity that will be the buyer, seller, lessor, or lessee.
- Whether the licensee's license is on active or inactive status

Listing Content

The real estate licensee completing a listing agreement is responsible to make reasonable efforts to verify the accuracy and content of the listing.

Net listings

An employment contract in which the broker receives as commission all excess monies over and above the minimum sales price agreed on by the broker and seller. Because of the danger of unethical practices in such a listing, its use is prohibited.

Advertising

This rule applies to all advertising materials, including newspaper, magazine, Internet, e-mail, radio, and television advertising, direct mail promotions, business cards, door hangers, signs, and other electronic communication.

Name of Brokerage: Any advertising or real estate services or property by active licensees or their employees must include the name of the real estate brokerage as shown on Division records in a clear and conspicuous manner.

Ownership Interest: If the licensee advertises property in which he has an ownership interest and the property is not listed, the ad need not appear over the name of the real estate brokerage if the ad includes the phrase "owner-agent" or the phrase "owner-broker".

Electronic Advertisement: Some electronic mediums limit the amount of information that can be conveyed, such as social media. In electronic advertisements where it is not reasonable for the commercial message to include the brokerage name, then the message must directly link to a display that clearly and conspicuously identifies the name of the brokerage.

Real Estate Teams: Advertising teams, groups, or other marketing entities which are not licensed as brokerages is permissible in advertising so long as they follow the same requirements and restrictions as individual agents:

1. The **brokerage must be identified** in a clear and conspicuous manner; and
2. In electronic advertisements where it is not reasonable to include the brokerage name, there must be a direct link to a display that includes the brokerage name in a clear and conspicuous manner.

Written Consent: Under no circumstances may a licensee advertise or offer to sell or lease property without the written consent of the owner of the property or the listing broker. Under no circumstances may a licensee advertise or offer to sell or lease property at a lower price than that listed without the written consent of the seller or lessor.

Advertisements to Purchase or Rent: All advertising to sell or rent by a licensee must contain the name of the licensees' real estate brokerage as shown on Division records.

Guaranteed Sales Plan: If a licensee advertises a guaranteed sales plan, they must include a statement that costs and conditions may apply in a clear and conspicuous manner. Any radio advertisement must also include a statement of any conditions and limitations. They must also include information on how to contact the licensee to obtain any required disclosures.

Double Commissions

In order to avoid subjecting the seller to paying double commissions, licensees must not sell listed properties other than through the listing broker. A licensee shall not subject a principal to paying a double commission without the principal's informed consent.

Adverse Double Agency

A licensee shall not enter or attempt to enter into a concurrent agency representation agreement with a buyer or a seller, a lessor or a lessee, when the licensee knows or should know of an existing agency representation agreement with another licensee. This practice is also referred to as double listing.

Retention of Buyer's Deposit

A principal broker holding an earnest money deposit shall not be entitled to any of the deposit without the written consent of the buyer and the seller.

Finder's Fees

A licensee may not pay a finder's fee or give any valuable consideration to an unlicensed person or entity for referring a prospect in a real estate transaction, except as provided in this rule.

Token Gifts

A licensee may give a gift valued at $150 or less to an individual in appreciation for an unsolicited referral of a prospect that resulted in a real estate transaction.

Referral Fees

Referral fees are not in and of themselves improper. The problem arises when a referral fee passes between two entities that should remain neutral in a transaction. Entities such as Title Companies and Lenders would compromise the neutrality that should exist with an agent and his client. An agent has a duty to be loyal to his client and do nothing that is not in his clients' best interest. Referral fees fly in the face of that loyalty. A licensee may not receive a referral fee from a lender or title company. A licensee may not pay a referral fee to a lender or title company

Using Two Licenses

A licensee may not act as a real estate agent or broker in the same transaction in which the licensee also acts as a mortgage loan officer or loan originator, appraiser, escrow officer, or provider of title services.

Failure to have written agency agreement

To avoid representing more than one party without the informed consent of all parties, principal brokers and licensees acting on their behalf shall have written agency agreements with their principals. The failure to define an agency relationship in writing will be considered **unprofessional conduct** and **grounds for disciplinary action** by the Division

Any agency relationship with a buyer or seller shall be in writing. The written agreement must outline the scope of the agency relationship.

When an agency relationship develops between both the buyer and the seller in one transaction written agency agreements must be obtained with both buyer and seller. The agreement must clarify the scope of the *limited agency* and demonstrate that the principal broker has obtained the *informed consent* of both buyer and seller to the limited agency.

Limited Agency Prohibited: A licensee may not act nor attempt to act as a limited agent in any transaction in which:
- The licensee is a principal in the transaction
- Any entity in which the licensee is an officer, director, partner, member, employee, or stockholder is a principal in the transaction.

Sub-agency

A licensee affiliated with a brokerage other than the listing brokerage who wishes to act as a *sub-agent* for the seller, shall, prior to showing the seller's property:
1) Obtain permission from the principal broker with whom he is affiliated to act as a sub-agent;
2) Notify the listing brokerage that sub-agency is requested;
3) Enter into a written agreement with the listing brokerage consenting to the sub-agency and defining the scope of the agency; and
4) Obtain from the listing brokerage all information about the property that the listing brokerage has obtained.

A principal broker and licensees acting on his behalf who act as sub-agents owe the same fiduciary duty to a principal as the brokerage retained by the principal.

Agency relationships with owners and landlords requiring the agent to perform property management functions shall be governed by a written *property management agreement* that spells out the duties, responsibilities and authority of the property manager. The same is required when an agency relationship is established with a *tenant*.

Signing without legal authority

A licensee shall not sign or initial any document for a principal unless the licensee has prior written authorization in the form of a duly executed power of attorney from the principal authorizing the licensee to sign or initial documents for the principal. A copy of the power of attorney shall be attached to all documents signed or initialed for the principal by the licensee.

- When signing a document for a principal, the licensee shall sign as follows: "(Principal's Name) by (Licensee's Name), Attorney-in-Fact."
- When initialing a document for a principal, the licensee shall initial as follows: "(Principal's Initials) by (Licensee's Name), Attorney-in-Fact for (Principal's Name)."

Counteroffers

A licensee shall not make a counteroffer by making changes, whiting out, or otherwise altering the provisions of the Real Estate Purchase Contract or the language that has been filled in on the blanks of the Real Estate Purchase Contract. All counteroffers to a Real Estate Purchase Contract shall be made using the State-Approved Addendum form.

Copies of Agreement

After both the buyer and seller properly sign a purchase agreement, it is the responsibility of each participating licensee to cause copies thereof, bearing all signatures, to be delivered or mailed to the buyer and seller with whom the licensee is dealing. The licensee preparing the document shall not have the parties sign for a final copy of the document prior to all parties signing the contract evidencing agreement to the terms thereof. It is the duty of the property manager to ensure that signed copies of a lease are delivered to the parties of the document.

Residential Construction Agreement

The Earnest Money Sales Agreement for Residential Construction must be used for all transactions for the construction of dwellings to be built or presently under construction for which a Certificate of Occupancy has not been issued.

Real Estate Auctions

The principal broker is responsible to assure that all aspects any auction conducted by the brokerage comply with Utah real estate law. Auctioneers and auction companies who are not licensed may conduct auctions of real property located within this state upon the following conditions:

- Advertising: All advertising and promotional materials associated with an auction must conspicuously disclose that the auction is conducted under the supervision of a named principal broker licensed in this state; and
- Supervision: The auction must be conducted under the supervision of a principal broker licensed in this state who must be present at the auction; and
- Use of Approved Forms: Any purchase agreements used at the auction must meet the requirements of Section 61-2-20 and must be filled out by a Utah real estate licensee; and
- Placement of Deposits: All monies deposited at the auction must be placed either in the real estate trust account of the principal broker who is supervising the auction or in an escrow depository agreed to in writing by the parties to the transaction.
- Closing Arrangements: The principal broker supervising the auction shall be responsible to assure that adequate arrangements are made for the closing of each real estate transaction arising out of the auction.

Guaranteed Sales

Guaranteed Sales Plan means:
a. Any plan in which a seller's real estate is guaranteed to be sold or;
b. Any plan whereby a licensee or anyone affiliated with a licensee will purchase a seller's real estate if a third party does not purchase it in the specified period of a listing or within some other specified period.

In any real estate transaction involving a guaranteed sales plan, the licensee shall provide full disclosure as provided herein regarding the guarantee:

Written Advertising: Any written advertisement by a licensee of a "guaranteed sales plan" shall include a statement advising the seller that if the seller is eligible, costs and conditions may apply and advising the seller to inquire of the licensee as to the terms of the guaranteed sales agreement. This information shall be set forth in print at least one-fourth as large as the largest print in the advertisement.

Radio/Television Advertising: Any radio or television advertisement by a licensee of a "guaranteed sales plan" shall include a conspicuous statement advising if any conditions and limitations apply.

Guaranteed Sales Agreements: Guaranteed sales agreements must be in writing and include all terms of the guarantee including conditions of the guarantee, costs for the service, guaranteed sale or purchase price, and approximate net proceeds the seller may expect to receive.

Agency Disclosure

In every real estate transaction involving a licensee, as agent or principal, the licensee shall clearly disclose in writing to his respective client(s) or any un-represented parties, his agency relationship(s). The disclosure shall be made prior to the parties entering into a binding agreement with each other. The disclosure shall become part of the permanent file.

- When a binding agreement is signed in a sales transaction, the **prior agency disclosure shall be confirmed** in the currently approved Real Estate Purchase Contract or, with substantially similar language, in a separate provision incorporated in or attached to that binding agreement.
- When a lease or **rental agreement** is signed, a separate provision shall be incorporated in or attached to it confirming the prior agency disclosure. The agency disclosure shall be in the form used in the approved Real Estate Purchase Contract, but shall substitute terms applicable for a rental transaction for the terms "buyer", "seller", "listing agent", and "selling agent".

- Disclosure to other agents: An agent who has established an agency relationship with a principal shall disclose whom he or she represents to another agent upon initial contact with the other agent.

Duty to Inform

Sales agents and associate brokers must keep their principal broker or branch broker informed on a timely basis concerning all real estate transactions in which the licensee is involved, as agent or principal, in which the licensee has received funds on behalf of the principal broker or in which an offer has been written.

Broker Supervision

Principal brokers and associate brokers who are branch brokers shall be responsible for exercising active supervision over the conduct of all licensees affiliated with them.

A broker will not be held responsible for inadequate supervision if:

- An affiliated licensee violates real estate law or the rules created by the Real Estate Commission, in contravention of the supervising broker's specific written policies or instructions; and
- Reasonable procedures were established by the broker to ensure that licensees receive adequate supervision and the broker has followed those procedures; and
- Upon learning of the violation, the broker attempted to prevent or mitigate the damage; and
- The broker did not participate in the violation
- The broker did not ratify the violation; and
  The broker did not attempt to avoid learning of the violation.
- The existence of an independent contractor relationship or any other special compensation arrangement between the broker and affiliated licensees shall not release the broker and licensees of any duties, obligations, or responsibilities.

Disclosure of Fees

If a real estate licensee who is acting as an agent in a transaction will receive any type of fee in connection with a real estate transaction in addition to a real estate commission, that fee must be disclosed in writing to all parties to the transaction.

Fees from Builders

All fees paid by builders for referral of prospects must be paid directly to principal broker with whom he is licensed and affiliated. The principal broker can then pay the fee to the licensee according to Utah law. All fees paid in connection with a transaction must be disclosed to the buyer.

Fees from Manufactured Housing Dealers

If a licensee refers a prospective buyer to a manufactured home dealer or a mobile home dealer, the dealer may pay a referral fee but only to the Principal broker. The principal broker with whom the licensee is licensed may then pay the licensee for the referral.

Gifts and Inducements

Gifts given by a principal broker to a buyer, seller, lessor or lessee, in a real estate transaction as an inducement to use or in appreciation for having used the services of a brokerage is permissible and is not an illegal sharing of commission. If an inducement is to be offered to a buyer or seller, lessor or lessee, who will not be obligated to pay a real estate commission in a transaction, the principal broker must obtain from the party who will pay the commission written consent that the inducement be offered.

Due-On-Sale Clauses

Real state licensees have an affirmative duty to disclose in writing to buyers and sellers the existence or possible existence of a "due-on-sale" clause (known as "Alienation Clause" in mortgage documents) in an underlying encumbrance on real property. The potential consequences of selling or purchasing a property without obtaining the authorization of the holder of the underlying encumbrance must be discussed with the buyer and seller.

Personal Assistants

With the permission of the principal broker with whom the licensee is affiliated, the licensee may employ an unlicensed individual to provide services in connection with real estate transactions, which do not require a real estate license, including the following examples:

- **Clerical duties**, including making appointments for prospects to meet with real estate licensees, but only if the contact has been initiated by the prospect and not by the unlicensed person;
- At an **open house**, distributing preprinted literature written by a licensee, so long as a licensee is present and the unlicensed person furnishes no additional information concerning the property or financing and does not become involved in negotiating, offering, selling or filling in contracts;
- Acting only as a **courier service** in delivering documents, picking up keys, or similar services, so long as the courier does not engage in any discussion of, or filling in of, the documents;
- Placing **brokerage signs** on listed properties;
- Having **keys made** for listed properties; and
- Securing **public records** from the County Recorders' offices, zoning offices, sewer districts, water districts, or similar entities
- If personal assistants are compensated for their work, they shall be **compensated at a predetermined rate**, which is not contingent upon the occurrence of real estate transactions. Licensees may not share commissions with unlicensed persons who have assisted in transactions by performing the services listed in this rule.
- The licensee who hires the unlicensed person will be responsible for **supervising** the unlicensed person's activities, and shall ensure that the unlicensed person does not perform activity, which requires a real estate license.
- Unlicensed individuals may not engage in **telephone solicitation** or other activity calculated to result in securing prospects for real estate transactions, except as a receptionist answering incoming calls and scheduling appointments for their supervisor as a part of their receptionist duties.

Fiduciary Duties

A principal broker and licensees acting on his behalf owe fiduciary duties to the principal in an agency relationship. The principal is the person who has appointed the agent to act for them. A principal may be a seller or buyer, a landlord or tenant. The principal may also be the principal broker to the sales agents and associate brokers licensed with them. All agency relationships place certain fiduciary duties on the agent. The duties are:

Loyalty, which obligates the agent to act in the best interest of the buyer or lessee instead of all other interests, including the agent's own;

Obedience, which obligates the agent to obey all lawful instructions from the buyer or lessee;

Full Disclosure, which obligates the agent to tell the buyer or lessee all material information, which the agent learns about the property or the seller or lessor's ability to perform his obligations;

Confidentiality, which prohibits the agent from disclosing any information given to the agent by their principal, (buyer, seller landlord tenant) which would likely weaken the principals' bargaining position if it were known, unless the agent has permission from the principal to disclose the information. This duty does not permit the agent to misrepresent, affirmatively or by omission, the principals' financial condition or ability to perform; nor does it allow the agent to withhold any known material fact concerning a defect in the property.

Reasonable care and diligence, licensees are obligated to be thorough and complete in the acquisition and distribution of pertinent information. Making statements that are not founded in known fact could harm the client or customer in a transaction. Agents are expected by the public to be knowledgeable and informed. We need to meet this expectation or, at the very least be sure that they do not believe we are informed and knowledgeable when we in fact are not. When asked if the roof leaks, if the true answer known, the best answer would be to say, "I am not sure".

Holding safe and accounting for all money or property entrusted to the agent; and any additional duties created by the agency agreement.

Duties of a limited agent

A principal broker and licensees acting on his behalf who act as agent for both seller and buyer, or lessor and lessee, commonly referred to as "dual agents," are limited agents since the fiduciary duties owed to seller and to buyer, or to lessor and lessee, are inherently contradictory. A principal broker and licensees acting on his behalf may act in this limited agency capacity only if the informed consent of both buyer and seller, or lessor and lessee, is obtained.

- In order to obtain **informed consent**, the principal broker or a licensee acting on his behalf shall clearly explain to both buyer and seller, or lessor and lessee, that they are each entitled to be represented by their own agent if they so choose, and shall obtain written agreement from both parties that they will each be giving up performance by the agent of the following fiduciary duties:
- The principal broker or a licensee acting on his behalf must explain to buyer and seller, or lessor and lessee, that they are **giving up their right to demand undivided loyalty** from the agent. The agent, acting in this neutral capacity, shall advance the interest of each party so long as it does not conflict with the interest of the other party. In the event of conflicting interests, the agent will be held to the standard of **neutrality**; and
- The principal broker or a licensee acting on his behalf must explain to buyer and seller, or lessor and lessee, that there will be a **conflict as to a limited agent's duties of confidentiality** and full disclosure.
  - Under un̲limited agency, the parties would expect full disclosure of any information the agent has become aware of.
  - Under limited agency, the agent could have become aware of information from either party that could be harmful to the other party if known.
  - The limited agent **may not disclose** any information given to the agent by either principal which would likely weaken that party's bargaining position if it were known, **unless** the

agent has permission from the principal to disclose the information; and

- The licensee shall explain to the buyer and seller, or lessor and lessee, that the limited agent will be required to disclose information given to the agent in confidence by one of the parties if **failure to disclose the information would be a material misrepresentation** regarding the property or regarding the abilities of the parties to fulfill their obligations.

In addition, a limited agent owes the following fiduciary duties to all parties:

- **Obedience**, which obligates the limited agent to obey all lawful instructions from either the buyer or the seller, lessor and lessee, consistent with the agent's duty of neutrality;
- **Reasonable care and diligence,** licensees are obligated to be thorough and complete in the acquisition and distribution of pertinent information. Making statements that are not founded in known fact could harm the client or customer in a transaction.;
- **Holding safe all money** or property entrusted to the limited agent; and
- Any additional duties created by the agency agreement.

Stigmatized Property in Utah

Many states require disclosure of stigmatized property to potential buyers. Utah and some other states have chosen not to.

Failure to disclose not a basis for liability

- The failure of an owner of real property to disclose that the property being offered for sale is stigmatized is not a material fact that must be disclosed in the transaction of real property.
- Neither an owner nor his agent is liable for failing to disclose that the property is stigmatized.
- Federal law prohibits any reference to AIDS or those who might have lived in the property with HIV virus.

Definition of Stigmatized Property: A property regarded as undesirable because of events that occurred there: Some conditions that typically stigmatize a property are a murder, gang activity, suicide, and even alleged presence of ghosts.

Review Questions

Match the Principal with the Definition by placing *A, B, C,* etc. in the appropriate box.

Principle		Match Principle	Definition	
A	Double Contract		1	Licensee must not sell listed property except through the listing broker or they would subject the owner to…
B	Sign			
C	Licensee's Interest In Transaction			
D	Net Listing		2	Holding weekly meetings in which the policy of the brokerage are discussed is an example of_____
E	Clear and conspicuous			
F	Brokerage name			
G	Advertising		3	Sales agents have a _____ the broker of all pending transactions.
H	Double Commission			
I	Token gifts		4	Advertising that includes an agent's name must also include the _____
J	Written Agency Agreement			
K	Duty to inform		5	All materials including newspaper, magazines, Internet, e-mail, radio, television, direct mail promotions, business cards, door hangers and signs.
L	Broker Supervision			
M	Inducements and Thank You Gifts			
N	Personal Assistant			
O	Fiduciary Duty		6	Unprofessional conduct would include representing persons as an agent without….
P	Limited Agent			
Q	Licensed Assistant		7	Installation prohibited without written consent.
			8	A licensee shall not buy, sell or rent any real property as a principal without disclosing _____.
			9	Loyalty, Obedience, Accounting, Disclosure, Care
			10	The brokerage name in advertising must be identified in a _____ manner
			11	The illegal use of two or more purchase agreements to defraud lender
			12	An agreement paying the agent all monies above a fixed price
			13	Unlicensed and limited to clerical duties, courier services, picking up keys and paid based on hourly wage.
			14	$150 or less only
			15	Dual Agent
			16	Spending $100 on canned goods to stock a new home for a buyer This is an example of legal _____
			17	Licensed with Broker though time is spent exclusively assisting sales agent

18. K a Utah sales agent helped her friend buy a home. She agreed to be her representative in negotiations with the seller. K chose not to charge a commission (with the permission of her broker) but her friend insisted that she accept a cash gift for her help of $500.
    a. K may accept the gift (tip); after all, she did earn it.
    b. K may accept the gift (tip) because it was between friends.
    c. K must turn over the gift to her broker so that she might be paid based on her employment agreement and Utah law.
    d. K must turn over the gift to her broker because she negotiated directly with the seller.

19. T a licensed sales agent, was showing a home when he was asked if the roof leaks. T stated that the roof was sound. The home was sold to the prospect. After the buyer moved in a heavy rainstorm occurred and the roof leaked over the kitchen. Which of the following is true?
    a. The seller told T the roof did not leak so T has no financial exposure for the roof leak.
    b. Buyers buy used homes in an "as is" condition. Neither the seller nor the sellers' agent has any obligation to disclose a roof leak.
    c. The buyer chose not to have the house inspected by a licensed inspector so they may not seek damages from anyone.
    d. Agents need to be careful to determine the facts before they make statements. T may have some financial liability.

20. T a newly licensed agent, is involved with a complicated transaction involving things he has never dealt with before. He wants to impress his new client with his abilities so he is inclined to "wing it". Making up what he does not know. This could lead to losing his license because:
    a. New agents lose their licenses more easily than more seasoned agents do.
    b. He is obligated to be competent so as to safeguard the public
    c. Only brokers can handle complicated transactions
    d. Only Commercial Agents should handle complicated transaction.

21. The seller refused to pay the commission as agreed. The sales agent's principal broker refused to pay the commission until the seller paid. The sales agent may:
    a. Place a lien on the sold property for the amount of the debt
    b. Sue the Seller to enforce the listing agreement
    c. Sue the Buyer for the financial shortfall
    d. Encourage the Broker to comply with the sales agent's employment agreement

22. Copies of the REPC must be provided to all of the following except;
    a. Broker
    b. Signatories
    c. County recorder
    d. Buyer

23. P obtained a listing to lease a retail property, which included permission to place a sign on the premises. When the Sign Company came to install the sign, they were afraid to cut holes in the asphalt parking lot. They instead placed the sign in the grass strip between the sidewalk and the curb of the street.
    a. The agent is not responsible for the actions of the Sign Company.
    b. The agent needs to be certain that the grass strip is a part of the listed property. If not, the agent must obtain separate permission to place a sign on the grass strip
    c. This was wise because parking lot damage is considered a violation of the fiduciary trust placed in an agent.
    d. The grass strip is always a better location for a sign.

24. T obtained an offer that was later accepted. When his clients applied for a loan to purchase the property, they were told they did not have enough down payments. Which of the following choices would not be a legal option for T to do?
    a. Take the buyers to another lender to apply
    b. After full disclosure to the lender give the buyers money from his commission to help with the down payment
    c. Work out a deal between the buyer and seller to show the price a little higher than agreed on a new contract thus showing more equity for the buyer when they applied for the loan
    d. Suggest that the buyer contact his parents and ask for a gift to help with the down payment.

25. O obtained a listing agreement that provided payment of commissions of all amounts over $160,000. This type of listing
    a. Requires principal broker approval
    b. Is an open listing and is illegal in Utah
    c. May only be sold with full disclosure to all parties
    d. Is a net listing and is illegal in Utah

26. R is an auctioneer hired to conduct an auction to sell a large farm. He has invited several large farm owners who he believes may be interested in purchasing the property because they border the property.
    a. R may only conduct the auction legally if he is hired by and supervised by a licensed broker, and include in all advertising that the broker is responsible for the sale.
    b. R may only conduct the auction if he is a licensed real estate agent acting under a broker's direction.
    c. Real estate may not be sold at auction in Utah except foreclosure sales.
    d. Only licensed real estate brokers and their agents may invite the neighboring farmers.

27. The office staff prepared the following advertisement. They have given you the opportunity to edit the text. Under Utah law what must be changed from the copy shown.

> Beautiful Avenues Home
> 2bd 2bt 2cg lg yd $149,000
> office 555-2396 or cell 555-6123

   a. Must include the terms if the price is included
   b. Must include the agent's name
   c. Must include brokerage name
   d. Must use abbreviations that can be understood

28. J an unlicensed individual helped his neighbor sell his house by finding a buyer and helping the buyer fill out an offer on a state approved Real Estate Purchase Contract form. His neighbor decided to pay J 4% of the purchase price as a commission because J had been so helpful. J violated the law when he:
   a. Helped his neighbor find a buyer because finding a buyer requires a real estate sales agent license
   b. Helped the buyer fill out an offer because he was not a licensed attorney
   c. Accepted payment for his services because one act for compensation qualifies a person as a broker or sales agent under Utah Law resulting in J acting as a sales agent without a license
   d. J did not violate the law because it as a single transaction and was therefore exempt.

29. K wants to purchase 5 acres of pasture from a neighbor that has refused to sell to K. K prepares an offer to purchase signed by a corporate officer of a corporation owned by K. When the offer is presented through his neighbors' agent, K indicates that he represents the corporation as an agent. K is:
   a. Guilty of failing to disclose his interest in the purchase
   b. Able to disguise his purchase legally using this method
   c. Breaching a fiduciary responsibility to the seller
   d. Not required to disclose his ownership because a corporate officer signed the offer

30. G was approached by a good friend and asked to help her sell her house. G was confident that their relationship was so strong and enduring that a handshake was all that was needed between such good friends.
   a. Common law sets a business relationship standard that will govern this situation.
   b. The Real Estate Purchase Contract will establish a written record of the transaction. No other agreement is needed in writing.
   c. Only sales contracts need be in writing.
   d. All agency relationships must be defined in writing.

31. Bill has been asked to list an older home. Bill has heard rumors that the previous owner had committed suicide in the home and that the current owner bought the home at the estate sale after the death. Bill should:
   a. Fully disclose the Stigma to all potential buyers.
   b. Only disclose the stigma to Bills broker who will prepare a stigma disclosure form for distribution
   c. Instruct the seller that the stigma must be disclosed to avoid liability
   d. Utah law does not require disclosure of stigma.

7. Enforcement

Learning Objectives:

Upon completion of this chapter, the student should be able to:

- Describe the differences between the Real Estate Commission and the Division of Real Estate
- Description the differences between the Division of Real Estate and the Utah Association of REALTORS
- Explain the process of a complaint against a licensee.
- Explain the "due process"
- Define at least three possible disciplinary sanctions against a licensee.
- Explain the function of the Recovery Fund.

Division of Real Estate & Real Estate Commission

The Division of Real Estate is created by statute to supervise and regulate the real estate industry. The Division is a sub division of the Department of Commerce. The Director who is appointed by the Executive Director of the Department of Commerce manages the Division of Real Estate.

Division
Administers the Law and Rules
Investigates consumer complaints
Conducts audits of trust accounts

The Director is charged with administering the laws of the State of Utah concerning real estate matters, preparing the Division budget and delivering an annual report to the legislature. The Division administers licensing laws, supervises education requirements and education providers, and investigates consumer complaints concerning real estate matters.

The Real Estate Commission assists the Division.

- The Real Estate Commission is made up of five persons appointed by the Governor and confirmed by the Senate.
- These five individuals serve four-year terms.
- Each term is staggered to expire at different times so that no two commissioners' terms end at the same time.
- A commissioner shall not serve more than one additional term consecutively.
- Four of the Commissioners must be licensed real estate agents with at least 5 years' experience. They need not be Brokers.
- The fifth member of the commission is selected from the public. No real estate experience is required.
- Each member of the Commission must reside in different counties of the state so that the representation of the commission is diverse.
- The commissioners are unpaid voluntary servants of the public receiving only a per diem reimbursement for some of their expenses.
- The commission meets at least monthly and frequently more often.

The Commission works hand in hand with the Division. The Division investigates consumer complaints. The commission holds hearings to determine if the law has been broken and to determine disciplinary sanction for licensees. The commission makes rules to provide the Division with a standard format for administering the Utah Law including the contents of the Licensing exams and educational requirements of license candidates.

The Director and some of his staff attend the Commission hearings and provide support services to the commission such as minute taking and providing information. The Director works intimately with the Commission. The Commission consults with the Director on Division matters such as the annual budget and policy and rule changes.

The Real Estate Commission then sets policy by establishing rules. It works closely with the Division to protect the public and strengthen the real estate profession. They may be overruled in their decisions in some circumstances. For instance, if a licensee disagrees with the findings of the commission relating to a disciplinary hearing he may appeal their decision to the Executive Director of the Department of Commerce or to the courts.

Other Organizations Concerned With Real Estate in Utah

The profession of real estate has fostered many professional organizations that serve the real estate community of professional. They provide a more pleasant working environment, education opportunities, networking opportunities and a general strengthening of the industry. Two of those organizations are the Utah Association of Realtors and the Wasatch Front Regional Multiple Listing Service. These private organizations are strictly voluntary. Membership is voluntary. They have no standing as a regulator. Their only power over their members is to expel them from the organization.

Utah Association of Realtors: This association is an organization established to strengthen the industry and the profession. It promotes ethical standards of conduct, continued learning and professional development. Membership is voluntary. Many of the best real estate agents are members and subscribe to the principals proffered. If a broker is a member of the association, then all licensees licensed under the bOther than its influence on the thinking of the industry, it has no role in regulation of anyone but its own members.

Wasatch Front Regional Multiple Listing Service: UtahRealEstate.com, This organization has been established to provide a way for member brokerages to share information about their listings. It is an excellent way to interact with other brokers and agents in providing information and sharing commissions through joint transactions. It too is voluntary. If a broker is a member, affiliated licensees must also be members.

Enforcement

The Division of Real Estate is charged with investigation of all consumer complaints relating to the real estate industry. They fill the role of investigator much the same as a police officer would. The following rules were established to direct the Division of Real Estate in their investigation process, to outline the hearing process and the hearing participants and potential outcomes.

Filing of Complaint

An aggrieved person may file a complaint in writing against a licensee; or the Division or the Commission may initiate a complaint upon its own motion for alleged violation of the provisions of these rules or Real Estate License Law. The Division will not entertain complaints between licensees regarding claims to commissions.

Notice of Complaint

When the Division notifies a licensee of a complaint against him or requests information from the licensee, the licensee must respond to the notice within **ten business days** after receipt of the notice from the Division. Failure to respond to the notice of complaint or any subsequent requests for information from the Division within the required time will be considered an additional violation of these rules and separate grounds for disciplinary action against the licensee.

Investigation and Enforcement

The Division of Real Estate investigates and regulates the following matters:
- investigate information provided on new license applications;
- evaluation and investigation of complaints;
- audit licensees' business records, including trust account records;
- meet with complainants, respondents, witnesses and attorneys;
- make recommendations for dismissal or prosecution;
- preparation of cases for formal or informal hearings,
- restraining orders or injunctions;
- work with the assistant attorney general and representatives of other state and federal agencies;
- entering into stipulations for presentation to the Commission and the director

Corrective Notice

In addition to disciplinary action, the Division may give a licensee written notice of specific violations of these rules and may grant a licensee a reasonable period, not exceeding 30 days, to correct a defect in that licensee's practices or operations. The licensee's failure to correct the defect within the time granted shall constitute separate grounds for disciplinary action against the licensee. The Division is not required to give a corrective notice and allow an opportunity to correct a defect before it may commence disciplinary action against a licensee.

1. Disciplinary hearings are held before the _____ Estate _____

2. The Commission may (suspend)(revoke)(sentence to jail) (order additional education)(charge a fine) cross out false answers

3. Disciplinary decisions of the Real Estate Commission may be appealed to the _____ _____.

4. Real Estate Commissioners are_____ paid for their service but are reimbursed for some of their _____.

5. The _____ of _____ Estate investigates consumer complaints and prepare evidence to be presented before the Real Estate _____.

6. The Utah Association of Realtors and the Wasatch Front Regional Multiple Listing Service are _____ organizations and have no statutory regulatory authority

7. The Real Estate Commission is made up of representatives from how many counties? _____

8. The Real Estate Commission determines: (indicate all that apply)
   a. License qualifications
   b. Disciplinary sanctions
   c. Salaries of the Division personnel
   d. Term of office of the Director

9. The _____ of the Division of Real Estate is not a member of the Real Estate Commission but attends its meetings.

10. The _____ and the _____ _____ Commission consults together but the Director prepares the Real Estate Division budget.

11. The Director prepares an Annual _____ for the Governor and the legislature each year concerning the activities of the Division

12. The Division (will / will not) entertain complaints between licensees regarding claims to commissions.

8. Prelicense Education

Learning Objectives:

Upon completion of this chapter, the student should be able to:
- Explain the certification process of a prelicense school.
- Outline the rules of conduct of certified schools
- Determine if a candidate to be an instructor would qualify

Prelicense Education

Prelicense education credit shall be given to students only for courses provided by schools that are certified by the Division at the time the courses are taught. Applicant schools shall apply for certification by submitting all forms and fees required by the Division not less than 90 days prior to a course being taught. Applications shall include at minimum the following information, which will be used in determining approval:

School Application for Certification

- Name, phone number and address of the school, the school director, and all owners of the school;
- The school director shall obtain approval of the school name from the Division prior to registering that name with the Division of Corporations and Commercial Code in the Department of Commerce as a real estate education provider.
- Provide a description of the type of school and a description of the school's physical facilities. Except for distance education courses, all courses must be taught in an appropriate classroom facility and not in any private residence.
- A comprehensive course outline including a description of the course, the length of time to be spent on each subject area broken into class periods, and a minimum of three to five learning objectives for every three hours of class time;

- Provide the name and certification number of each certified instructor
- Provide the name and resume documenting the knowledge and expertise of each guest lecturer who will teach the course. A college or university may use any faculty member to teach an approved course provided the instructor demonstrate to the satisfaction of the Division academic training or experience qualifying him to teach the course.
- An identification of whether the method of instruction will be traditional education or distance education;

All courses of study shall meet the minimum standards set forth in the State of Utah Standard Course Outline provided for each approved course. The school may alter the sequence of presentation of the required topics. The school director shall certify that:

- All courses of study will meet the minimum hourly requirement of that course.
- That the school will not give a student credit for more than eight credit hours per day

A school seeking certification of distance education prelicensing courses shall:

- submit to the Division a complete description of all course delivery methods and all media to be used;
- provide course access to the Division using the same delivery methods and media that will be provided to the students;
- description specific and regularly scheduled interactive events included in the course and appropriate to the delivery method that will contribute to the students' achievement of the stated learning objectives;
- description how the students' achievement of the stated learning objectives will be measured at regular intervals;
- description how and when prelicense instructors will be available to answer student questions;
- Provide an attestation from the school director of the availability and adequacy of the equipment, software, and other technologies needed to achieve the course's instructional claims.

- A copy of at least two final examinations of the course and the answer keys, which are used to determine if the student has passed the exam.
- Provide an explanation of procedure if the student fails the final examination and thereby fails the course.
- A maximum of 10% of the required class time may be spent in testing, including practice tests and the final examination. A student cannot challenge a course or any part of a course of study in lieu of attendance or active participation.
- A list of the titles, authors and publishers of all required textbooks;
- All texts, workbooks, supplements, and any other materials must be appropriate and current in their application to the required course outline.
- List the days, times and locations of classes. A college or a university may schedule its courses within the criteria of its regular schedule, for example, quarter, semester, or other. A college quarter hour credit is the equivalent of 10 classroom hours. A college semester hour credit is the equivalent of 15 classroom hours.
- A copy of the statement which shall be provided for each student outlining the days, times and locations of classes; the number of quizzes and examinations; the grading system, including methods of testing and standards of grading; the requirements for attendance; the school's evidence of notification to candidates of the qualifying questionnaire; and the school's refund policy;
- A copy of the statement which shall be provided to each student in capital letters no smaller than 1/4 inch containing the following language: "A student attending the (school name) is under no obligation to affiliate with any of the real estate brokerages that may be soliciting for agents at this school;" and
- Any other information as the Division may require.

Certification Determining Fitness for School

The Division, with the concurrence of the Commission, shall certify schools based on the honesty, integrity, truthfulness, reputation and competency of the school director and school owners.

School Certification and Renewal

The term of a school certification is twenty-four months. A certification may be renewed by submitting all forms and fees required by the Division prior to the expiration date of the current certification. School certifications not properly renewed shall expire on the expiration date.

A certification may be reinstated for a period of thirty days after expiration by complying with all requirements for a timely renewal and paying a non-refundable late fee.

A certification may be reinstated after thirty days and within six months after expiration by complying with all requirements for a timely renewal and payment of a non-refundable reinstatement fee.

A certification that has been expired for more than six months may not be reinstated and an applicant must apply for a new certification following the same procedure as an original certification.

School Conduct and Standards of Practice

In order to maintain good standing and renew a certification, a course sponsor shall:
- teach the approved course of study as outlined in the State Approved Course Outline;
- require each student to attend the required number of hours and pass a final examination;
- maintain a record of each student's attendance for a minimum of three years after enrollment;
- not accept a student for a reduced number of hours without first having a written statement from the Division which defines the exact number of hours the student needs;
- Not make any misrepresentation in its advertising about any course of instruction, and shall be able to provide substantiation of any claims made. All advertising and public notices shall be free of statements or implications, which do not enhance the dignity and integrity of the real estate profession. A school shall not make disparaging remarks about a competitor's services or methods of operation;
- Limit approved guest lecturers who are experts in related fields to 20% of the instructional hours per approved

course. A guest lecturer shall provide evidence of professional qualifications to the Division prior to being used as a guest lecturer;

- within 15 calendar days after the occurrence of any material change in the school which would affect its approval, the school shall give the Division written notice of that change;

- not attempt by any means to obtain or use the questions on the prelicensing examinations unless the questions have been dropped from the current exam bank;

- Not give any valuable consideration to a real estate brokerage for having referred students to the school. A school shall not accept valuable consideration from a brokerage for having referred students to the brokerage;

- If the school agrees, real estate brokerages may be allowed to solicit for agents at the school. No solicitation may be made during the class time or during the student break time. Solicitation may be made only after the regularly scheduled class so that no student will be obligated to stay for the solicitation;

- use only certified instructors or guest lecturers who have been registered with the Division;

- provide the instructor with the approved content outline for each course and shall assure the content has been taught;

- provide a course completion certificate in the form approved by the Division to each student upon the student's completion of the prelicensing course;

- Furnish to the Division a current roster of the school's approved instructors and guest lecturers. A school shall provide an updated roster to the Division each time there is a change in school instructors or guest lecturers;

- give no more than eight credit hours per day to any student;

- Prior to accepting payment from a prospective student for a pre-licensing education course, a certified school shall provide a written disclosure to the prospective student stating:

    a) applicants for licensure must disclose any criminal history by answering a questionnaire as part of the pre-license exam;

b) applicants for licensure must submit fingerprint cards to the Division and consent to a criminal background check;

c) licenses issued by the Division are conditional pending the completion of the background check and that failure to accurately disclose a criminal history will result in an immediate and automatic license revocation;

d) applicants with a criminal history of felonies within 5 years and/or misdemeanors for dishonest acts within 3 years do not qualify for a license; and Applicants with a criminal history other than as described above will be considered on a case-by-case basis and may be required to appear at an administrative hearing to determine qualifications for licensure.

The school shall be required to obtain the student's signature on the written criminal history/ background check disclosure acknowledging receipt of the disclosure. The disclosure form and acknowledgement shall be retained in the school's records and made available for inspection by the Division for a minimum of three years following the date upon which the student completed the prelicensing course; and

A school's owners and directors shall be responsible for the quality of instruction in the school and for adherence to the state statutes and administrative rules regarding school and instructor certification.

Instructor Application for Certification

An instructor shall not teach a prelicensing course without having been certified by the Division prior to teaching. Applicants shall apply for instructor certification by submitting all forms and fees required by the Division not less than 30 days prior to the course being taught. Applications shall include at minimum the following information, which will be used in determining approval:

- Name and certification number of the certified prelicense school for which the applicant will work;
- Evidence of a minimum educational level of graduation from high school or its equivalent;

- Evidence of any combination of at least five years of full time experience and/or college-level education related to the course subject;
- Evidence of a minimum of twelve months of fulltime teaching experience or an equivalent number of months of part time teaching experience, or attendance at Division Instructor Development Workshops totaling at least two days in length; and
- Evidence of having passed an examination designed to test the knowledge of the subject matter proposed to be taught;
- A signed statement agreeing to allow the instructor's courses to be randomly audited on an unannounced basis by the Division or its representative;
- A signed statement agreeing not to market personal sales product; and
- To teach the sales agent prelicensing course, evidence of being a licensed sales agent or broker;
- To teach the broker prelicensing course, evidence of being a licensed associate broker, branch broker, or principal broker
- Any other information as the Division may require.

An applicant may qualify to teach a sub course of the broker-prelicensing course by meeting the following criteria:

i. Brokerage Management: The instructor applicant must be a licensed real estate broker and have managed a real estate office, or hold a CRB or equivalent professional designation in real estate brokerage management. The instructor applicant must have at least two years practical experience as an active real estate principal broker.

ii. Advanced Real Estate Law: The instructor applicant must be a licensed real estate broker or is a current member of the Utah State Bar or have graduated from an American Bar Association accredited law school and have at least two years real estate law experience.

iii. Advanced Appraisal: The instructor applicant must be a licensed real estate broker, or be a state-licensed or state-certified appraiser.

iv. Advanced Finance: The instructor applicant must be a licensed real estate broker, have been associated with a

> lending institution as a loan officer, or have a degree in finance. The instructor applicant must have at least two years practical experience in real estate finance.
>
> v.   Advanced Property Management: The instructor applicant must be a real estate licensee. The instructor applicant must have at least two years property management experience or hold a CPM or equivalent professional designation. The instructor applicant must have at least two years full-time experience as a property manager.

Determining Fitness for Instructor Certification

The Division, with the concurrence of the Commission, shall certify instructors based on the applicant's honesty, integrity, truthfulness, reputation, and competency.

Instructor Certification Renewal

The term of a prelicensing education instructor certification is twenty-four months. A certification may be renewed by submitting all forms and fees required by the Division prior to the certification's expiration date. Certifications not properly renewed shall expire on the expiration date.

- A certification may be reinstated for a period of thirty days after expiration by complying with all requirements for a timely renewal and paying a non-refundable late fee.
- A certification may be reinstated after thirty days and within six months after expiration by complying with all requirements for a timely renewal and payment of a non-refundable reinstatement fee.
- A certification that has been expired for more than six months may not be reinstated and an applicant must apply for a new certification following the same procedure as an original certification.

To renew an instructor certification an instructor shall, during the two years prior to renewal:
- teach at least 20 hours of in-class instruction in a certified real estate course; and
- Attend an instructor development workshop sponsored by the Division.

Review Questions

1. A school must apply for certification at least _____ days prior to teaching the first class.
   a. 30
   b. 60
   c. 90
   d. 120

2. A school must submit how many final exams for Division of Real Estate review?
   a. 1
   b. 2
   c. 3
   d. 4

3. The maximum percentage of course class time that may be spent on testing may not exceed:
   a. 5%
   b. 7%
   c. 10%
   d. 15%

4. A school applying for a prelicensing school certification must do which of the following?
   a. Provide a copy of all text books to be used in the course
   b. Prevent recruiters from contacting students outside of the classroom
   c. Provide college credit for each 15 hours of class
   d. Provide a test out method for prepared students to take a test instead of attending class.

5. A one hour class time requires that students be in attendance for at least:
   a. 45 minutes
   b. 50 minutes
   c. 55 minutes
   d. 60 minutes

9. Continuing Education

Learning Objectives:

Upon completion of this chapter, the student should be able to:

- Outline the continuing education course approval process
- Select from a list the classes that may be certified as a CE class
- List at least 3 standard practices expected of CE course providers

Continuing Education

Continuing education credit shall be given to students only for courses that are certified by the Division at the time the courses are taught. Course sponsors shall apply for course certification by submitting all forms and fees required by the Division not less than 30 days prior to the course being taught. Applications shall include at a minimum the following information, which will be used in determining approval:

Course Application for Certification

- Name and contact information of the course sponsor and the name of the entity through which the course will be provided;
- Address of the physical facility where the course will be taught; Except for distance education courses, all courses must be taught in an appropriate classroom facility and not in a private residence
- The title of the course;
- The proposed amount of credit hours for the course;
    a. A credit hour is defined as 50 minutes within a 60-minute time period;
    b. The minimum length of a course shall be one credit hour;
- A statement defining how the course will meet the objectives of continuing education by increasing the

licensee's knowledge, professionalism, and ability to protect and serve the public;

- A course outline including, for each segment of no more than 15 minutes, a of the subject matter;
- A minimum of three learning objectives for every three hours of class time;
- The name and certification number of each certified instructor who will teach the course;
- Identification of whether the method of instruction will be traditional education or distance education;
- A sponsor seeking certification of a distance education course shall:
  Submit to the Division a complete of all course delivery methods and all media to be used:
- provide course access to the Division using the same delivery methods and media that will be provided to the students;
- description specific and regularly scheduled interactive events included in the course and appropriate to the delivery method that will contribute to the students' achievement of the stated learning objectives;
- description how and when instructors will be available to answer student questions; and
- Provide an attestation from the sponsor of the availability and adequacy of the equipment, software, and other technologies needed to achieve the course's instructional claims.
- Copies of all materials to be distributed to the participants;
- The procedure for pre-registration, the tuition or registration fee and a copy of the cancellation and refund policy;
- Except for courses approved for distance education, the procedure for taking and maintaining control of attendance during class time, which procedure shall be more extensive than having the student sign a class roll;
- A sample of the completion certificate which shall bear the following information:
  a. A Space for the licensee's name, type of license and license number, date of course;
  b. The name of the course provider, course title, hours of credit, certification number, and certification expiration date; and

      c. A Space for signature of the course sponsor and a space for the licensee's signature

- A signed statement agreeing not to market personal sales products;
- A signed statement agreeing to allow the course to be randomly audited on an unannounced basis by the Division or its representative;
- A signed statement agreeing to upload, within 10 days after the end of a course offering, to the database specified by the Division: the course name, course certificate number assigned by the Division, the date the course was taught, the number of credit hours, and the names and license numbers of all students receiving continuing education credit. A course sponsor is not responsible for uploading information for students who fail to provide an accurate name or license number registered with the Division. Continuing education credit will not be given to any student who fails to provide to a course sponsor an accurate name or license number registered with the Division within 7 days of attending the course;
- Any other information as the Division may require.

Determining Fitness for Course Certification

The Division shall certify courses based on intellectual and practical content and whether the course increases the licensee's knowledge, professionalism and ability to protect and serve the public.

Courses in the following subjects may be certified as "**core**":
- state approved forms/contracts,
- other industry forms/contracts,
- property management and leases,
- short sales,
- REO sales,
- Environmental hazards including meth, mold, asbestos and radon,
- ethics,
- fair housing,
- agency,
- prevention of real estate and mortgage fraud,
- federal and state real estate laws,
- Brokers' trust accounts,
- Water law, rights and transfer.

Courses in the following subjects may be certified as "**elective**":

- Real estate financing, including mortgages and other financing techniques; real estate investments;
- real estate market measures and evaluation;
- real estate appraising;
- accounting and taxation as applied to real property;
- estate building and portfolio management for clients;
- settlement statements;
- real estate mathematics;
- Real estate law;
- contract law;
- real estate securities and syndications;
- regulation and management of timeshares,
- condominiums and cooperatives;
- resort and recreational properties;
- farm and ranch properties;
- real property exchanging;
- legislative issues that influence real estate practice;
- real estate license law and administrative rules;
- Land development; land use, planning and zoning; construction; energy conservation in buildings; water rights; real estate environmental issues and hazards including lead-based paint, underground storage tanks, radon, etc., and how they affect real estate; real estate inspections;
- Americans with Disabilities Act; affirmative marketing;
- Commercial real estate;
- Tenants-in-Common;
- Using the computer, the Internet, business calculators, and other technologies to directly increase the licensee's knowledge, professionalism and ability to protect and serve the public;
- Professional development, business success, customer relation skills, or sales promotion, including salesmanship, negotiation, sales psychology, marketing techniques related to real estate knowledge, servicing clients, communication skills;
- Personal and property protection for licensees and their clients; and

- Any other topic that directly relates to the real estate brokerage practice and directly contributes to the objective of continuing education.

Non-acceptable course subject matter includes topics such as:

- Offerings in mechanical office and business skills, such as typing, speed reading, memory improvement, language report writing, advertising, or similar offerings;
- Physical well-being, personal motivation, stress management, dress-for-success, or similar offerings;
- Meetings held in conjunction with the general business of the licensee and his broker, employer or trade organization, such as sales meetings, in-house staff or licensee training meetings, or member orientation for professional organizations;
- Courses in wealth creation or retirement planning for licensees; and
- Courses that are specifically designed for exam preparation

Course Certification Renewal

Course certifications are valid for a period of two years. A certification may be renewed by submitting all forms and fees required by the Division prior to the expiration date of the current certification. Certifications not properly renewed shall expire on the expiration date.

- A certification may be reinstated for a period of thirty days after expiration by complying with all requirements for a timely renewal and paying a non-refundable late fee.
- A certification may be reinstated after thirty days and within six months after expiration by complying with all requirements for a timely renewal and payment of a non-refundable reinstatement fee.
- A certification that has been expired for more than six months may not be reinstated and an applicant must apply for a new certification following the same procedure as an original certification.

Conduct and Standards of Practice

In order to maintain good standing and renew a certification, a course sponsor shall:

- Upon completion of a course offering, provide a certificate of completion, in the form required by the Division, to those students who attend a minimum of **90%** of the required class time;
- Maintain for **three years** a record of registration of each person completing an offering and any other prescribed information regarding the offering, including exam results, if any;
- For distance education courses, give education credit only to students who complete the course within one year of the registration date;
- Notify the Division in writing **within 15 days of any material change** in a certified course, for example, curriculum, course length, instructor, refund policy, etc.;
- Upon completion of a course offering, provide to each student a course evaluation, in the form required by the Division, and submit the completed course evaluations to the Division within 10 days.

Instructor Application for Certification

Continuing education credit shall be given to students only for courses that are taught by an instructor who is certified by the Division at the time the courses are taught. Applicants shall apply for instructor certification by submitting all forms and fees required by the Division not less than 30 days prior to the course being taught. Applications shall include at a minimum the following information, which will be used in determining approval:

- Name and contact information of the applicant;
- Evidence of a minimum education level of graduation from high school or its equivalent;
- Evidence of any combination of at least three years of full time experience and/or college-level education related to the course subject;
- Evidence of at least twelve months of fulltime teaching experience or an equivalent number of months of part time teaching experience, or attendance at the Division's Instructor Development Workshops totaling at least two days in length;

- A signed statement agreeing to allow the instructor's courses to be randomly audited on an unannounced basis by the Division or its representative;
- A signed statement agreeing not to market personal sales products; and
- Any other information as the Division may require.

Determining Fitness for Instructor Certification

The Division with the concurrence of the Commission shall certify instructors based on the applicant's honesty, integrity, truthfulness, reputation, and competency.

Instructor Certification Renewal

Instructor certifications are valid for a period of two years. A certification may be renewed by submitting all forms and fees required by the Division prior to the expiration date of the current certification. Certifications not properly renewed shall expire on the expiration date.

- A certification may be reinstated for a period of thirty days after expiration by complying with all requirements for a timely renewal and paying a non-refundable late fee.
- A certification may be reinstated after thirty days and within six months after expiration by complying with all requirements for a timely renewal and paying a non-refundable reinstatement fee.
- A certification that has been expired for more than six months may not be reinstated and an applicant must apply for a new certification following the same procedure as an original certification.

To renew an instructor certification an instructor must teach, during the previous renewal period, a minimum of 12 continuing education credit hours.

If the instructor has not taught a minimum of 12 hours during the previous renewal period, written explanation outlining the reason for not meeting the requirement and satisfactory documentation of the applicant's present level of expertise shall be provided to the Division.

Marketing of Continuing Education Courses

A course sponsor may not advertise or market a continuing education course where Division continuing education course credit will be offered or provided to a licensed attendee unless the course:

a) Is approved and has been issued a current continuing education course certification number by the Division; and

b) Is advertised with the continuing education course certification number issued by the Division displayed in all advertising materials

A course sponsor may not advertise, market, or promote a continuing education course with language, which indicates Division continuing education course approval is "pending" or otherwise forthcoming.

Review Questions

1. A continuing education course provider must upload course completion information for banking within:
   a. 24 hours
   b. 5 days
   c. 10 days
   d. 15 days

2. Which of the following course topics may be certified as a core class?
   a. Real estate appraisal
   b. Real estate mathematics
   c. Commercial real estate practices
   d. Short sales

3. Which of the following courses is eligible for continuing education certification?
   a. Tenant in Common rules
   b. Business skills
   c. Dress for success
   d. Real estate exam preparation

4. Student records are to be stored and made available to state investigators on request for at least:
   a. 1 year
   b. 2 years
   c. 3 years
   d. 4 years

5. If course content is changed the school is required to provide a written notice to the Division of Real Estate within:
   a. 3 days
   b. 10 days
   c. 15 days
   d. 30 days

10. Administrative Procedures

Learning Objectives:

Upon completion of this chapter, the student should be able to:

- Identify the types of hearings held in disciplinary proceedings.
- Characterize the types of matters that can be addressed in an informal hearing
- List potential penalties for law violations
- Name the entity who could hear an appeal of a hearing outcome

Administrative Procedures

Formal Adjudicative Proceedings

Certain matters must be addressed in a formal hearing before the Real Estate Commission while others are more of a day-to-day nature and require the attention of the Division only. The licensee has rights including representation by an attorney, confronting their accuser, questioning witnesses, and presenting witnesses and evidence in defense. A licensee has all the rights expected in a traditional court of law. Thus, *due process* is afforded a licensee when they are accused.

Even after a hearing is held, there are appeal rights. The licensee may request a review of the Real Estate Commissions decision by the Director of the Department of Commerce. This is the most frequently used appeal process. The Executive Director reviews the entire hearing record, compares the outcome to Utah law and Real Estate Rules and weighs the severity of sanctions imposed to determine if the entire process is fair, according to law, and just. The licensee may also appeal to the courts. An appeal to the courts requires that the licensee follow all the legal filing requirements just as with any other legal appeal involving matters originally heard in a trial court setting.

The following matters are addressed on a formal basis requiring that the hearing be held before the Real Estate Commission

- Except as otherwise expressly provided herein, **the revocation, suspension or probation of a real estate license**, school or instructor certification or fine levied against a licensee
- The revocation, suspension or probation of any **registration issued pursuant to the Timeshare and Camp Resort Act.**
- Any proceedings conducted subsequent to the issuance of **cease and desist orders**

The Division staff handles these issues:

- The **issuance of a real estate license**, the renewal of an active, inactive or expired license, or the activation of an inactive license
- Any action on a sales agent's license based upon the **revocation or suspension of a principal broker's license** or the failure of the principal broker to renew his license.
- The issuance of renewal or **certification of real estate schools** or instructors
- The revocation of a real estate license due to payment made from the **Real Estate Recovery Fund**.
- The issuance, renewal, suspension or revocation of registration pursuant to the **Land Sales Practices Act**
- The **exemption** from, or the amendment of, registration pursuant to the **Land Sales Practices Act**
- The issuance or renewal of any registration pursuant to the **Time-Share and Camp Resort Act**
- Any waiver of, or exemption from, registration requirements pursuant to the **Time-Share and Camp Resort Act**

Penalty for violation of Utah License Law

- The post-revocation hearing for failure to accurately disclose a **criminal history**
- A hearing on whether or not a licensee or certificate holder whose license or certificate was issued or renewed on **probationary status** has violated the condition of that probation.

(1) Any individual violating Utah License Law is subject to the following potential penalties:
  - $5,000 fine for each violation, or increased to amount of any gain derived from each violation.
  - If first violation, deemed guilty of a class A misdemeanor resulting in imprisonment up to six months.

(2) Upon conviction of a second or subsequent violation, an individual would be guilty of a third degree felony. Imprisonment could be up to two years. If a corporation is convicted of a second or subsequent violation, it is guilty of a third degree felony.

(3) Any officer or agent of a corporation, or any member or agent of a partnership or association, who personally participates in or is an accessory to any violation is subject to the penalties prescribed for individuals.

(4) If any person receives any money or its equivalent, as commission, compensation, or profit by or in consequence of a violation, that person is liable for an additional penalty of not less than the amount of the money received and not more than three times the amount of money received, as may be determined by the court. This penalty may be sued for in any court of competent jurisdiction, and recovered by any injured party and may use such award for his own use and benefit.

(5) All fines imposed by the commission and the director under this chapter shall be deposited into the Real Estate Education, Research, and Recovery Fund to be used in a manner consistent with the requirements of the Real Estate Recovery Fund Act.

Hearing Procedures

- The Commission and the Division may delegate a hearing to an Administrative Law Judge or hear the case themselves

- The Division may issue subpoenas or other orders to compel production of necessary and relevant evidence. The Parties have access to information gathered during an investigation by the Division. The Division will provide the information within 15 days of receipt of the written request.

- Notice of hearing: Upon the scheduling of a hearing by the Division, the Division shall mail written notice of the date, time, and place scheduled for the hearing. If the respondent in a proceeding commenced by the Division is an actively licensed sales agent or associate broker, the Division shall mail a copy of the notice of hearing to the principal broker with whom the respondent is licensed.

- **Hearings** shall be open to all parties unless it is expected that there will be discussion of the character, professional competence, or physical or mental health of an individual.

- **Witnesses** may be called by the defendant. The Division will assist the defendant in subpoenaing witnesses

- **Representation by counsel**: The defendant may be represented by counsel and have the opportunity to testify, present witnesses and other evidence, and comment on the issues.

- Record: The Division will keep a record of the hearing

- Orders: Within a reasonable time after the close of a proceeding, the presiding officer shall issue a signed order in writing that states the decision, the reasons for the decision, a notice of any right of administrative or judicial review available to the parties, and the time limits for filing an appeal or requesting a review.

- Orders typically take effect 30 days following the decision. The Commission could impose an earlier date to protect the public.

Review Questions

1. Which of the following conditions would require that a hearing be a formal hearing?
   a. A fine may be imposed
   b. A license may be revoked
   c. A license may be suspended
   d. A registration may be suspended
   e. A cease and desist order may be issued
   f. All are correct.

2. T or F   Forced inactivation due to an error of the Broker does not require a formal hearing.

3. T or F   Recovery fund distributions are only considered by the courts, no hearing is required.

4. Which of the following is not one of the appeal rights?
   a. Request a formal review of the matter by the Director of the Division of Real Estate
   b. Request a formal review of the matter by the Executive Director of the Department of Commerce
   c. Appeal to the courts

5. T or F   The first violation of Utah License law carries a maximum penalty of 2 years.

6. John was convicted of a violation of Utah license law for the first time. Which of the following is an accurate statement?
   a. John is guilty of a third degree felony
   b. John is guilty of a class A misdemeanor
   c. John is facing jail time
   d. John's broker is also automatically convicted.

11. Fractionalized Estates

Learning Objectives:

At the conclusion of this class, the student will be able to:
- Define an undivided long-term fractionalized estate.
- List three required sales marketing disclosures
- List 3 required leasing marketing disclosures.

Definitions:

- Affiliate: An individual or entity that directly or indirectly through one or more intermediaries controls or is controlled by, or is under common control with, a specified individual or entity.
- Entity: Any Corporation, Limited Liability Company, General or Limited Partnership, company association, joint venture, business trust, trust, or other organization.
- Sponsor: The party that is the seller of an undivided fractionalized long-term estate.
- Undivided fractionalized long-term estate: an ownership interest in real property by two or more persons that is a:
    1. Tenancy in common (TIC); or
    2. Any other legal form of undivided estate in real property including:
        a. A fee estate
        b. A life estate
        c. Other long-term estate

3. "Undivided fractionalized long-term estate" does not include a joint tenancy.

Required Marketing Disclosures

All real estate licensees who market an undivided fractionalized long-term estate shall obtain from the sponsor (seller) the following information. They shall provide it to purchasers in the form of written disclosures provided in a reasonable amount of time in advance of closing to allow adequate review:

1. Information concerning the sponsor and the sponsor's affiliates:

   a. The financial strength of the sponsor and all affiliates, as evidenced by current certified financial statements and current credit reports, and information concerning any bankruptcies or civil suits;

   b. Whether any affiliate of the sponsor is a third party service provider in the transaction, including mortgage brokers, mortgage lenders, loan originators, title service providers, attorneys, appraisers, document preparation services, providers of credit reports, property condition inspectors, settlement agents, real estate brokers or other marketing agents, insurance providers, and providers of any other services for which the investor will be required to pay.

   c. Whether any affiliate of the sponsor is a master lease tenant or whether the sponsor is an affiliate of any master lease tenant.

   d. Any use that will be made of purchaser proceeds.

2. Information concerning the real property in which the undivided fractionalized long-term estate is offered:

   a. Material information concerning any leases or subleases affecting the real property;

   b. Material information concerning any environmental issues affecting the real property;

   c. A preliminary title report on the real property;

110

d. If available, financial statements on any tenants for the life of the entity or the last five years, whichever is shorter;

e. If applicable, rent rolls and operating history;

f. If applicable, loan documents;

g. The Tenants in Common agreement, or any agreement that forms the substance of the undivided fractionalized long-term estate, including definition of the undivided fractionalized interest;

h. All third party reports acquired by the sponsor;

i. A narrative appraisal report, with an effective date no more than 6 months prior to the date the offer of sale is made, that includes at minimum pictures, type of construction, age of building, and site information such as improvements, parking, cross easements, site and location maps;

j. All material information concerning the market conditions for the property class; and

k. All material information concerning the demographics of the general market area.

3. Information concerning the asset managers and the property managers of the real property in which the undivided fractionalized long-term estate is offered:

a. Contact information for any existing or recommended asset managers and property managers;

b. Any relationship between the asset managers and the sponsor;

c. Any relationship between the property managers and the sponsor; and

d. Copies of any existing asset management agreements and any property management agreements.

All real estate licensees who market an undivided fractionalized long-term estate that is subject to a master lease shall obtain from the sponsor financial statements of the master lease tenant, audited according to generally accepted accounting principles. They shall provide them to purchasers in a reasonable amount of time in advance of closing to allow adequate review by the purchaser. If the master lease tenant is an entity formed for the sole purpose of acting as the master lease tenant, then the financial statements of the owners of that entity shall be furnished.

All real estate licensees who market an undivided fractionalized long-term estate, in a reasonable amount of time in advance of closing to allow adequate review by the purchaser, shall:

1. Disclose in writing to purchasers:

   a. That there may be tax consequences for a failure to close on the purchase

   b. That there may be risks involved in the purchase

2. Advise purchasers that they should consult with tax advisors and other professionals for advice concerning these matters.

Regulation D Offering

The Division and the Commission shall consider any offering of a fractionalized undivided long- term estate in real property that is compliant with Securities and Exchange Commission Regulation D, to be in compliance with these rules.

Review Questions

1. Which of the following is an example of a form of ownership available under the undivided fractionalized long term estate? Select all that apply.
   a. Joint tenancy
   b. Life estate
   c. Tenant in Common (TIC)
   d. Tenant by the entireties

2. Utah undivided fractionalized long term estate law is primarily a:
   a. Disclosure law
   b. Licensing law
   c. Prohibition law
   d. Facilitation law

3. Rule 11 of the Division of Real Estate rules, Fractionalized Long Term Estates, places requirements on which of the following? Select all that apply.
   a. Sales agent/broker
   b. Seller
   c. Buyer
      d. Sponsor

4. Select the disclosures required when selling the Fractionalized Long Term Estate. Select all that apply.
   a. Sponsor/seller and property disclosures including risks and material facts
   b. Affiliates, environment issues and leases of the property and its owners
   c. Financial statements of the seller and the property including all detail
   d. Details of all risks of purchasing the Fractionalized Long Term Estate

5. Which of the following is a Fractionalized Long Term Estate? Select all that apply.
   a. A Tenant In Common ownership interest in real property by two or more persons
   b. A joint Tenancy ownership interest in real property by two or more persons
   c. A Life Estate interest by one owner of real property with 3 or more years remaining
      d. A Long Term Lease interest by two or more tenants in separate portions of real property

6. Which of the following must be disclosed to a buyer of a Fractionalized Long Term Estate? Select all that apply.
   a. Any principal of the seller and service provider to the property
   b. All experience of the property managers to document capacity to manage
   c. The sales history of the property over the last 10 years naming each buyer and the price paid
   d. Audited financial statements of the sponsor and all affiliates

12. Real Estate Recovery Fund

Learning Objectives:

At the conclusion of this class the student will be able to:

- List the three purposes of the fund
- Identify who will pay into the fund
- Explain the claim process for the fund.
- Explain the distribution requirements of the fund

Real Estate Education, Research and Recovery Fund Act

Purpose

The Real Estate Education, Research, and Recovery Fund was established to reimburse the public out of the fund for damages up to $15,000 caused by real estate licensees in a real estate transaction. The fund is only available for damages caused by individual licensees. Reimbursement may not be made for judgments against corporations, partnerships, associations, or other legal entities.

The fund was also established to provide revenue for improving the real estate profession through education and research with the goal of making real estate salespersons more responsible to the public.

Size of Fund	The actual interest earned on the Real Estate Education, Research, and Recovery Fund shall be deposited into the fund. At the commencement of each fiscal year, **$100,000** shall be available in the fund for satisfying judgments rendered against licensees.
Fees paid into the Fund	Each person who applies for or renews a real estate principal broker or associate broker license shall pay, in addition to the application or renewal fee, a reasonable annual fee of up to $18, as determined by the Division of Real Estate with the concurrence of the Real Estate Commission.
	Each person who applies for or renews a real estate sales agent license shall pay in addition to the application or renewal fee a reasonable annual fee of up to $12, as determined by the division with the concurrence of the commission.
Claim Procedure	A person may bring a claim against the Real Estate Education, Research, and Recovery Fund only if he provides written notice to the Division of Real Estate at the time he files an action against a real estate licensee alleging fraud, misrepresentation, or deceit. Within 30 days of receipt of the notice, the division shall have an unconditional right to intervene in the action. Once judgment is obtained the claimant, may file a petition in court for an order directing payment from the Fund for the uncollected actual damages included in the judgment that remain unpaid.
Maximum Payment from the Fund	Recovery from the fund may not include punitive damages, attorney's fees, interest, or court costs. Regardless of the number of claimants or parcels of real estate involved in a transaction, the liability of the fund may not exceed **$15,000** for a single transaction and **$50,000** for any one licensee. A copy of the petition must be served upon the Division of Real Estate of the Department of Commerce, and an affidavit of the service shall be filed with the court.
Court Process	The court shall conduct a hearing on the petition within 30 days after service. The petitioner shall recover from the fund only if he shows all of the following:

a. He is not the spouse of the judgment debtor or the personal representative of the spouse.

b. He has complied with all provisions of this statute.

c. He has obtained a final judgment

d. He has proved the amount still owing on the judgment at the date of the petition.

e. He has had a writ of execution issued upon the judgment, and the officer executing the writ discovered no property subject to execution in satisfaction of the judgment. If execution is levied against the property of the judgment debtor, the petitioner shall show that the amount realized was insufficient to satisfy the judgment, and shall indicate the amount realized and the balance remaining on the judgment after application of the amount realized.

f. He has made reasonable searches and inquiries to ascertain whether the judgment debtor has any interest in property, real or personal, that may satisfy the judgment, and he has exercised reasonable diligence to secure payment of the judgment from the assets of the judgment debtor.

If the petitioner satisfies the court that it is not practicable for him to comply with one or more of the requirements, the court may waive those requirements.

A judgment that is the basis for a claim against the fund may not have been discharged in bankruptcy. In the case of a bankruptcy, preceding that is still open or that is commenced during the time a claim is pending, the claimant shall obtain an order from the bankruptcy court declaring the judgment and debt to be non-dischargeable.

Excess Funds Used for Education & Research

Money in excess of $100,000 that has accumulated in the fund is to be set aside and segregated. The excess money is to be used by the Real Estate Division in the advancement of education and research in the field of real estate. This includes educational courses sponsored or offered by the division, offered by the division in conjunction with any university or college in the state, or by contracting for a particular research project in the field of real estate.

If the division makes payment from the fund to a judgment creditor, the division has the right to seek repayment to the fund from the licensee. The license of any real estate licensee for whom payment from the fund is made shall be automatically revoked. The licensee may not apply for a new license until the amount paid out on his account, plus interest has been repaid in full.

Review Questions

1. The purpose of the Real Estate Recovery Fund is:

   a. Reimburse damaged consumers.
   b. Reimburse unpaid commissions from consumers
   c. Compensate owners for property damages due to contamination
   d. Compensate apartment owners for methamphetamine contamination cleanup

2. The fund shall have a minimum balance at the beginning of each fiscal year of:

   a. 1,000,000
   b. 10,000
   c. 10,000,000
   d. 100,000

3. Maximum payment from the Real Estate Recovery Fund for any one transaction shall not exceed:

   a. $15,000
   b. $20,000
   c. $30,000
   d. $50,000

4. If the Real Estate Recovery Fund pays a claim the associated licensee shall:

   a. Automatically be fined the maximum amount of $2,500
   b. Automatically have their license revoked.
   c. Automatically have their license placed on probation
   d. Automatically have their license suspended

5. The first step a complainant must take in order to ensure eligibility for payment from the fund is:

   a. Document the collection process
   b. Demonstrate financial hardship
   c. Notify the Division in writing
   d. File a law suit

13. Utah Water Law

Learning Objectives

At the conclusion of this class, the student will be able to:
- Define appropriation
- Identify the department of government where water is appropriated.
- List the eligibility requirements for obtaining water appropriation.
- Explain the consequences of water abandonment.

Water Rights in Utah Historical Background

The Utah law of water rights evolved from the early irrigation practices initiated by the first Mormon pioneers who arrived in the Great Salt Lake Valley in July 1847. These pioneers were the first Anglo-Saxons in the United States to practice irrigation on a large scale. Because of the arid nature of the area, the diversion and application of water to the surrounding land for agricultural purposes made the adoption of the appropriation doctrine a necessity in order to accomplish the settlement of the area.

The pioneers during the first 50 years appropriated water by diverting the water from stream channels and applying it to beneficial use. From 1852 to 1880, the appropriator was required to bring a petition before the county court for a water privilege, which the court could either grant or reject. The appropriator had to have his petition granted prior to any development and subject to any terms imposed in the grant.

In 1880 a statute was enacted which replaced the county court's procedure with an ex officio water commissioner of the county.

He had the authority to measure stream-flow, to determine all claims of right to the use of water, to issue certificates on water rights to parties found to possess vested water rights, and to record certificates and to distribute the water accordingly. However, the 1880 law contained no procedure for making new appropriations. Therefore, in order to appropriate water a person need only divert and apply the water to beneficial use and thereby establish their right. Utah was admitted to the Union as a State on January 4, 1896. The Utah Constitution recognized and confirmed all existing rights to the use of water for any useful and beneficial purpose. **The Legislature subsequently declared all water in the State** *(1903)***, whether above or under the ground** *(1935)***, to be the property of the public, and that beneficial use shall be the basis, the measure, and the limit of all rights to the use of water in this State.** (Utah Code Chapter 73)

In 1897, the Legislature enacted a specific statutory procedure for the future appropriations of water in Utah, which provided for posting of notices, filing them with the county recorder, and commencing and prosecuting the work to completion with reasonable diligence. If the appropriator met all statutory requirements in initiating and consummating his appropriation, the priority related back to the date of the posting notice. However, with the Act of 1897, few appropriators posted notice or filed them with the county recorder, thus making the law useless. Also in 1897, the State Engineer's Office was created, but it had only limited responsibility—mainly in the area of water measurements and distribution.

Current Water Law and Procedures

In 1903, the present method of appropriating water was adopted by the Legislature. Since that time, the Legislature has made minor revisions to the water law. The 1903 Act provided that an appropriation could only be acquired through filing an application with the State Engineer. Due to the development of problems in the use of groundwater, and since the 1903 Act only applied to surface water, in 1935 the Utah Legislature if rights to appropriate groundwater could only be acquired by filing an application with the State Engineer. Since that date both surface and groundwater applications are handled in the same manner.

Application Process

Upon receipt of an application, the State Engineer causes notice to be published in the county where the point of diversion is located. Protests against the application may be submitted within 30 days following the last publication date. If a protest is filed, the State Engineer sets the application for hearing.

Before approving an application, the State Engineer must find that:

a. There is un-appropriated water in the proposed sources
b. The proposed use will not impair existing rights or interfere with the more beneficial use of the water
c. The proposed plan is physically and economically feasible
d. The applicant has the financial ability to complete the proposed works, and the application was filed in good faith and not for purposes of speculation or monopoly.

The State Engineer may reject an application if he determines it will interfere with the more beneficial use of water for other purposes or will prove detrimental to the public welfare or the natural stream environment.

Once an application is approved, the applicant is given a specific time within which to place the water to beneficial uses and submits written proof of appropriation. After the water is placed to beneficial use and the applicant submits proof, the State Engineer issues a certificate of appropriation, which is recorded in the county recorder's office.

The Utah statute allows changes in the point of diversion, place of use, and nature of use of appropriated water. To accomplish such a change, the water user must file a change application with the State Engineer and receive his approval. The approval or rejection of a change application depends on whether or not the proposed change will impair other vested rights.

Recent Additions to Utah Water Law

There have been two recent, and perhaps very important, additions to the Utah water law. The first grants the State Engineer the responsibility to control geothermal development in the State. The second grants the State Engineer the authority to grant applications to appropriate for industrial purposes (energy development) for a fixed period. This fulfills the purpose of the original appropriation, and at the end of which time the water reverts to the State for allocation to other uses. Besides the duties stated above, the State Engineer is to assure proper distribution of existing water rights. In addition, in Utah there is a statutory procedure for the adjudication of existing rights to a stream or other source, including groundwater. Once such an action is initiated, it is the State Engineer's responsibility to investigate the claims, to prepare a hydrographic survey of the area involved, and to assemble the information gathered into a proposed determination of water rights for submission to the court and the individual water users.

Any person aggrieved by a decision of the State Engineer may bring a civil action in the district court for plenary review thereof, within 30 days after notice of the decision.

Available Water Rights Information

In Utah, the Division of Water Rights (the State Engineer's Office) is the office of record for water rights, and a central records and file section is maintained which is public record. The State has been divided into 47 hydrologic basins or sub-basins, and the water rights are filed in the central files, numerically, within the hydrologic basin where they are located.

The water rights on file show the following basic information:
- the applicant's name and address,
- the source of water,
- the flow of C.F.S. (cubic feet per second) or the quantity in acre-feet (43,560 cubic feet),
- the point of diversion and diverting works,
- a description of the use or uses,
- the place of use, the period of use,
- the priority date of the right,
- the status of the right.

The water rights are contained on several different types of forms, but all show the above basic information.

The Division has an extensive database, and water rights can be identified if the file number, the applicant's name, and/or the location of the water right are known. It is possible to identify the water rights in a specific or general area, and to identify those water rights owned by a certain party. Water rights evidenced by decrees, certificates of appropriation, diligence claims, and underground water claims, or by water user's claims filed in a general adjudication, proceeding shall be transferred by deed in the same manner as real estate inasmuch as they are considered real property. *When water rights are represented by shares of stock in a corporation, they are considered personal property and are not appurtenant to the land.* A certified copy of such deed or other instrument transferring title of water rights shall be promptly transmitted to the State Engineer for filing.

There were many decrees entered by the courts during the early 1900's, which define water rights on several river systems in Utah. Copies of the court decrees are on record with the Division of Water Rights. Many of these rights originated prior to the Act of 1903; however, as long as the water user continues to make beneficial use of the water, he is able to maintain a use right with the priority date of when the water was first put to use.

Engineers Determination of Water Availability

As noted earlier, the State Engineer prepares a Proposed Determination of Water Rights for a given hydrologic area for submission to the court in an adjudication proceeding. The proposed determinations are in booklet form, and contain basic information of the water rights in the area. There are approximately 130 completed, partially completed, or proposed determinations, and these are available to the public. Proposed determinations contain alphabetical, numerical and source indexes, in addition to the completed description of the water rights of the water users in the area. In conjunction with a proposed determination, hydrographic survey maps are compiled, showing the points of diversion and irrigated acreage's of the various water rights. In areas where a proposed determination has been prepared, the decreed rights mentioned earlier, and any other diligence rights for which a claim has not been filed, are identified, given a file number, and become part of the proposed determination and central records.

Other information available from the State Engineer's Office concerning water right information includes water well logs and water distribution reports. Well drillers in the State of Utah must be licensed with the Division of Water Rights and are required to file a well log of all water wells drilled. These well logs are kept on the water right file, which covers the well drilled, and they are filed according to the section, township, and range in which the well is located.

To insure that existing water rights are distributed properly, the State Engineer has appointed water commissioners on several rivers and underground sources in the State. These commissioners make measurements of water diverted to each water user in accordance with established rights and submit reports annually to the State Engineer. The commissioners' reports are available for inspection at the Division of Water Rights.

Abandoned Water Rights

Water rights are considered abandoned if they are not used continuously over a 5-year period. Abandoned water reenters the public domain and becomes available for others to use.

Definitions Concerning Water

- **Accretion**: Gradual addition of soil by deposits through natural causes
- **Alluvion:** The actual increase of soil deposited on a shore or bank of a river through the process of accretion
- **Avulsion:** The sudden or violent loss of soil caused by the action of water
- **Riparian:** Person owns the land where the water right is either on, or under or adjacent to the land adjacent to a river.*
- **Littoral:** Person owns the land where the water right is either under or adjacent to a lake or ocean.*

Utah water riparian and littoral rights extend only to the land but not the water. Water is prior appropriated in Utah. A person with property adjacent to a water body only has rights to the land by the appropriate definition; no water rights are connected to these definitions in Utah.

- **Acre-Foot:** An acre of water one-foot deep, 43,560 cubic feet this unit of measure is used to measure irrigation water. The quantity needed to water an acre of ground with 12 inches of water per year.
- **CFPS** Cubic feet per second of water passing a given location this unit of measure is used to measure the volume of a flowing stream.

Review Questions

1. Application for water rights in Utah must be made to the State _____.

2. To be eligible for water rights you must show that the water will be put to a _____ use.

3. The state Engineer must determine what quantities of water are _____ for appropriation.

4. Once water has been appropriated the right to the water may be lost if its use is _____.

5. The state Engineer needs to determine if all the water in the source you are requesting water from has been _____ _____.

14. Land Sales Practices

Learning Objectives:

Upon completion of this chapter, the student should be able to:

- State the general purpose the Land Sales Practices Act.
- List at least three exceptions to the act.
- Name the registration agency for property regulated by the act.
- List at least four property conditions that must be disclosed in compliance with the act.

Utah Uniform Land Sales Practices Act

This could have been called the "Subdivision Act." It covers any land being offered as a subdivision by a single developer or group of developers of 10 or more lots. Subdivisions of nine or less lots would not be covered by this act. The best way to describe what circumstances are covered by this act is to list its exceptions.

Exemptions

- The Land Sales Practices Act does not apply to land sales:
- By a purchaser of subdivided lands for his own account in a single or isolated transaction;

- On each unit of which there is a residential, commercial, or industrial building, or on each unit of which there is a legal obligation on the part of the seller to complete construction of such a building within two years from date of disposition;
- To any person who acquires the land for use in the business of constructing residential, commercial, or industrial buildings, or to any person buying the land with the intention of selling to a person engaged in that business, unless the person who acquires land for these purposes sells that land to individuals as unimproved lots with no legal obligation on the part of the seller to construct a residential, commercial, or industrial building on that lot within two years from the date of disposition;
- Pursuant to court order;
- By any government or government agency;
- If the land lies within the boundaries of a first, second, or third class city or a county which:
  a) Has a planning and zoning board utilizing or employing at least one professional planner;
  b) Enacts ordinances that require approval of planning, zoning, and plats, including the approval of plans for streets, culinary water, sanitary sewer, and flood control; and
  c) In which the interest in land will have the improvements described in b) above plus telephone and electricity;
- In an industrial park;
- As cemetery lots; or
- If the interest is offered as part of a camp resort or a timeshare development

Registration

If the property is not exempt then the seller must **register** the property with the Division of Real Estate prior to offering the land for sale. The Division will issue a permit to sell the land to the registrant. The application for Registration must contain the following documents:

1. Irrevocable appointment of the Division to receive service of any lawful process against the applicant or his representatives

2. Legal description together with map, streets, improvements and units
3. States or jurisdictions where the application was filed
4. Applicants name, address, jurisdiction of organization, address of each of its offices, and the representative designated for communication
5. Statement of the condition of the title including encumbrances
6. Copies of all documents a purchaser will sign.
7. Copies of all document creating easements, restrictions and encumbrances.
8. Statement of zoning and other governmental regulation
9. Statement of provisions for water, sewage and other public utilities
10. Statement of any improvements and estimated costs to the purchaser
11. Description of the promotional plan including all advertising material
12. Copy of the proposed public offering statement

Public Offering Statement

The Division of Real Estate must approve the Public Offering Statement

- The statement must **disclose the physical characteristics** of the offered subdivided land.
- The statement must always be **used in its entirety**.
- The statement must be **given to every potential buyer**. The agent must obtain a receipt from the buyer as proof that the statement was provided. This receipt must be kept on file for two years.
- The Public Offering Statement shall include the following statement:

Right To Cancel
YOU HAVE THE OPTION TO CANCEL YOUR CONTRACT OR AGREEMENT OF DISPOSITION BY NOTICE TO THE SELLER UNTIL MIDNIGHT OF THE FIFTH CALENDAR DAY FOLLOWING THE SIGNING OF THE CONTRACT OR AGREEMENT. WRITTEN NOTICE OF CANCELLATION MUST BE PERSONALLY DELIVERED OR SENT BY CERTIFIED MAIL, POSTMARKED BY MIDNIGHT OF THE FIFTH CALENDAR DAY FOLLOWING THE SIGNING OF THE CONTRACT OR AGREEMENT, TO THE SELLER AT:
(Address of Seller)

Penalties

Any person who willfully violates this act or makes an untrue statement of material fact is subject to the following:

- Division investigation in order to protect the public interest and issue a 'Cease and Desist" order.
- Fine up to $1,000 or double the amount of gain from the transaction but not to exceed $50,000, imprisonment for not more than (2) years, or both.

1. The act affects _____ sales with _____ or more lots.

2. Examples of properties not subject to the act are:

    a) Lots with _____ on them at the time of sale.

    b) Lots with a contract to build buildings on the land within _____ year of purchase.

    c) Property located in _____, _____, or _____ class cities.

    d) Ind _____ parks.

    e) C_____ lots

3. The _____ _____ statement must be included as part of the application. This statement discloses to the potential buyer the details of the property.

4. All buyers or potential buyers must be given the Public _____ _____ , which includes the _____ day right to _____ statement.

5. Properties under this act must be registered with the _____ ___ _____

6. The Land Sales Practices Act was designed to provide
   a. Protection to the public through disclosure
   b. Detailed procedures to be followed in the sales of business and industrial property
   c. Penalties for selling to persons not represented by competent legal counsel
   d. Specific practices required for the development of 1 to 5 parcels of land

7. The Land Sales Practices Act does not cover
   a. Property that already has all of the improvements the seller intends to provide
   b. Property purchased by a developer intending to build cabins for sale to the public.
   c. Property located outside of second class cities
   d. Property located in any city boundary

8. The Land Sales Practices Act was intended to regulate;
   a. The sale of cemetery lots
   b. Property sold to government agencies
   c. Properties located in first, second or third class cities.
   d. Property sold in largely unregulated locales.

9. The Five Day Right of Rescission is a feature in all of the following circumstances except:
    a. Purchase of a time-share RV space
    b. One acre lot offered in a development of 100 lots located in a county with no planning and zoning board or with a professional planner
    c. Purchase of time-share condominiums
    d. The purchase of a warehouse

10. A public offering statement is associated with;
    a. Land Sales Practices Act
    b. Marketable Records Title Act
    c. Utah Exemptions Act
    d. Mechanic's lien Law

11. Buyers of parcels that are governed by the Land Sales Practices Act are entitled to
    a. The guaranteed installation of roads and sewers
    b. A process to file grievances against agents who represent sellers of protected property
    c. A five-day right of rescission
    d. Restrictions on the size of parcels sold without water

12. The Land Sales Practices Act does not cover
    a. Property of 20 acres or more
    b. Property divided into 10 or more lots
    c. Property located in Ogden City
    d. Property outside city boundaries

13. K bought a property on Friday of Labor Day weekend and it was subject to the Land Sales Practices Act. K may cancel the sale by sending a letter postmarked
    a. The second Monday from the date of purchase
    b. Wednesday next after purchase
    c. Tuesday next after purchase
    d. The second Tuesday after the date of purchase

15. Time Share/ Camp Resort

Learning Objectives:	Upon completion of this chapter, the student should be able to: • Explain which properties are subject to the Timeshare and Camp Resort Act. • Identify who must register with the Division of Real Estate under the act. • Define the purchasers' right to cancel. • List three items that must be disclosed when presenting property under the act.
Timeshare and Camp Resort ACT	"Timeshare interest" means a right to occupy accommodations during three or more separate times over a period of at least three years, including renewal options, whether or not coupled with an estate in land. It includes what is commonly known as a "timeshare estate," which is a small-undivided fractional fee interest in real property by which the purchaser does not receive any right to use accommodations except as provided by contract, declaration, or other instrument defining a legal right. Camp Resorts are similar to Time Shares except for the right to allow a campsite.
Unregistered sales prohibited.	Except for exempt transactions, it is unlawful for any person to offer or sell in this state an interest in a project unless the project is registered under this chapter.

Registration

A person may apply for registration of a project by filing with the Director of the Department of Real Estate. The application must include:

1. The written disclosure required to be furnished to prospective purchasers.
2. Financial statements and other information that the director may require
3. Interests in a project which are encumbered by liens, mortgages, or other encumbrances may not be accepted for registration or offered for disposition to the public unless adequate release or non-disturbance clauses are contained in the encumbering instruments to reasonably assure that the purchaser's interest in the project will not be defeated

Each application for registration of a project shall be accompanied by:

1. A filing fee of $500 for up to 100 interests, plus an additional $3 per interest for each interest over 100, up to a maximum of $2,500 for each application; and
2. A deposit of $300 to cover all on-site inspection costs and expenses incurred by the division

Disclosure required

A written disclosure must be provided to any potential purchaser before any money changes hands. The written disclosure must be on the property report form required by the division and shall include:

1. The name and address of the developer;
2. A statement whether or not the developer has ever been:
   a. Convicted of a felony, or any misdemeanor involving theft, fraud, or dishonesty; or
   b. Enjoined from, assessed any civil penalty for, or found to have engaged in the violation of any law designed to protect consumers;
3. A brief description of the developer's experience in timeshare, camp resort, or any other real estate development;
4. A brief description of the interest which is being offered in the project;
5. A description of any provisions to protect the purchaser's interest from loss due to foreclosure on any underlying financial obligation of the project;

136

6. A statement of the maximum number of interests in the project to be marketed, and a commitment that this maximum number will not be exceeded unless disclosed by filing an amendment to the registration prior to offering additional interests for sale;

7. Any event which has occurred as of the date of the offer which may have a material adverse effect on the operation of the project;

8. Any other information the director considers necessary for the protection of purchasers.

Purchaser's right to cancel

An agreement to purchase an interest in a project may be cancelled, at the option of the purchaser, if:

- The purchaser provides to the developer, by hand delivery or certified mail, written notice of the cancellation; and

- The notice is delivered or postmarked no later than midnight of the fifth calendar day following the day on which the agreement is signed.

In computing the number of calendar days for purposes of this section, the day on which the agreement was signed and legal holidays are not included as "calendar days."

Within 30 days after receipt of timely notice of cancellation, the developer shall refund any money or other consideration paid by the purchaser.

Every agreement to purchase an interest in a Timeshare or Camp Resort Property shall include the following statement in at least ten-point bold upper-case type, immediately preceding the space for the purchaser's signature:

Right to Cancel

YOU MAY CANCEL THIS AGREEMENT WITHOUT ANY CANCELLATION FEE OR OTHER PENALTY BY HAND DELIVERING OR SENDING BY CERTIFIED MAIL WRITTEN NOTICE OF CANCELLATION TO: (NAME AND ADDRESS OF DEVELOPER). THE NOTICE MUST BE DELIVERED OR POSTMARKED BY MIDNIGHT OF THE FIFTH CALENDAR DAY FOLLOWING THE DAY ON WHICH THE AGREEMENT IS SIGNED. IN COMPUTING THE NUMBER OF CALENDAR DAYS, THE DAY ON WHICH THE CONTRACT IS SIGNED AND LEGAL HOLIDAYS ARE NOT INCLUDED:

(Address of Seller)

**Registration
Of
Salesperson**

It is unlawful for any person to act as a salesperson marketing a project in this state without first registering under this chapter as a salesperson.

The division waives the fee for registration as a salesperson for licensed Real Estate Agents

Exemptions

Unless entered into for evading the provisions requiring registration, the following transactions are exempt:

- **Isolated transactions** by an owner of an interest in a project or by a person holding such an owner's executed power of attorney;
- An offer or sale by a **governmental entity**; and
- **A bona fide pledge** of interest in a project

Review Questions

1. Sales agents, whether licensed or not, must _____ with the Division of Real Estate.

2. Buyers have a _____ day

   _____ __

   _____ just like buyers under the Land Sales Practices Act.

3. Sales agents selling time-share condominiums must
   a. Be licensed with the state if the sales will take place on the premises
   b. Be registered with the state
   c. Be resident agents
   d. Be certified by a separate test

4. To offer Time-share properties for sale in the state you must
   a. Hire only licensed sales agents
   b. Own all property offered for sale without debt
   c. Provide crossover agreements for use of other time-share properties
   d. Register the property with the state and provide an offering statement

16. Mechanic's Liens

Learning Objectives

Upon completion of this chapter, the student should be able to:

- Explain the definition of a mechanic.
- List those who may qualify as a mechanic.
- List several time frames in connection with Utah Mechanic's Lien law.
- Identify the lien rights of a contractor working of a single-family residence under a contract that has been paid in full.

Mechanic's Lien Law

This law is a law of equity (justice). When work is done or materials furnished the owner of property benefits in that the value of the property is better than before the work or materials were furnished. The owner therefore gets the benefit of the contribution. It is only just that the contribution be paid for. No one is entitled to take from another without just payment. Inadvertent failure to pay such as a new owner that was not aware of the work or need to pay, still receives the benefit. It is only just that those who supply the benefit should be paid.

Documenting the payment of suppliers and contractors is the only way to avoid the penalties of liens that were filed unjustly. All payments given should be exchanged for a **lien waiver** in which would effectively remove the lien rights of any provider by their admitting that they have been paid for their services. Lien wavers are standard practice in the construction industry.

Sometimes liens are filed due to delays in payment. To document the payment in full of these providers the owner should obtain a lien release in exchange for payment. The lien release then is delivered to the County Recorder's office to document the satisfaction of the lien. The County Recorder will then indicate in the property record that the lien has been satisfied.

Contractors and subcontractors

Any person who does work or furnishes materials by contract, express or implied, with the owner, as provided in this chapter, shall be considered an original contractor and all other persons doing work or furnishing materials shall be considered subcontractors. A subcontractor has its contract with the contractor not the owner.

Those entitled to lien

1. Contractors, subcontractors, and all persons performing any services or furnishing or renting any materials or equipment used in the construction, alteration, or improvement of any building or structure
2. Architects and engineers and artisans who have furnished designs, plats, plans, maps, specifications, drawings, estimates of cost, surveys or superintendence, or who have rendered other like professional service, or bestowed labor
3. Except as the Residence Lien Restriction and Lien Recovery Fund Act bar the lien

Priority over other encumbrances

1. The liens take effect as of, the time of the commencement to do work or furnish materials on the ground for the structure or improvement.
2. Take priority over any lien, mortgage or other encumbrance, which may have attached subsequently to the time when the building, improvement or structure was commenced, work begun, or first material furnished on the ground.
3. Take priority over any lien, mortgage or other encumbrance of which the lien holder had no notice and which was unrecorded at the time the building, structure or improvement was commenced, work begun, or first material furnished on the ground.

Priority over claims of creditors of original contractor or subcontractor

Claims against an original contractor may not attach to or prevent liens filed by:

1. Subcontractors
2. Material men
3. Design services

Claims against subcontractors may not prevent liens filed by laborers employed by the day or piece. Laborers by the day or piece are entitled to lien in their own right. A subcontractor may not attempt to circumvent that right by attempting to attach the laborers lien.

State Construction Registry

During the 2004 State legislative session, House Bill 136, Sixth Substitute, Electronic Filing of Preliminary Lien Documents was passed and put into law. The new legislation modified the Mechanics' Lien statute and called for the development of a standardized, statewide system for filing and managing preliminary notices, as well as notices of commencement and notices of completion.

The Utah Construction Registry is an online project "bulletin board" providing full disclosure to property owners, contractors, and other interested parties, of people providing goods and services to a construction project. By providing a centralized resource for project participant information, the State Construction Registry (REGISTRY) will help property owners minimize unknown project liability and risk.

Another function of the REGISTRY program is to implement an efficient and standardized system for protecting lien rights associated with all types of construction projects - residential, public and commercial projects. The REGISTRY will be the exclusive system for filing and managing preliminary notices and will provide a suite of automated and streamlined services.

A designated agent, Utah Interactive, under the oversight of the Division of Occupational and Professional Licensing, administers the full Utah Construction Registry system.

The Registry Web address is http://www.scr.utah.gov.

The initial entry of a project on the Construction Registry may be made by:
- The owner of record
- The general contractor
- The government agency issuing the building permit will enter the project on the Registry as a part of the permit process.

The Registry is indexed by:
- owner name;
- original contractor name;
- subdivision, development, or other project name, if any;
- project address;
- lot or parcel number;
- unique project number assigned by the designated agent; and
- Any other identifier that the division considers reasonably appropriate in collaboration with the designated agent

The Registry is classified as a public record. It has the following provisions:

- Privately owned as well as all state and local government owned construction projects require the filing of preliminary notices and allow for the filing of notices of commencement and notices of completion.
- Notices of Commencement will be automatically filed by the Registry upon permit data submission from each city or county permitting office for projects requiring a building permit. Permitting agencies are required to submit building permit information to the Registry within 15 days of issuing a permit. For projects in which a Notice of Commencement is not automatically filed, owners and original contractors may file a Commencement in order to enforce the preliminary notice requirement. Examples: state projects in which permits are not issued, exempt projects, projects in which a municipality fails to transmit permit data.
- Preliminary notices must be filed through the Registry system in order to preserve lien rights. Parties required to file preliminary notices may not maintain a valid lien

if a preliminary notice was not filed through the Registry within the proper timeframe.

- First tier subcontractors (as well as lower tier subcontractors) must file preliminary notices in order to protect lien rights.
- Upon completion of a construction project, a notice of completion may be filed through the Construction Registry. Once a notice of completion is filed, participating parties have only 10 days to file preliminary notices. If a valid Notice of Completion is filed through the Registry, the window for filing a lien is 90 days. If a valid Notice of Completion is not filed the window for filing a lien is extended to 180 days. This applies to both residential and commercial construction projects.

Time Line

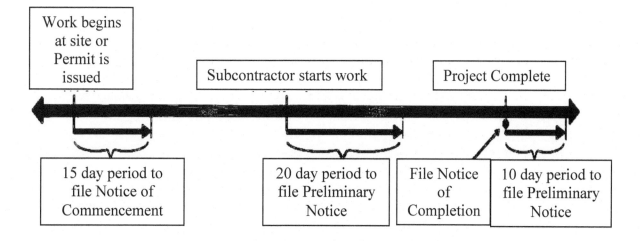

Notices of Commencement

Key Dates & Details:

Notices of Commencement must be filed within 15 days of commencement of physical work or the issuance of a building permit. If a Notice of Commencement is not filed within the 15-

day window, the preliminary notice requirement is voided and lien rights are automatically preserved.

For the majority of projects, Notices of Commencement are automatically filed in the SCR based on permit data received from the issuing municipalities. For projects in which a Notice of Commencement is not automatically filed, owners and original contractors may file a Commencement in order to enforce the preliminary notice requirement. Examples: state projects in which permits are not issued, exempt projects, projects in which a municipality fails to transmit permit data.

Preliminary Notices

Preliminary notices must be filed within 20 days of furnishing labor, service, material and/or equipment OR within 20 days of the filing of the notice of commencement, whichever comes later.

The timeline for filing a preliminary notice is affected by the filing of a Notice of Completion. The window for filing Preliminary Notices is closed 10 days after the filing of a Notice of Completion. Therefore, parties providing goods and services at the end of a project may have less than 20 days to file their Preliminary Notice (party providing materials 2 days prior to the filing of a Notice of Completion only have 12 days total to file a Preliminary Notice).

A party that misses their initial 20-day window may still file a Preliminary Notice to protect future work and / or materials. If a Preliminary Notice is filed after the initial 20-day period passes, there is a 5-day penalty and any material and / or service provided after the penalty period is protected.

Notices of Completion

Notices of completion may be filed by owners, original contractors, lenders, surety or title companies any time after one of the following conditions has been met:

- A permanent certificate of occupancy has been issued
- A final inspection has been completed
- All substantial work has been completed

Notice of Claim

A person claiming benefits under this chapter shall file for record with the county recorder of the county in which the property, or some part of the property, is situated, a written notice to hold and claim a lien:

6. within 90 days of "Notice of Completion" listed in the Construction Registry
7. within 180 days from last performed labor or service or last furnished equipment or material on a project

Work performed or materials supplied on a project that has not been listed on the Construction Registry are still lean able based on last date of work on the project.

Projects that are listed on the Construction Registry have lien rights available only to those workmen or suppliers who have entered data into the registry in connection with a project.

Enforcement

A mechanic's lien is enforced by petitioning the court for the right to sell the property. A lien claimant shall file an action to enforce the lien filed under this chapter within:

180 days from the filing of
"Notice of Claim"

Lis Pendens (action pending notice)

Within the time period provided for filing the lien claimant shall file for record with the county recorder of each county in which the lien is recorded a notice that an action is pending or the lien shall be void.

Burden of Proof

The burden of proof lies with the claimant. (Contractor, laborer, material man, designer, etc)

Abuse of Lien Right

Any person entitled to record or file a lien is guilty of a class B misdemeanor who intentionally causes a claim of lien against any property, which contains a greater demand than the sum due to be recorded or filed:

1. With the intent to cloud the title;
2. To exact from the owner or person liable by means of the excessive claim of lien more than is due; or
3. To procure any unjustified advantage or benefit.

Residence Lien Restriction and Lien Recovery Fund

In 1994, the Utah Legislature passed the Residence Lien Restriction and Lien Recovery Fund Act. The Act was amended and funded in 1995, became effective on May 1, 1995, was amended again in 1996, 1997, and 1998, and is currently being implemented and enforced by the Utah Department of Commerce's Division of Occupational and Professional Licensing.

The Act has two primary functions

1. The Act prohibits anyone who provides services or materials for residential housing construction from:
   - maintaining a mechanic's lien against a residence
   - obtaining a civil judgment against a homeowner for construction expenses
   - provided the homeowner complies with the following requirements:
     a. The homeowner must enter into a written contract with a licensed contractor, a contractor exempt from licensure, or a real estate developer for construction on or the purchase of a single family or duplex residence

      b. The homeowner must pay the contractor or real estate developer in full according to the terms of the written contract and any amendments to the contract.

2. Act creates the Residence Lien Recovery Fund. The Fund is a last-resort source of payment for persons, including subcontractors, suppliers, and laborers, who can no longer recover for goods and services by bringing mechanic's liens against residential property or by bringing civil action against the homeowner.

1. Indicate which of the following may file a mechanic's lien:

   Yes   No
   ___   ___   a) Material men
   ___   ___   b) Real Estate Agents
   ___   ___   c) General Contractors
   ___   ___   d) Brokers
   ___   ___   e) Laborers
   ___   ___   f) Architects
   ___   ___   g) Subcontractors

2. These liens may only be filed against a property that actual _____, _____ or professional design services were supplied.

3. Mechanic's liens take priority over _____ recorded after work on the property commenced.

4. Mechanic's liens must be filed within ____ days after Certificate of Completion has been issued on a job that has been listed on the State Construction Registry.

5. Prosecution in court of the lien must begin within ____ days of Notice of Lien.

6. If payment is made after the lien is filed the person filing the lien must provide a Lien _____.

7. On any construction project, when work is paid for the owner should request a _____ Waiver.

8. Filing a lien that exceeds the actual debt constitutes a _____.

9. The only method of enforcement for mechanic's liens is to _____ in court.

17.   Utah Homestead Law

Learning objectives:

Upon completion of this chapter, the student should be able to:

- Determine who is eligible to file a Declaration of Homestead
- List the types of properties eligible to be exempt.
- Explain what Exempt properties are protected from.

Utah Exemptions Homestead Exemption Act

Definitions:

- **Household** means a group of persons related by blood or marriage living together in the same dwelling as an economic unit, sharing furnishings, facilities, accommodations, and expenses;
- **Primary personal residence** means a dwelling or mobile home and the land surrounding it, not exceeding one acre, as is reasonably necessary for the use of the dwelling or mobile home, in which the individual and the individual's household reside; and
- **Property means:**
- A primary personal residence
- Real property
- An equitable interest in real property awarded to a person in a divorce decree by a court.

Entitlement

An individual is entitled to a homestead exemption consisting of property in this state in an amount not exceeding:

- **Non-personal residence:** $5,000 in value if the property consists in whole or in part of property which is not the primary personal residence of the individual; or jointly owned property up to $10,000 per household.
- **Personal Residence:** $30,000 in value if the property claimed is the primary personal residence of the individual or jointly owned property up to $60,000 per household.
- **Multiple parcels allowed:** A person may claim a homestead exemption in one or more parcels of real property together with appurtenances and improvements.

Exemption from what?:

A homestead is exempt from judicial lien and from levy, execution, or forced sale except for:

- Statutory liens for property taxes and assessments on the property;
- Security interests in the property and judicial liens for debts created for the purchase price of the property;
- Judicial liens obtained on debts created by failure to provide support or maintenance for dependent children; and
- Consensual liens obtained on debts created by mutual contract.

Water Rights: Water right may be included in the claim of exemption so long as the water right is necessarily employed in supplying water to the homestead for domestic and irrigation purposes. Water rights held through the ownership of stock in a water corporation are not exempt from legal actions against the corporation issuing the stock.

Conveyance of exempt property:

- When the owner of the property conveys a homestead, the conveyance may not subject the property to any lien to which it would not be subject in the hands of the owner.

The proceeds of any sale, to the amount of the exemption existing at the time of sale, is exempt from levy, execution, or other process for one year after the receipt of the proceeds by the person entitled to the exemption.

Perpetual Homestead Right

The sale and disposition of one homestead does not prevent the selection or purchase of another.

Status of Homestead with Internal Revenue Service

For purposes of any claim or action for taxes brought by the United States Internal Revenue Service, a homestead exemption claimed on real property in this state is considered to be a property right.

Declaration of Homestead

An individual may select and claim a homestead by complying with the following requirements:
(1) Filing a signed and acknowledged declaration of homestead with the recorder of the county or counties in which the homestead claimant's property is located or serving a signed and acknowledged declaration of homestead upon the sheriff or other officer conducting an execution prior to the time stated in the notice of such execution.
(2) The declaration of homestead shall contain a statement that the claimant is entitled to an exemption and if the claimant is married a statement that the claimant's spouse has not filed a declaration of homestead:
- A description of the property subject to the homestead;
- An estimate of the cash value of such property; and
- A statement specifying the amount of the homestead claimed and stating the name, age, and address of any spouse and dependents claimed to determine **the value of the homestead.**

If a declaration of homestead is not filed or served as provided in this section, title shall pass to the purchaser upon execution free and clear of all homestead rights.

If an individual is married, both spouses must join in the declaration of homestead interest Property that includes a homestead cannot be sold in a court ordered sale if there is no bid, which exceeds the amount of the declared homestead exemption

Review Questions

1. Homestead Exemption may be claimed on both _____ and non-residential property.

2. Property held in joint ownership is eligible for:
    a. up to $60,000 if primary residence per household
    b. up to $60,000 regardless of property type.
    c. up to $30,00 if primary residence per household
    d. up to $10,000 if primary residence per household.

3. In order to claim the exemption for a particular property you must file a

_____ _____.

4. Homestead Declarations must be filed with the _____ _____ office.

5. The Utah Exemptions Act protects property from: (True or False)

   ____ Mortgage Liens
   ____ Recorded Easements
   ____ Judicial Liens (Court Judgments)
   ____ Child support payments
   ____ 2nd Mortgage Liens
   ____ Mechanic's liens

18. Marketable Records Act

Learning Objectives:	Upon completion of this chapter, the student should be able to: • Recite the time required for the act to affect a property. • Name the Primary Base Line and the Primary Meridian used for most of Utah • List key dates in the property tax law of Utah
Learning Objectives	Upon completion of this chapter, the student should be able to: • Recite the time required for the act to affect a property. • Name the Primary Base Line and the Primary Meridian used for most of Utah • List key dates in the property tax law of Utah.
Utah Marketable Records Title Act	Marketable title is a good or clear salable title reasonably free from risk of litigation over possible defects. Marketable title does not necessarily mean a perfect title, just one that is free from plausible or reasonable objection. A seller under contract of sale is required to deliver marketable title. Over time, defects can attach to a title due to acts of the owner or others. Some of these defects may no longer be justified due to the passage of time or a change in circumstances that make them unnecessary, inappropriate or unjust. Utah has a law intended to remove defects that have been many years in affect but not enforced or utilized.

What constitutes marketable record title?

Any person having the legal capacity to own land in this state, who has an unbroken chain of title of record to any interest in land for **forty years** or more, shall be deemed to have a *marketable record title* to such interest. A property must be held by one entity for the entire 40-year period to establish the *marketable record title.*

This act extinguishes (makes void) encumbrances that existed at least 40 years previous. Only encumbrances that have been dormant the entire 40-year period are subject to become extinguished. The purpose of this act is to clear old encumbrances thus making the title records easier to research, and to put a limit on the length of time an encumbrance can affect the title of the property. Encumbrances that have been an integral part of the property from the beginning of the 40-year period are not affected. Examples of this type of encumbrance are utility, pipeline, highway, and railroad easements. These types of encumbrance are entered in the title record once and would not show any activity but would most likely be in use. They qualify as an exception to this act for that reason. Other encumbrances would be extinguished however. Such things as liens recording a lender interest as the result of a loan for example may never have been released after the debt was paid. This act extinguishes those liens because they have not been enforced in a timely manner. Another example would be a party that claims they hold an interest in the property because of some circumstance or action that occurred over 40 years ago would also be extinguished by this act.

This act has no effect on landlord / tenant agreements. A landlord may lease a property for over 40 years but when the lease expires, the property would still revert to the landlord. This act would have no affect even though a lease qualifies as an encumbrance. Landlord / tenant agreements are exempt.

Utah Base Line and Prime Meridian

Legal Descriptions in Utah are based on the rectangular survey method. When Brigham Young entered the valley, one of the first tasks he set out to do was identify the reference point for a land survey. He wanted land identified by an accurate legal description to avoid confusion and conflict. He marked the intersection point of the Base Line and Prime Meridian in the soil with a stone monument. The stone monument has since been replaced by a brass marker set in the concrete of the sidewalk. The monument was located at what is now known as the North West corner of South Temple and Main Street in downtown Salt Lake City. The Base Line is known as the **Salt Lake Base Line**. The Prime Meridian is known as the **Salt Lake Prime Meridian**.

Utah Property Taxes

Utah property tax is collected at the county level. Each county has an assessor. The assessor is responsible for valuing property parcels and assessing a fair and appropriate tax on each. Property is valued and assessed on January 1 of each year. The anticipated assessment is mailed to each property owner in July of the year previous. This allows disputes to be resolved prior to the assessment date.

Taxes are assessed on January 1st and payable no later than November 30 of the same year. Taxes become delinquent on December 1. Each county assessor's office closes to public access on December 1 through January 2. A list of delinquent taxes and the owners associated with the delinquency is published in local papers in January.

Review Questions

1. The statutory period that must pass before the act becomes effective is _____ years.
    a. 20
    b. 50
    c. 40
    d. 30

2. The act was created to clear old encumbrances from title records.
        True   False

3. The central monument marking the intersection of the Salt Lake Prime Meridian and the Salt Lake Base Line is located at:
    a. South Temple and Main Street, Salt Lake City
    b. South East Corner of Utah State Capital Building
    c. State Street and South Temple, Salt Lake City
    d. Main Street and North Temple, Salt Lake City

4. Property Taxes become delinquent on:
    a. December 1
    b. November 30
    c. December 31
    d. January 1

5. The Marketable Records Title Act would extinguish which of the following:
    a. 51 year old mortgage
    b. Railroad easement
    c. Pipeline easement
    d. Ingress/egress right of way

19. Utah Landlord Tenant Law

Learning Objectives

At the Conclusion of this chapter, the student will be able to:
- Identify three duties of a landlord to provide fit premises.
- List two tenant responsibilities.
- List the four steps to eviction.

Fit Premises Act Definitions

Owner	The owner, lessor, or sublessor of a residential rental unit. A managing agent, leasing agent, or resident manager is also considered an owner for purposes of notice and other communication unless the agent or manager specifies otherwise in writing in the rental agreement.
Rental agreement	Any agreement, written or oral, which establishes or modifies the terms, conditions, rules, or any other provisions regarding the use and occupancy of a residential rental unit.
Renter	Any person entitled under a rental agreement to occupy a residential rental unit to the exclusion of others.
Residential rental unit	A renter's principal place of residence including appurtenances, grounds, and facilities held out for the use of the residential renter generally, and any other area or facility provided to the renter in the rental agreement. It does not include facilities contained in a boarding or rooming house or similar facility.

Duties of owners and renters – Generally

Each owner and his agent renting or leasing a residential rental unit shall maintain that unit in a condition fit for human habitation and in accordance with local ordinances and rules. Each residential rental unit shall have electrical systems, heating, plumbing, and hot and cold water.

- Each renter shall cooperate in maintaining his residential rental unit in accordance with this chapter.
- This chapter does not apply to breakage, malfunctions, or other conditions, which do not materially affect the physical health or safety of the ordinary renter.
- Any duty in this act may be allocated to a different party by explicit written agreement signed by the parties.

Owner's duties

To protect the physical health and safety of the ordinary renter, each owner shall:
- Only rent the premises when they are safe, sanitary, and fit for human occupancy
- Maintain common areas of the residential rental unit in a sanitary and safe condition
- Maintain electrical systems, plumbing, heating, and hot and cold water
- Maintain other appliances and facilities as specifically contracted in the lease agreement
- For buildings containing more than two residential rental units, provide and maintain appropriate receptacles for garbage and other waste and arrange for its removal, except to the extent that renters and owners otherwise agree.

In the event the renter believes the residential rental unit does not comply with the standards for health and safety required under this chapter, the renter shall:
- Give written notice of the noncompliance to the owner.
- Within a reasonable time, as determined by the court,
- After receipt of this notice, the owner shall commence action to correct the condition of the unit.

Renter Caused condition

The owner need not correct or remedy **any condition caused by the renter**, the renter's family, or the renter's guests or invitees by inappropriate use or misuse of the property during the rental term or any extension of it.

The owner may refuse to correct the condition of the residential rental unit and terminate the rental agreement if the unit is unfit for occupancy. If the owner refuses to correct the condition and intends to terminate the rental agreement, he shall:

- Notify the renter in writing
- Within a reasonable time after receipt of the notice of noncompliance.
- If the rental agreement is terminated, the rent paid shall be prorated to the date the agreement is terminated, and any balance shall be refunded to the renter along with any deposit due.
- The owner is not liable under this chapter for claims for mental suffering or anguish.

Renter's duties

Each renter shall:

- Comply with the rules of the board of health having jurisdiction in the area in which the residential rental unit is located which materially affect physical health and safety
- Maintain the premises occupied in a clean and safe condition and shall not unreasonably burden any common area
- Dispose of all garbage and other waste in a clean and safe manner
- Maintain all plumbing fixtures in as sanitary a condition as the fixtures permit
- Use all electrical, plumbing, sanitary, heating, and other facilities and appliances in a reasonable manner
- Occupy the residential rental unit in the manner for which it was designed, but the renter may not increase the number of occupants above that specified in the rental agreement without written permission of the owner
- Be current on all payments required by the rental agreement
- Comply with all appropriate requirements of the rental agreement between the owner and the renter, which may include a prohibition on, or the allowance of, smoking tobacco products within the residential rental unit, or on the premises, or both.

Renter Don'ts

The Renter may not:
- Intentionally or negligently destroy, deface, damage, impair, or remove any part of the residential rental unit or knowingly permit any person to do so
- Interfere with the peaceful enjoyment of the residential rental unit of another renter
- Unreasonably deny access to, refuse entry to, or withhold consent to enter the residential rental unit to the owner, agent, or manager for the purpose of making repairs to the unit

Crime victim's right to new locks

For purposes of this section, "crime victim" means a victim of:
- Domestic violence
- Stalking
- Sexual Offenses
- Burglary or aggravated burglary
- Dating violence, consisting of verbal, emotional, psychological, physical, or sexual abuse of one person by another in a dating relationship

An acceptable form of documentation would include:
- A protective order protecting the renter issued pursuant the Cohabitant Abuse Act
- A copy of a police report documenting a crime listed above

A renter who is a crime victim may require the rental unit owner to install a new lock to the renter's residential rental unit if the renter:
- Provides the owner with an acceptable form of documentation
- Pays for the cost of installing the new lock

An owner may comply by:
- Rekeying the lock if the lock is in good working condition
- Changing the entire locking mechanism with a locking mechanism of equal or greater quality than the lock being replaced

An owner who installs a new lock may retain a copy of the key that opens the new lock.

Notwithstanding any rental agreement, an owner who installs a new lock shall refuse to provide a copy of the key that opens the new lock to the perpetrator of the crime triggering the lock change. This includes refusing to provide a key to a perpetrator who also happens to be entitled to access under any lease agreement. If an owner refuses to provide a copy of the key to a perpetrator who is not barred from the residential rental unit by a protective order but is a renter on the rental agreement, the perpetrator may file a petition with a court of competent jurisdiction within 30 days to:

- Establish whether the perpetrator should be given a key and allowed access to the residential rental unit
- Whether the perpetrator should be relieved of further liability under the rental agreement because of the owner's exclusion of the perpetrator from the residential rental unit
- A perpetrator may not be relieved of further liability under the rental agreement if the perpetrator is found by the court to have committed the act upon which the landlord's exclusion of the perpetrator is based.

Renter's remedies

A renter is not entitled to the remedies set forth in this section unless the renter complies with all provisions the relevant lease agreement

If a reasonable time has elapsed after the renter has served written notice on the owner and the condition described in the notice has not been corrected, the renter may cause a "notice to repair or correct condition" to be prepared and served on the owner. This notice shall:

- Recite the previous notice served
- Recite the number of days that have elapsed since the notice was served and state that under the circumstances such a period of time constitutes the reasonable time allowed
- State the conditions included in the previous notice which have not been corrected
- Make demand that the uncorrected conditions be corrected
- State that in the event of failure of the owner to commence reasonable corrective action within three days the renter will seek redress in the courts.

If the owner has not corrected or used due diligence to correct the conditions following the notice under this section, the renter is entitled to bring an action in district court.

Upon a showing of an unjustified refusal to correct or the failure to use due diligence to correct a condition described in this chapter, the renter is entitled to damages and injunctive relief as determined by the court including:

- Rent improperly retained or collected.
- Injunctive relief includes a declaration of the court terminating the rental agreement and an order for the repayment of any deposit and rent due.

The prevailing party shall be awarded attorney fees commensurate with the cost of the action brought.

If the renter is notified that the owner intends to terminate the rental agreement the renter is entitled to receive the balance of the rent due and the deposit on the rental unit within ten days of the date the agreement is terminated.

No renter may be required to move sooner than ten days after the date of notice.

Rental Deposits

Return or explain

Owners or designated agents requiring deposits from renters shall either return those deposits at the termination of the tenancy or provide the renter with written notice explaining why any deposit refundable under the terms of the lease is being retained.

Non-refundable deposit

If there is a written agreement and if any part of the deposit is to be made non-refundable, it must be so stated in writing to the renter at the time the deposit is taken by the owner or designated agent.

Deductions from deposit

Upon termination of the tenancy, property or money held as a deposit may be applied, at the owner's option,
- To the payment of accrued rent,
- Damages to the premises beyond reasonable wear and tear,
- Other costs provided for in the contract and cleaning of the unit

The balance of any deposit and prepaid rent, if any, and a written itemization of any deductions from the deposit, with explanation, shall be delivered or mailed to the renter within 30 days after termination of the tenancy except:
- If the renter has delayed providing a new mailing address, the time for paying the deposit is within 15 days after receipt of the renter's new mailing address.
- If there is damage to the rented premises, this period shall be extended to 30 days.

Penalties

If the owner of a residential unit or his agent in bad faith fails within 30 days after termination of the tenancy or within 15 days after receipt of the renter's new mailing address, whichever is later, to provide the renter the notice required, the renter may recover the full deposit, a civil penalty of $100, and court costs. Receipt of new address must occur within 30 days of termination of tenancy

Abandoned premises

In the event of abandonment, the owner may retake the premises and attempt to rent them at a fair rental value and the tenant who abandoned the premises shall be liable:

- for the entire rent due for the remainder of the term
- for rent accrued during the period necessary to re-rent the premises at a fair rental value, plus the difference between the fair rental value and the rent agreed to in the prior rental agreement, plus a reasonable commission for the renting of the premises and the costs, if any, necessary to restore the rental unit to its condition when rented by the tenant less normal wear and tear.

How can you know that a unit is abandoned.

- It's Vacant with no personal property inside.
- You were notified of the abandonment by the tenant.
- The tenant is unexplainably absent for several days and rent is due. This situation requires caution. In this case, it would be more defensible if taken to court if notice was posted that the unit would be considered abandoned if the owner was not contacted within 10 days.

If the tenant has abandoned the premises and has left personal property on the premises, the owner is entitled to remove the property from the dwelling, store it for the tenant, and recover actual moving and storage costs from the tenant.
- The owner shall make reasonable efforts to notify the tenant of the location of the personal property.
- If the property has been in storage for over 30 days and the tenant has made no reasonable effort to recover it, the owner may:
  - sell the property and apply the proceeds toward any amount the tenant owes; or
  - Donate the property to charity if the donation is a commercially reasonable alternative.
  - Any money left over from the sale of the property shall be handled as specified is abandoned property and must be turned over to the State Treasurer's Office.

An Overview of the Eviction Process

The eviction process in Utah is a four-step process.

A landlord must follow the law closely in order to evict a tenant. A notice must say exactly the right thing, and must be served on the tenant in the right way. If the landlord makes a mistake, a tenant may be able to get the case dismissed.

1. First, the landlord must actually end the tenancy, by delivering to the tenant the appropriate "Notice to Quit," sometimes called a "Notice to Vacate" and often referred to as an "eviction notice." Any defects in the notice may cause dismissal of the case, requiring the landlord to begin the process again. The type of eviction notice and how much notice (time) is required is determined by the tenant's status (i.e., a tenant at will, a tenant on a month-to-month oral tenancy, or a tenant under a lease). Regardless of the type of tenancy, though, the law requires the use of the statutory process to evict.

2. After the time in the eviction notice has expired, the landlord then completes the Summons and Complaint for an "Unlawful Detainer" (eviction) lawsuit. The Complaint is filed in the district court (court of general jurisdiction for Utah). The Summons and Complaint must be served on each tenant being evicted by a constable, deputy sheriff, or a person over the age of 18 years who is not a party to the action.

3. After being served with the Summons and Complaint, the tenant must file an "Answer" with the court within three business days. The Answer allows the tenant to explain to the court and the landlord why he or she should not be evicted, to raise defenses against the court action, and to bring any claims the tenant may have against the landlord. If the tenant cannot answer within three days, the tenant must file a written motion with the court objecting to the three days and asking for more time to answer. The judge will decide if under

the facts of the tenant's case the tenant should have more time to answer. Whether or not the tenant is given more time, if the Answer is not filed on time the landlord may ask for a default judgment and "Order of Restitution" against the tenant. The "Order of Restitution" directs the sheriff or constable to forcefully remove the tenant from the rental property. If the tenant files a timely Answer, the case will proceed as a civil case under the Utah Rules of Civil Procedure (discovery, trial, etc.).

4. After the complaint has been filed, the case may be moved along more quickly by:
   a. If the eviction is only for non-payment of rent, either the landlord or tenant can request a hearing at any time after the complaint is filed. The hearing will be set within ten days of the tenant filing an answer.
   b. If the eviction is for criminal nuisance, the court will automatically set a hearing, to be held within ten days of the filing of the complaint.
   c. The landlord may file an "Owner's Possession Bond" with the court and serve notice of the bond upon the tenant. The landlord can file a Possession Bond at any time after the complaint is filed, but it is most frequently done when the tenant has answered the Complaint because answering the Complaint eliminates the possibility of the landlord obtaining a default judgment. The Owner's Possession Bond must be approved by the court in an amount equal to the probable amount of costs of suit and actual damages to the tenant if the eviction action was brought improperly.

You may complete the documents required to initiate an eviction by using the Online Court Assistance Program using the following address:

http://www.utcourts.gov/ocap/

Review Questions

1. Which of the following is an owner's duty under Utah's Landlord Tenant Laws when renting a residential rental unit?
   a. Provide a security system
   b. Provide adequate parking for all the tenant's cars
   c. Ensure the property is fit for human occupancy
   d. Provide air conditioning systems to properly cool the rental unit

2. If the rental unit becomes damaged and the owner chooses not to make repairs because the unit has become unfit for human occupancy the owner must:
   a. Pay relocation expenses of the tenant
   b. Notify the tenant in writing
   c. Pay damages for mental suffering of the tenant
   d. Refund all rent for the month the damage occurred.

3. The tenant is required to do which of the following?
   a. Comply with the rules of the Board of Health
   b. Discontinue any sound outside the premises after 8 PM
   c. Provide written notice to the landlord of any other tenant's violation of the landlord rules
   d. Provide access to the owner or the owner's representative at all times for any reason.

4. Which of the following, if properly documented would qualify a tenant to have new or rekeyed locks installed?
   a. Road rage
   b. Divorce
   c. Burglary
   d. Oral threats

5. An owner must change locks for a crime victim. Which of the following statements is true.
   a. The owner should not provide a key to the primary signatory on the lease because they were the perpetrator of the crime.
   b. When a perpetrator is refused a key, they are automatically release of any liability on the lease.
   c. The replacement locks cannot be the same lock rekeyed.
   d. The owner is required to install deadbolts in addition to any existing locks the unit had before the crime.

6. The owner must begin repairs on a rental unit after notice from the tenant of the problem. How much time does the owner have to begin?
   a. 24 hours
   b. A reasonable time
   c. 3 days
   d. 10 days

7. An owner has a duty by law to return or explain the rental deposit of a former tenant within how many days?
   a. 5 days
   b. 10 days
   c. 20 days
   d. 30 days

8. The landlord is obligated to store abandoned property for how many days following the departure of the tenant?
   a. 30 days
   b. 45 days
   c. 60 days
   d. 90 days

9. The first step in the eviction process is which of the following?
   a. Ask for payment
   b. File a lawsuit
   c. Correct all defects in the premises
   d. Terminate the lease in writing

10. The purpose of the Owner's Possession Bond is to:
    a. Prove the owner's solvency
    b. Induce the court to expedite the hearing process
    c. Guarantee payment of the owner's court expenses
    d. Overpower the tenant with obligations they cannot match

20. Utah Statute of Frauds

Learning Objectives:

Upon completion of this chapter, the student should be able to:

- Identify which contracts must be in writing.
- Define the Electronic Transactions Act.

Estate or interest in real property.

No estate or interest in real property, shall be created, granted, assigned, surrendered or declared except by one of the two following actions:
- By act or operation of law
- By deed or conveyance in writing:
    a. By the party creating, granting, assigning, surrendering or declaring the same
    b. By his lawful agent under a written special power of attorney, trustee agreement.

Exceptions to this restriction are:
- Leases for a term not exceeding one year
- Any trust or power over or concerning real property or in any manner relating thereto
- A testator in the disposition of his real estate by last will and testament
- Any trust arising or being extinguished by implication or operation of law.

Leases and contracts for interest in lands.

Leases and contracts of interest in lands shall be void unless the contract, or some note or memorandum thereof, is in writing including:

- Every contract for the leasing for a longer period than one year
- The sale of any lands, or any interest in lands

Agreements deemed void unless written and signed.

The following agreements are void unless the agreement, or some note or memorandum of the agreement, is in writing, signed by the party to be charged with the agreement:

- Every agreement that by its terms is not to be performed within **one year** from the making of the agreement
- Every promise to answer for the **debt**, default, or miscarriage of another
- **Marriage**, except mutual promises to marry An example of this provision would be a prenuptial agreement.
- Every special promise made by an executor or administrator to answer in damages for the liabilities, or to pay the debts, of the testator or intestate out of his own estate
- Every agreement authorizing or **employing an agent or broker** to purchase or sell real estate for compensation;
- Every **credit agreement**.
    a. "Credit agreement" means an agreement by a financial institution to lend, delay, or otherwise modify an obligation to repay money, goods, or things in action, to otherwise extend credit, or to make any other financial accommodation. "Credit agreement" does not include the usual and customary agreements related to deposit accounts or overdrafts or other terms associated with deposit accounts or overdrafts.
    b. "Creditor" means a financial institution, which extends credit or extends a financial accommodation under a credit agreement with a debtor.
    c. "Debtor" means a person who seeks or obtains credit, or seeks or receives a financial accommodation, under a credit agreement with a financial institution.

d. "Financial institution" means a state or federally chartered bank, savings and loan association, savings bank, industrial loan corporation, credit union, or any other institution under the jurisdiction of the commissioner of Financial.

Agent may sign for principal

Every instrument required by the provisions of this chapter to be subscribed by any party may be subscribed by the lawful agent of such party.

Uniform Electronic Transactions Act

Under the Utah Electronic Transactions Act, the parties in the transaction may agree to conduct the transaction and the transmission and storage of documents by electronic means. Electronic means include:

- Fax
- Wire
- Telegraph
- Email
- Any means that a record can be created, generated, sent, communicated, received, or stored by electronic means

This chapter does not apply to a transaction to the extent it is governed by a law governing the creation and execution of wills, codicils, or testamentary trusts

County recorders are not required to accept electronic documents for the purpose of recording in land title records.

An electronic document can also have an electronic signature, which could become attached to the document in the form of an electronic sound, symbol, or process attached to or logically associated with a record and executed or adopted by a person with the intent to sign the record.

The Uniform Electronic Transactions Act States that:

- A record or signature may not be denied legal effect or enforceability solely because it is in electronic form.
- A contract may not be denied legal effect or enforceability solely because an electronic record was used in its formation.
- If a law requires a record to be in writing, an electronic record satisfies the law.

- If a law requires a signature, an electronic signature satisfies the law.

If parties have agreed to conduct a transaction by electronic means and a law requires a person to provide, send, or deliver information in writing to another person, the requirement is satisfied if the information is provided, sent, or delivered, as the case may be, in an electronic record capable of retention by the recipient at the time of receipt.

If a law other than this chapter requires a record to be posted or displayed in a certain manner, to be sent, communicated, or transmitted by a specified method, or to contain information that is formatted in a certain manner, the following rules apply:

- The record must be posted or displayed in the manner specified in the other law
- The record must be sent, communicated, or transmitted by the method specified in the other law; and
- The record must contain the information formatted in the manner specified in the other law.

Electronic documents can be notarized in Utah so long as the notary stamp is achieved electronically onto the document.

Review Questions

1. T or F. All contracts are enforceable, in in writing or not.

2. T or F. The transfer of an interest in real property, since it is recorded, need not be in writing.

3. Which of the following contracts need not be in writing?
   A. Month to month lease
   B. Agency agreement
   C. Real Estate purchase contract
   D. Prenuptial agreement
   E. Credit guarantee

4. T or F. If the parties agree, a fax or email is considered an original document.

5. T or F. Documents that must be notarized cannot be transmitted electronically.

21. Utah Forms

Learning Objectives:

Upon completion of this chapter, the student should be able to:
- Describe the legal process of using contracts as a real estate licensee
- Identify which forms must be used by a Utah real estate licensee

Utah Approved Forms

Contracts are an integral part of the real estate profession. Utah law prohibits licensees from practicing law, yet we need to use contracts to do what our clients expect of us. This is a delicate matter therefore with the regulation of real estate licensees. To make it possible for us to do the things we need to do, the Division has provide us with approved forms that we can fill in. this enables us to put our buyers wishes into contract form without creating the contract language. Real Estate licensees may only use approved forms. The following forms and special circumstances, therefore, bridge the need to use contracts in our profession without crossing over into the practice of law.

The Utah Real Estate Commission and the Office of the Attorney General have approved the following standard forms for the use of licensees:
1. Real Estate Purchase Contract
2. Uniform Real Estate Contract, or Land Contract
3. All Inclusive Trust Deed
4. All Inclusive Promissory Note Secured by All Inclusive Trust Deed
5. Addendum/Counteroffer to Real Estate Purchase Contract
6. Seller Financing Addendum to Real Estate Purchase Contract

7. Buyer Financial Information Sheet
8. FHA/VA Loan Addendum to Real Estate Purchase Contract (HUD)
9. Assumption Addendum to Real Estate Purchase Contract
10. Lead-based Paint Addendum to Real Estate Purchase Contract
11. Disclosure and Acknowledgment Regarding Lead-based Paint and/or Lead-based Paint Hazards

The Attorney General, Division of Real Estate, and the Real Estate Commission have also approved the use of unapproved forms that meet the following conditions.

- **Forms Required for Closing**. Principal brokers and associate brokers may fill out forms in addition to the standard state-approved forms if the additional forms are necessary to close a transaction. Examples include closing statements, and warranty or quitclaim deeds. Sales agents are not permitted to fill out these forms. The training required of those applying to be brokers and associate brokers prepare the broker and associate broker to fill out these forms.

- **Forms Prepared by an Attorney**. Any licensee may fill out forms prepared by the attorney for the buyer or lessee or the attorney for the seller or lessor to be used in place of any form listed in #1 through #7 listed on the previous page. The use of these forms must be based on a request by the buyer or lessee or the seller or lessor that other forms be used. The licensee must verify that an attorney has in fact drafted the forms for the buyer or lessee, or the attorney for the seller or lessor.

- **Additional Forms:** If it is necessary for a licensee to use a form for which there is no state-approved form, for example a lease, the licensee may fill in the blanks on any form, which has been prepared by an attorney.

REAL ESTATE PURCHASE CONTRACT

This is a legally binding Real Estate Purchase Contract ("REPC"). Utah law requires real estate licensees to use this form. Buyer and Seller, however, may agree to alter or delete its provisions or to use a different form. If you desire legal or tax advice, consult your attorney or tax advisor.

EARNEST MONEY DEPOSIT

On this _____ day of _____, 20____ ("Offer Reference Date") _____ ("Buyer") offers to purchase from _____ ("Seller") the Property described below and **agrees to deliver no later than four (4) calendar days after Acceptance (as defined in Section 23)**, an Earnest Money Deposit in the amount of $_____ in the form of_____. After Acceptance of the REPC by Buyer and Seller, and receipt of the Earnest Money by the Brokerage, the Brokerage shall have four (4) calendar days in which to deposit the Earnest Money into the Brokerage Real Estate Trust Account.

OFFER TO PURCHASE

1. PROPERTY: _____

City of _____, County of _____, State of Utah, Zip _____ Tax ID No. _____ (the "Property"). Any reference below to the term "Property" shall include the Property described above, together with the Included Items and water rights/water shares, if any, referenced in Sections 1.1, 1.2 and 1.4.

    1.1   Included Items. Unless excluded herein, this sale includes the following items if presently owned and in place on the Property: plumbing, heating, air conditioning fixtures and equipment; solar panels; ovens, ranges and hoods; cook tops; dishwashers; ceiling fans; water heaters; water softeners; light fixtures and bulbs; bathroom fixtures and bathroom mirrors; all window coverings including curtains, draperies, rods, window blinds and shutters; window and door screens; storm doors and windows; awnings; satellite dishes; all installed TV mounting brackets; all wall and ceiling mounted speakers; affixed carpets; automatic garage door openers and accompanying transmitters; security system; fencing and any landscaping.

    1.2   Other Included Items. The following items that are presently owned and in place on the Property have been left for the convenience of the parties and are also included in this sale **(check applicable box): [ ] washers [ ] dryers [ ] refrigerators [ ] microwave ovens [ ] other (specify)** _____

The above checked items shall be conveyed to Buyer under separate bill of sale with warranties as to title. In addition to any boxes checked in this Section 1.2 above, there **[ ] ARE [ ] ARE NOT** additional items of personal property Buyer intends to acquire from Seller at Closing by separate written agreement.

    1.3   Excluded Items. The following items are excluded from this sale: _____

    1.4   Water Service. The Purchase Price for the Property shall include all water rights/water shares, if any, that are the legal source for Seller's current culinary water service and irrigation water service, if any, to the Property. The water rights/water shares will be conveyed or otherwise transferred to Buyer at Closing by applicable deed or legal instruments. The following water rights/water shares, if applicable, are specifically excluded from this sale: _____

2. PURCHASE PRICE.

    2.1   Payment of Purchase Price. The Purchase Price for the Property is $ _____. Except as provided in this Section, the Purchase Price shall be paid as provided in Sections 2.1(a) through 2.1(e) below. Any amounts shown in Sections 2.1(c) and 2.1(e) may be adjusted as deemed necessary by Buyer and the Lender (the "Lender").

$_____	(a)	**Earnest Money Deposit.** Under certain conditions described in the REPC, this deposit may become totally non-refundable.
$_____	(b)	**Additional Earnest Money Deposit** (see Section 8.4 if applicable)
$_____	(c)	**New Loan.** Buyer may apply for mortgage loan financing (the "Loan") on terms acceptable to Buyer: If an FHA/VA loan applies, see attached FHA/VA Loan Addendum.
$_____	(d)	**Seller Financing** (see attached Seller Financing Addendum)
$_____	(e)	**Balance of Purchase Price in Cash at Settlement**
$_____		**PURCHASE PRICE. Total of lines (a) through (e)**

    2.2   Sale of Buyer's Property. Buyer's ability to purchase the Property, to obtain the Loan referenced in Section 2.1(c) above, and/or any portion of the cash referenced in Section 2.1(e) above **[ ] IS [ ] IS NOT** conditioned upon the sale of real estate owned by Buyer. If checked in the affirmative, the terms of the attached subject to sale of Buyer's property addendum apply.

3. SETTLEMENT AND CLOSING.

    3.1   Settlement. Settlement shall take place no later than the Settlement Deadline referenced in Section 24(d), or as otherwise mutually agreed by Buyer and Seller in writing. "Settlement" shall occur only when all of the following have been completed: (a) Buyer and Seller have signed

Page 1 of 6 pages   Buyer's Initials_____ Date_____   Seller's Initials_____ Date_____

and delivered to each other or to the escrow/closing office all documents required by the REPC, by the Lender, by the title insurance and escrow/closing offices, by written escrow instructions (including any split closing instructions, if applicable), or by applicable law; (b) any monies required to be paid by Buyer or Seller under these documents (except for the proceeds of any Loan) have been delivered by Buyer or Seller to the other party, or to the escrow/closing office, in the form of cash, wire transfer, cashier's check, or other form acceptable to the escrow/closing office.

   3.2   Closing. For purposes of the REPC, "Closing" means that: (a) Settlement has been completed; (b) the proceeds of any new Loan have been delivered by the Lender to Seller or to the escrow/closing office; and (c) the applicable Closing documents have been recorded in the office of the county recorder ("Recording"). The actions described in 3.2 (b) and (c) shall be completed no later than four calendar days after Settlement.

   3.3   Possession. Except as provided in Section 6.1(a) and (b), Seller shall deliver physical possession of the Property to Buyer as follows: [   ] **Upon Recording;** [   ] _____ **Hours after Recording;** [   ] ___ **Calendar Days after Recording.** Any contracted rental of the Property prior to or after Closing, between Buyer and Seller, shall be by separate written agreement. Seller and Buyer shall each be responsible for any insurance coverage each party deems necessary for the Property including any personal property and belongings. The provisions of this Section 3.3 shall survive Closing.

4.   PRORATIONS / ASSESSMENTS / OTHER PAYMENT OBLIGATIONS.
   4.1   Prorations. All prorations, including, but not limited to, homeowner's association dues, property taxes for the current year, rents, and interest on assumed obligations, if any, shall be made as of the Settlement Deadline referenced in Section 24(d), unless otherwise agreed to in writing by the parties. Such writing could include the settlement statement. The provisions of this Section 4.1 shall survive Closing.

   4.2   Special Assessments. Any assessments for capital improvements as approved by the homeowner's association ("HOA") (pursuant to HOA governing documents) or as assessed by a municipality or special improvement district, prior to the Settlement Deadline shall be paid for by: [   ] **Seller** [   ] **Buyer** [   ] **Split Equally Between Buyer and Seller** [   ] **Other (explain)** _____.
The provisions of this Section 4.2 shall survive Closing.

   4.3   Fees/Costs/Payment Obligations.
      (a)   Escrow Fees. Unless otherwise agreed to in writing, Seller and Buyer shall each pay their respective fees charged by the escrow/closing office for its services in the settlement/closing process. The provisions of this Section 4.3(a) shall survive Closing.

      (b)   Rental Deposits/Prepaid Rents. Rental deposits (including, but not limited to, security deposits, cleaning deposits and prepaid rents) for long term lease or rental agreements, as defined in Section 6.1(a), and short-term rental bookings, as defined in Section 6.1(b), not expiring prior to Closing, shall be paid or credited by Seller to Buyer at Settlement. The provisions of this Section 4.3(b) shall survive Closing.

      (c)   HOA/Other Entity Fees Due Upon Change of Ownership. Some HOA's, special improvement districts and/or other specially planned areas, under their governing documents charge a fee that is due to such entity as a result of the transfer of title to the Property from Seller to Buyer. Such fees are sometimes referred to as transfer fees, community enhancement fees, HOA reinvestment fees, etc. (collectively referred to in this section as "change of ownership fees"). Regardless of how the change of ownership fee is titled in the applicable governing documents, if a change of ownership fee is due upon the transfer of title to the Property from Seller to Buyer, that change of ownership fee shall, at Settlement, be paid for by: [   ] **Seller** [   ] **Buyer** [   ] **Split Equally Between Buyer and Seller** [   ] **Other (explain)** _____.
The provisions of this Section 4.3(c) shall survive Closing.

      (d)   Utility Services. Buyer agrees to be responsible for all utilities and other services provided to the Property after the Settlement Deadline. The provisions of this Section 4.3(d) shall survive Closing.

      (e)   Sales Proceeds Withholding. The escrow/closing office is authorized and directed to withhold from Seller's proceeds at Closing, sufficient funds to pay off on Seller's behalf all mortgages, trust deeds, judgments, mechanic's liens, tax liens and warrants. The provisions of this Section 4.3(e) shall survive Closing.

5.   CONFIRMATION OF AGENCY DISCLOSURE. Buyer and Seller acknowledge prior written receipt of agency disclosure provided by their respective agent that has disclosed the agency relationships confirmed below. At the signing of the REPC:
Seller's Agent(s) _____, represent(s) [   ] **Seller** [   ] **both Buyer and Seller as Limited Agent(s);**

Seller's Agent(s) Utah Real Estate License Number(s):_____.

Seller's Brokerage_____, represents [   ] **Seller** [   ] **both Buyer and Seller as Limited Agent;**

Seller's Brokerage Utah Real Estate License Number:_____.

Buyer's Agent(s) _____, represent(s) [   ] **Buyer** [   ] **both Buyer and Seller as Limited Agent(s);**

Buyer's Agent(s) Utah Real Estate License Number(s):_____.

Buyer's Brokerage_____, represents [   ] **Buyer** [   ] **both Buyer and Seller as a Limited Agent.**

Buyer's Brokerage Utah Real Estate License Number:_____.

6.   TITLE & TITLE INSURANCE.
   6.1   Title to Property. Seller represents that Seller has fee title to the Property and will convey marketable title to the Property to Buyer at Closing by general warranty deed. Buyer does agree to accept title to the Property subject to the contents of the Commitment for Title Insurance (the "Commitment") provided by Seller under Section 7, and as reviewed and approved by Buyer under Section 8.

      (a)   Long-Term Lease or Rental Agreements. Buyer agrees to accept title to the Property subject to any long-term tenant lease or rental agreements (meaning for periods of thirty (30) or more consecutive days) affecting the Property not expiring prior to Closing. Buyer also agrees to accept title to the Property subject to any existing rental and property management agreements affecting the Property not expiring prior to Closing.

Page 2 of 6 pages   Buyer's Initials_____ Date_____   Seller's Initials_____ Date_____

The provisions of this Section 6.1(a) shall survive Closing.

(b) Short-Term Rental Bookings. Buyer agrees to accept title to the Property subject to any short-term rental bookings (meaning for periods of less than thirty (30) consecutive days) affecting the Property not expiring prior to Closing. The provisions of this Section 6.1(b) shall survive Closing.

6.2 Title Insurance. At Settlement, Seller agrees to pay for and cause to be issued in favor of Buyer, through the title insurance agency that issued the Commitment (the "Issuing Agent"), the most current version of the *ALTA Homeowner's Policy of Title Insurance* (the "*Homeowner's Policy*"). If the *Homeowner's Policy* is not available through the Issuing Agent, Buyer and Seller further agree as follows: (a) Seller agrees to pay for the *Homeowner's Policy* if available through any other title insurance agency selected by Buyer; (b) if the *Homeowner's Policy* is not available either through the Issuing Agent or any other title insurance agency, then Seller agrees to pay for, and Buyer agrees to accept, the most current available version of an *ALTA Owner's Policy of Title Insurance* ("*Owner's Policy*") available through the Issuing Agent.

7. SELLER DISCLOSURES. No later than the Seller Disclosure Deadline referenced in Section 24(a), Seller shall provide to Buyer the following documents in hard copy or electronic format which are collectively referred to as the "Seller Disclosures":

(a) a written Seller property condition disclosure for the Property, completed, signed and dated by Seller as provided in Section 10.3;
(b) a *Lead-Based Paint Disclosure & Acknowledgement* for the Property, completed, signed and dated by Seller (only if the Property was built prior to 1978);
(c) a Commitment for Title Insurance as referenced in Section 6.1;
(d) a copy of any restrictive covenants (CC&R's), rules and regulations affecting the Property;
(e) a copy of the most recent minutes, budget and financial statement for the homeowners' association, if any;
(f) a copy of any long-term tenant lease or rental agreements affecting the Property not expiring prior to Closing;
(g) a copy of any short-term rental booking schedule (as of the Seller Disclosure Deadline) for guest use of the Property after Closing;
(h) a copy of any existing property management agreements affecting the Property;
(i) evidence of any water rights and/or water shares referenced in Section 1.4;
(j) written notice of any claims and/or conditions known to Seller relating to environmental problems and building or zoning code violations;
(k) In general, the sale or other disposition of a U.S. real property interest by a foreign person is subject to income tax withholding under the *Foreign Investment in Real Property Tax Act of 1980* (FIRPTA). A "foreign person" includes a non-resident alien individual, foreign corporation, partnership, trust or estate. If FIRPTA applies to Seller, Seller is advised that Buyer or other qualified substitute may be legally required to withhold this tax at Closing. In order to avoid closing delays, if Seller is a foreign person under FIRPTA, Seller shall advise Buyer in writing; and
(l) Other (specify) _____

8. BUYER'S CONDITIONS OF PURCHASE.
8.1 DUE DILIGENCE CONDITION. Buyer's obligation to purchase the Property: [ ] IS [ ] IS NOT conditioned upon Buyer's Due Diligence as defined in this Section 8.1(a) below. This condition is referred to as the "Due Diligence Condition." If checked in the affirmative, Sections 8.1(a) through 8.1(c) apply; otherwise they do not.

(a) Due Diligence Items. Buyer's Due Diligence shall consist of Buyer's review and approval of the contents of the Seller Disclosures referenced in Section 7, and any other tests, evaluations and verifications of the Property deemed necessary or appropriate by Buyer, such as: the physical condition of the Property; the existence of any hazardous substances, environmental issues or geologic conditions; the square footage or acreage of the land and/or improvements; the condition of the roof, walls, and foundation; the condition of the plumbing, electrical, mechanical, heating and air conditioning systems and fixtures; the condition of all appliances; the costs and availability of homeowners' insurance and flood insurance, if applicable; water source, availability and quality; the location of property lines; regulatory use restrictions or violations; fees for services such as HOA dues, municipal services, and utility costs; convicted sex offenders residing in proximity to the Property; and any other matters deemed material to Buyer in making a decision to purchase the Property. Unless otherwise provided in the REPC, all of Buyer's Due Diligence shall be paid for by Buyer and shall be conducted by individuals or entities of Buyer's choice. Seller agrees to cooperate with Buyer's Due Diligence. Buyer agrees to pay for any damage to the Property resulting from any such inspections or tests during the Due Diligence.

(b) Buyer's Right to Cancel or Resolve Objections. If Buyer determines, in Buyer's sole discretion, that the results of the Due Diligence are unacceptable, Buyer may either: (i) no later than the Due Diligence Deadline referenced in Section 24(b), cancel the REPC by providing written notice to Seller, whereupon the Earnest Money Deposit shall be released to Buyer without the requirement of further written authorization from Seller; or (ii) no later than the Due Diligence Deadline referenced in Section 24(b), resolve in writing with Seller any objections Buyer has arising from Buyer's Due Diligence.

(c) Failure to Cancel or Resolve Objections. If Buyer fails to cancel the REPC or fails to resolve in writing with Seller any objections Buyer has arising from Buyer's Due Diligence, as provided in Section 8.1(b), Buyer shall be deemed to have waived the Due Diligence Condition, and except as provided in Sections 8.2(a) and 8.3(b)(i), the Earnest Money Deposit shall become non-refundable.

8.2 APPRAISAL CONDITION. Buyer's obligation to purchase the Property: [ ] IS [ ] IS NOT conditioned upon the Property appraising for not less than the Purchase Price. This condition is referred to as the "Appraisal Condition." If checked in the affirmative, Sections 8.2(a) and 8.2(b) apply; otherwise they do not.

(a) Buyer's Right to Cancel. If after completion of an appraisal by a licensed appraiser, Buyer receives written notice from the Lender or the appraiser that the Property has appraised for less than the Purchase Price (a "Notice of Appraised Value"), Buyer may cancel the REPC by providing written notice to Seller (with a copy of the Notice of Appraised Value) no later than the Financing & Appraisal Deadline referenced in Section 24(c); whereupon the Earnest Money Deposit shall be released to Buyer without the requirement of further written authorization from Seller.

(b) Failure to Cancel: If the REPC is not cancelled as provided in this section 8.2, Buyer shall be deemed to have waived the Appraisal

Page 3 of 6 pages   Buyer's Initials_____ Date_____   Seller's Initials_____ Date_____

Condition, and except as provided in Sections 8.1(b) and 8.3(b)(i), the Earnest Money Deposit shall become non-refundable.

8.3   FINANCING CONDITION. (Check Applicable Box)
     (a) [   ] No Financing Required. Buyer's obligation to purchase the Property **IS NOT** conditioned upon Buyer obtaining financing. If checked, Section 8.3(b) below does NOT apply.
     (b) [   ] Financing Required. Buyer's obligation to purchase the Property **IS** conditioned upon Buyer obtaining the Loan referenced in Section 2.1(c). This Condition is referred to as the "Financing Condition." If checked, Sections 8.3(b)(i), (ii) and (iii) apply; otherwise they do not. If the REPC is not cancelled by Buyer as provided in Sections 8.1(b) or 8.2(a), then Buyer agrees to work diligently and in good faith to obtain the Loan.
          (i)   Buyer's Right to Cancel Before the Financing & Appraisal Deadline. If Buyer, in Buyer's sole discretion, is not satisfied with the terms and conditions of the Loan, Buyer may, after the Due Diligence Deadline referenced in Section 24(b), if applicable, cancel the REPC by providing written notice to Seller no later than the Financing & Appraisal Deadline referenced in Section 24(c); whereupon $_____ of Buyer's Earnest Money Deposit shall be released to Seller without the requirement of further written authorization from Buyer, and the remainder of Buyer's Earnest Money Deposit shall be released to Buyer without further written authorization from Seller.
          (ii) Buyer's Right to Cancel After the Financing & Appraisal Deadline. If after expiration of the Financing & Appraisal Deadline referenced in Section 24(c), Buyer fails to obtain the Loan, meaning that the proceeds of the Loan have not been delivered by the Lender to the escrow/closing office as required under Section 3.2, then Buyer shall not be obligated to purchase the Property and Buyer or Seller may cancel the REPC by providing written notice to the other party.
          (iii) Earnest Money Deposit(s) Released to Seller. If the REPC is cancelled as provided in Section 8.3(b)(ii), Buyer agrees that all of Buyer's Earnest Money Deposit, or Deposits, if applicable (see Section 8.4 below), shall be released to Seller without the requirement of further written authorization from Buyer. Seller agrees to accept, as Seller's exclusive remedy, the Earnest Money Deposit, or Deposits, if applicable, as liquidated damages. Buyer and Seller agree that liquidated damages would be difficult and impractical to calculate, and the Earnest Money Deposit, or Deposits, if applicable, is a fair and reasonable estimate of Seller's damages in the event Buyer fails to obtain the Loan.

8.4   ADDITIONAL EARNEST MONEY DEPOSIT. If the REPC has not been previously canceled by Buyer as provided in Sections 8.1, 8.2 or 8.3, as applicable, then no later than the Due Diligence Deadline, or the Financing & Appraisal Deadline, whichever is later, Buyer: **[   ] WILL [   ] WILL NOT** deliver to the Buyer's Brokerage, an Additional Earnest Money Deposit in the amount of $_____. The Earnest Money Deposit and the Additional Earnest Money Deposit, if applicable, are sometimes referred to herein as the "Deposits". The Earnest Money Deposit, or Deposits, if applicable, shall be credited toward the Purchase Price at Closing.

9. ADDENDA. There **[   ] ARE [   ] ARE NOT** addenda to the REPC containing additional terms. If there are, the terms of the following addenda are incorporated into the REPC by this reference: **[   ] Addendum No. _____ [   ] Seller Financing Addendum [   ] FHA/VA Loan Addendum [   ] Other (specify) _____.**

10. HOME WARRANTY PLAN / AS-IS CONDITION OF PROPERTY.
     10.1   Home Warranty Plan. A one-year Home Warranty Plan **[   ] WILL [   ] WILL NOT** be included in this transaction. If included, the Home Warranty Plan shall be ordered by **[   ] Buyer [   ] Seller** and shall be issued by a company selected by **[   ] Buyer [   ] Seller.** The cost of the Home Warranty Plan shall not exceed $_____ and shall be paid for at Settlement by **[   ] Buyer [   ] Seller.**
     10.2   Condition of Property/Buyer Acknowledgements. Buyer acknowledges and agrees that in reference to the physical condition of the Property: (a) Buyer is purchasing the Property in its "As-Is" condition without expressed or implied warranties of any kind; (b) Buyer shall have, during Buyer's Due Diligence as referenced in Section 8.1, an opportunity to completely inspect and evaluate the condition of the Property; and (c) if based on the Buyer's Due Diligence, Buyer elects to proceed with the purchase of the Property, Buyer is relying wholly on Buyer's own judgment and that of any contractors or inspectors engaged by Buyer to review, evaluate and inspect the Property. The provisions of Section 10.2 shall survive Closing.
     10.3 Condition of Property/Seller Acknowledgements. Seller acknowledges and agrees that in reference to the physical condition of the Property, Seller agrees to: (a) disclose in writing to Buyer defects in the Property known to Seller that materially affect the value of the Property that cannot be discovered by a reasonable inspection by an ordinary prudent Buyer; (b) carefully review, complete, and provide to Buyer a written Seller property condition disclosure as stated in Section 7(a); (c) deliver the Property to Buyer in substantially the same general condition as it was on the date of Acceptance, as defined in Section 23, ordinary wear and tear excepted; (d) deliver the Property to Buyer in broom-clean condition and free of debris and personal belongings; and (e) repair any Seller or tenant moving-related damage to the Property at Seller's expense. The provisions of Section 10.3 shall survive Closing.

11. FINAL PRE-SETTLEMENT WALK-THROUGH INSPECTION. No earlier than seven (7) calendar days prior to Settlement, and upon reasonable notice and at a reasonable time, Buyer may conduct a final pre-Settlement walk-through inspection of the Property to determine only that the Property is "as represented," meaning that the items referenced in Sections 1.1, 1.2 and 8.1(b)(ii) ("the items") are respectively present, repaired or corrected as agreed. The failure to conduct a walk-through inspection or to claim that an item is not as represented shall not constitute a waiver by Buyer of the right to receive, on the date of possession, the items as represented.

12. CHANGES DURING TRANSACTION. Seller agrees that except as provided in Section 12.5 below, from the date of Acceptance until the date of Closing the following additional items apply:
     12.1   Alterations/Improvements to the Property. No substantial alterations or improvements to the Property shall be made or undertaken without prior written consent of Buyer.
     12.2   Financial Encumbrances/Changes to Legal Title. No further financial encumbrances to the Property shall be made, and no changes in

Page 4 of 6 pages   Buyer's Initials_____ Date_____   Seller's Initials_____ Date_____

the legal title to the Property shall be made without the prior written consent of Buyer.

12.3   Property Management Agreements. No changes to any existing property management agreements shall be made and no new property management agreements may be entered into without the prior written consent of Buyer.

12.4   Long-Term Lease or Rental Agreements. No changes to any existing tenant lease or rental agreements shall be made and no new long-term lease or rental agreements, as defined in Section 6.1(a), may be entered into without the prior written consent of Buyer.

12.5   Short-Term Rental Bookings. If the Property is made available for short-term rental bookings as defined in Section 6.1(b), Seller **MAY NOT** after the Seller Disclosure Deadline continue to accept short-term rental bookings for guest use of the property without the prior written consent of Buyer.

13. AUTHORITY OF SIGNERS. If Buyer or Seller is a corporation, partnership, trust, estate, limited liability company or other entity, the person signing the REPC on its behalf warrants his or her authority to do so and to bind Buyer and Seller.

14. COMPLETE CONTRACT. The REPC together with its addenda, any attached exhibits, and Seller Disclosures (collectively referred to as the "REPC"), constitutes the entire contract between the parties and supersedes and replaces any and all prior negotiations, representations, warranties, understandings or contracts between the parties whether verbal or otherwise. The REPC cannot be changed except by written agreement of the parties.

15. MEDIATION. Any dispute relating to the REPC arising prior to or after Closing: [ ] SHALL [ ] MAY AT THE OPTION OF THE PARTIES first be submitted to mediation. Mediation is a process in which the parties meet with an impartial person who helps to resolve the dispute informally and confidentially. Mediators cannot impose binding decisions. The parties to the dispute must agree before any settlement is binding. The parties will jointly appoint an acceptable mediator and share equally in the cost of such mediation. If mediation fails, the other procedures and remedies available under the REPC shall apply. Nothing in this Section 15 prohibits any party from seeking emergency legal or equitable relief, pending mediation. The provisions of this Section 15 shall survive Closing.

16. DEFAULT.

16.1 Buyer Default. If Buyer defaults, Seller may elect one of the following remedies: (a) cancel the REPC and retain the Earnest Money Deposit, or Deposits, if applicable, as liquidated damages; (b) maintain the Earnest Money Deposit, or Deposits, if applicable, in trust and sue Buyer to specifically enforce the REPC; or (c) return the Earnest Money Deposit, or Deposits, if applicable, to Buyer and pursue any other remedies available at law.

16.2 Seller Default. If Seller defaults, Buyer may elect one of the following remedies: (a) cancel the REPC, and in addition to the return of the Earnest Money Deposit, or Deposits, if applicable, Buyer may elect to accept from Seller, as liquidated damages, a sum equal to the Earnest Money Deposit, or Deposits, if applicable; or (b) maintain the Earnest Money Deposit, or Deposits, if applicable, in trust and sue Seller to specifically enforce the REPC; or (c) accept a return of the Earnest Money Deposit, or Deposits, if applicable, and pursue any other remedies available at law. If Buyer elects to accept liquidated damages, Seller agrees to pay the liquidated damages to Buyer upon demand.

17. ATTORNEY FEES AND COSTS/GOVERNING LAW. In the event of litigation or binding arbitration arising out of the transaction contemplated by the REPC, the prevailing party shall be entitled to costs and reasonable attorney fees. However, attorney fees shall not be awarded for participation in mediation under Section 15. This contract shall be governed by and construed in accordance with the laws of the State of Utah. The provisions of this Section 17 shall survive Closing.

18. NOTICES. Except as provided in Section 23, all notices required under the REPC must be: (a) in writing; (b) signed by the Buyer or Seller giving notice; and (c) received by the Buyer or the Seller, or their respective agent, or by the brokerage firm representing the Buyer or Seller, no later than the applicable date referenced in the REPC.

19. NO ASSIGNMENT. The REPC and the rights and obligations of Buyer hereunder, are personal to Buyer. The REPC may not be assigned by Buyer without the prior written consent of Seller. Provided, however, the transfer of Buyer's interest in the REPC to any business entity in which Buyer holds a legal interest, including, but not limited to, a family partnership, family trust, limited liability company, partnership, or corporation (collectively referred to as a "Permissible Transfer"), shall not be treated as an assignment by Buyer that requires Seller's prior written consent. Furthermore, the inclusion of "and/or assigns" or similar language on the line identifying Buyer on the first page of the REPC shall constitute Seller's written consent only to a Permissible Transfer.

20. INSURANCE & RISK OF LOSS.

20.1 Insurance Coverage. As of Closing, Buyer shall be responsible to obtain casualty and liability insurance coverage on the Property in amounts acceptable to Buyer and Buyer's Lender, if applicable.

20.2 Risk of Loss. If prior to Closing, any part of the Property is damaged or destroyed by fire, vandalism, flood, earthquake, or act of God, the risk of such loss or damage shall be borne by Seller; provided however, that if the cost of repairing such loss or damage would exceed ten percent (10%) of the Purchase Price referenced in Section 2, either Seller or Buyer may elect to cancel the REPC by providing written notice to the other party, in which instance the Earnest Money Deposit, or Deposits, if applicable, shall be returned to Buyer.

21. TIME IS OF THE ESSENCE. Time is of the essence regarding the dates set forth in the REPC. Extensions must be agreed to in writing by all parties. Unless otherwise explicitly stated in the REPC: (a) performance under each Section of the REPC which references a date shall absolutely be required by 5:00 PM Mountain Time on the stated date; and (b) the term "days" and "calendar days" shall mean calendar days and shall be counted beginning on the day following the event which triggers the timing requirement (e.g. Acceptance). Performance dates and times referenced herein shall not be binding upon title companies, lenders, appraisers and others not parties to the REPC, except as otherwise agreed to in writing by such non-party.

Page 5 of 6 pages   Buyer's Initials_____ Date_____   Seller's Initials_____ Date_____

22. ELECTRONIC TRANSMISSION AND COUNTERPARTS. The REPC may be executed in counterparts. Signatures on any of the Documents, whether executed physically or by use of electronic signatures, shall be deemed original signatures and shall have the same legal effect as original signatures.

23. ACCEPTANCE. "Acceptance" occurs **only** when **all** of the following have occurred: (a) Seller or Buyer has signed the offer or counteroffer where noted to indicate acceptance; and (b) Seller or Buyer or their agent has communicated to the other party or to the other party's agent that the offer or counteroffer has been signed as required.

24. CONTRACT DEADLINES. Buyer and Seller agree that the following deadlines shall apply to the REPC:

(a) Seller Disclosure Deadline   _____ (Date)

(b) Due Diligence Deadline   _____ (Date)

(c) Financing & Appraisal Deadline   _____ (Date)

(d) Settlement Deadline   _____ (Date)

25. OFFER AND TIME FOR ACCEPTANCE. Buyer offers to purchase the Property on the above terms and conditions. If Seller does not accept this offer by: _____ [ ] AM [ ] PM Mountain Time on_____ (Date), this offer shall lapse; and the Brokerage shall return any Earnest Money Deposit to Buyer.

_____   _____
(Buyer's Signature)   (Date)   (Buyer's Signature)   (Date)

ACCEPTANCE/COUNTEROFFER/REJECTION

CHECK ONE:
[ ] **ACCEPTANCE OF OFFER TO PURCHASE:** Seller Accepts the foregoing offer on the terms and conditions specified above.
[ ] **COUNTEROFFER:** Seller presents for Buyer's Acceptance the terms of Buyer's offer subject to the exceptions or modifications as specified in the attached ADDENDUM NO. _____.
[ ] **REJECTION:** Seller rejects the foregoing offer.

_____   _____
(Seller's Signature)   (Date)   (Time)   (Seller's Signature)   (Date)   (Time)

THIS FORM APPROVED BY THE UTAH REAL ESTATE COMMISSION AND THE OFFICE OF THE UTAH ATTORNEY GENERAL, EFFECTIVE SEPTEMBER 1, 2017. AS OF JANUARY 1, 2018, IT WILL REPLACE AND SUPERSEDE THE PREVIOUSLY APPROVED VERSION OF THIS FORM.

Page 6 of 6 pages   Buyer's Initials_____ Date_____   Seller's Initials_____ Date_____

CAUTION: READ BEFORE YOU SIGN

- *This is a legally binding contract; if you do not understand it, seek legal advice before you sign.*
- *This contract is intended to be filled in by lawyers or by real estate brokers. All others seek professional advice.*
- *To assure protection of certain priority rights in the property, it is recommended that this contract and any assignments, or addenda, be recorded in the office of the applicable County Recorder.*

UNIFORM REAL ESTATE CONTRACT

1.   **Parties.**   This contract, made and entered into this _____ day of _____ , 19 _____ is by and between _____
(hereafter collectively called "Seller"), whose address is _____
_____
and _____
(hereafter collectively called "Buyer"), whose address is _____
_____

2.   **Property.**   Seller agrees to sell and Buyer agrees to buy the real property (the "Property") located at _____
_____ (street address), in the City of _____
County of _____ , State of Utah, described as: _____
_____
_____
_____

3.   **Date of Possession.**   Seller agrees to deliver possession and Buyer agrees to enter into possession of the Property on the _____ day of _____ , 19 _____ .

4.   **Price and Payment.**

   A.   Buyer agrees to pay for the Property the purchase price of _____
_____ Dollars ($_____) payable at Seller's address above given, or to Seller's order on the following terms: _____
_____
_____ Dollars
($_____) down payment, receipt of which is hereby acknowledged, and the balance of _____
_____ Dollars
($_____) to be paid as follows:

   B.   Payments shall include interest at the rate of _____ percent (_____%) per annum on the unpaid principal balance from the date of _____ . Any payment not made within _____ (_____) days of its due date shall subject Buyer to a late payment charge of _____ percent (_____%) of such overdue payment, which charge must be paid before receiving credit for the late payment. The foregoing payments include a reserve for payment of [ ] taxes [ ] insurance [ ] condo fees [ ] other (explain) _____

Initially, the reserve amount per payment is _____ . In the event reserve payments on underlying obligations for the Property change, Seller shall give Buyer thirty (30) days written notice of change, and reserve payments herein shall be adjusted accordingly.

This form is approved by the Utah Real Estate Commission and the Office of the Attorney General. January 1, 1987.

C.   All payments made by Buyer shall be applied first to payment of late charges, next to Seller's payments under Section 12, with interest as provided therein, next to the payment of reserves if any, next to the payment of interest, and then to the reduction of principal. Buyer may, at Buyer's option, pay amounts in excess of the periodic payments herein provided, and such excess shall be applied to unpaid principal unless Buyer elects in writing at the time of such payment that it shall be applied as prepayment of future installments. In the event of any prepayment by Buyer, Buyer shall assume and pay all penalties incurred by Seller in making accelerated payments on any underlying obligations.

D.   When the unpaid principal balance owing under this contract is equal to or less than the total balance outstanding on the underlying obligation(s) shown in Section 8 below, then:

(1)   Upon (i) assumption by Buyer of the underlying obligation(s) and (ii) release of Seller from all liabilities and obligations thereunder, Buyer may request and Seller shall execute and deliver a Warranty Deed subject to the then existing underlying obligation(s) shown in Section 8 below; or

(2)   Provided there is no "due-on-sale" provision contained in any underlying obligation(s) shown in Section 8 below, Seller may execute and deliver to Buyer a Warranty Deed subject to the then existing underlying obligation(s) shown in Section 8 below, which Buyer agrees to assume and pay; or

(3)   In the event neither Buyer nor Seller exercises the options provided in (1) a d (2) of this sub-section, and this contract therefore remains in effect, then the payments and interest rate shown in this Section, to the extent they differ from the underlying obligations, shall immediately and automatically be adjusted to equal the payments and interest rate then required under the underlying obligations, and Buyer, in addition to such adjusted payments, shall also pay a monthly servicing fee to Seller in the amount of $_____.

5.   **No Waiver.**   If Seller accepts payments from Buyer on this contract in an amount less than or at a time later than herein provided, such acceptance will not constitute a modification of this contract or a waiver of Seller's rights to full and timely performance by Buyer.

6.   **Risk of Loss.**   All risk of loss and destruction of the Property shall be borne by Seller until the agreed date of possession.

7.   **Evidence of Title.**   Buyer has received a Commitment for Title Insurance (Commitment) on the Property at the time of or prior to execution of this contract. Seller shall, at his expense, furnish Buyer evidence of marketable title in the form of an Owner's Title Insurance Policy (Title Policy) insuring Buyer's interest in the Property under this contract for the amount of the purchase price. The Title Policy will be based on Commitment No. _____ issued by: _____. The Title Policy issued to Buyer will contain the following numbered exceptions shown on the Commitment: _____
_____

8.   **Underlying Obligations.**

A.   Seller warrants that the only underlying obligations against the Property are:
       (1)   Obligation in favor of _____

with an unpaid principal balance of _____ Dollars
($_____) as of _____, 19 _____ with monthly payments of $_____, with interest at _____
percent (_____%) per annum and balloon payments as follows: _____
_____

       (2)   Obligation in favor of _____

with an unpaid principal balance of _____ Dollars
($_____) as of _____, 19 _____ with monthly payments of $_____, with interest at _____
percent (_____%) per annum and balloon payments as follows: _____
_____

       (3)   Obligation in favor of _____

with an unpaid principal balance of _____ Dollars
($_____) as of _____, 19 _____ with monthly payments of $_____, with interest at _____
percent (_____%) per annum and balloon payments as follows: _____

     B.   **COPIES OF SUCH UNDERLYING OBLIGATIONS [ ] HAVE [ ] HAVE NOT BEEN DELIVERED TO BUYER AT OR PRIOR TO CLOSING. SUCH UNDERLYING OBLIGATIONS [ ] CONTAIN [ ] DO NOT CONTAIN DUE ON SALE OR DUE ON ENCUMBRANCE PROVISIONS.**

     C.   **IN THE EVENT THE HOLDER OF ANY UNDERLYING OBLIGATION(S) REFERRED TO IN SUB-SECTION A. CAUSES TO BE ISSUED A WRITTEN NOTICE OF ITS INTENT TO EXERCISE ANY OF THE DUE ON SALE REMEDIES, THEN BUYER AGREES TO EITHER PAY, ASSUME OR REFINANCE SUCH UNDERLYING OBLIGATION(S) IN THE MANNER PROVIDED BELOW, AND BUYER AGREES TO PAY ALL COSTS, FEES AND CHARGES INCURRED IN CONNECTION WITH SUCH PAYMENT, ASSUMPTION OR REFINANCING (INCLUDING, BUT NOT LIMITED TO, PREPAYMENT PENALTIES, LOAN POINTS, INCREASED INTEREST RATE, APPRAISAL AND CREDIT REPORT FEES, ESCROW AND TITLE CHARGES, TITLE INSURANCE PREMIUMS, AND RECORDING FEES). BUYER'S INABILITY OR FAILURE TO PAY, ASSUME, OR REFINANCE SUCH UNDERLYING OBLIGATION(S) WITHIN FORTY-FIVE (45) DAYS FROM THE DATE OF NOTICE TO BUYER OF SUCH WRITTEN NOTICE FROM THE HOLDER, SHALL CONSTITUTE A DEFAULT BY BUYER UNDER THIS CONTRACT.**

(1)   **Assumption.**   In the event buyer elects to assume such underlying obligation(s), Buyer shall be entitled to the delivery of a Warranty Deed executed by the Seller wherein the Buyer is the Grantee upon the satisfaction of the following conditions precedent: (i) Buyer is not then in default under the terms of this contract; (ii) Buyer has deposited with Seller written evidence from the holder of the underlying obligation(s) being assumed that such holder has approved Buyer's assumption; and (iii) if any portion of the Seller's equity under this contract remains unpaid, Buyer shall execute and deliver to Seller, Buyer's Trust Deed Note in a principal amount equal to the unpaid balance of Seller's equity under this contract, which shall include any accrued unpaid interest. Said note shall bear interest from the date thereof at the same rate at which interest accrues on the Seller's equity under this contract. Installments shall be made over the term then remaining and at the same time as provided for in this contract with the exact amount of the installments being calculated by re-amortizing the aforesaid

amount of the Trust Deed Note utilizing the interest rate at which interest accrues on Seller's equity under this contract, the schedule of payments, and term specified herein. Such note shall be secured by a Deed of Trust encumbering the property which shall be subordinate only to the Deed or Deeds of Trust securing the underlying obligation(s) and any obligations refinanced as provided in sub-section C.(2).

        (2) **Refinancing/Pay-Out.** In the event Buyer pays or obtains a new loan refinancing one or more of the underlying obligations, then buyer shall be entitled to the delivery of a Warranty Deed executed by the Seller wherein the Buyer is Grantee; provided, however, if any portion of the seller's equity remains unpaid, then the following conditions precedent shall have been satisfied: (i) Buyer is not then in default under any of the terms of this Contract; (ii) the principal amount of the new loan may exceed the unpaid balance of the underlying obligation(s) being refinanced only if all loan proceeds which exceed the unpaid balance of the underlying obligation(s) are paid to the Seller as a credit against the unpaid balance of Seller's equity in this Contract; and (iii) Buyer shall have executed and delivered to Seller, Buyer's Trust Deed Note in the form, the amount, and with the terms of the Trust Deed Note described in Section C(1)(iii). Such note shall be subordinate only to the Deed(s) of Trust securing the new loan(s) and any remaining Deed(s) of Trust securing the underlying obligation(s) which have not been reconveyed.

9.   **Taxes and Assessments.** Buyer agrees to pay all taxes and assessments of every kind which become due on the Property during the life of this contract. Seller covenants that there are no taxes, assessments, or liens against the Property not mentioned in Section 8 except:

_____

_____

_____

which will be paid by: [ ] Seller [ ]Buyer [ ] Other (explain) _____

_____

10.   **Covenant Against Liens.** Except for the liens and encumbrances listed in Sections 8 and 9, Seller covenants to keep the Property free and clear of all liens and encumbrances resulting from acts of Seller. So long as Buyer is current hereunder, Seller agrees to keep current the payments on all obligations to which Buyer's interest is subordinate. Should Seller default on the foregoing covenants on any one or more occasions, Buyer may, at Buyer's option, in whole or in part, make good Seller's default to Seller's obligee and deduct all expenditures so paid from future payments to Seller and Seller shall credit all Buyer's sums so expended to the indebtedness herein created just as if payment had been made directly to Seller under provisions of Section 4 above.

11.   **Insurance.** On and after the agreed date of possession, Buyer shall maintain at Buyer's expense, the following insurance policies naming the Seller as an additional insured and with a certificate of insurance provided to Seller that includes a ten (10) day notice of cancellation in favor of Seller: (i) insurance against loss by fire and other risks customarily covered by "All Risk" insurance on insurable buildings and improvements at 80% of replacement value; and (ii) general liability insurance having coverage of not less than $_____. All such insurance policies shall be in companies which are duly licensed by the State of Utah and are acceptable to Seller. Acceptance of such companies by Seller may not be unreasonably withheld.

12.   **Seller's Option To Discharge Obligations.** In the event Buyer shall default in the payment of taxes, assessments, insurance premiums or other expenses of the Property, Seller may, at Seller's option, pay said taxes, assessments, insurance premiums or other expenses, and if Seller elects so to do, Buyer agrees to repay Seller upon demand all such sums so advanced and paid by Seller together with interest thereon from date of payment of said sums at the rate of the greater of one (1%) or _____ percent (_____%) per month until paid, and when the principal sum provided in this contract is paid, if Buyer fails to also repay Seller such advances, Seller may refuse to convey title to the Property until such repayment is made.

13.   **Conveyance of Title.** Seller on receiving the payments herein reserved to be paid at the time and in the manner specified herein, agrees to execute and deliver to Buyer or assigns, a good and sufficient warranty deed conveying the title to the above described premises free and clear of all encumbrances except those which have accrued by or through the acts or neglect of Buyer and those which Buyer has specifically agreed to pay or assume under the terms of this contract, and subject to the following numbered exceptions to title that are contained in the commitment for title insurance described in Section 7 hereof: _____

_____

14.   **No Waste.** Buyer agrees that Buyer will neither commit nor suffer to be committed any waste, spoil or destruction in or upon the Property which would impair Seller's security, and that Buyer will maintain the Property in good condition.

15.   **Attorney's Fees.** Both parties agree that, should either party default in any of the covenants or agreements herein contained, the non-defaulting party or, should litigation be commenced, the prevailing party in litigation, shall be entitled to all costs and expenses, including a reasonable attorney's fee, which may arise or accrue from enforcing or terminating this contract, or in obtaining possession of the Property, or in pursuing any remedy provided hereunder or by applicable law.

16.   **Buyer's Default.** Should buyer fail to comply with any of the terms hereof, Seller may, in addition to any other remedies afforded the Seller in this contract or by law, elect any of the following remedies:

        A.   Seller shall give Buyer written notice specifically stating: (1) The Buyer's default(s); (2) that buyer shall have thirty (30) days from his receipt of such written notice within which to cure the default(s), which cure shall include payment of Seller's costs and reasonable attorney's fees; and (3) Seller's intent to elect this remedy if the Buyer does not cure the default(s) within the thirty (30) days. Should Buyer fail to cure such default(s) within the thirty (30) days, then Seller shall give to Buyer another written notice informing Buyer of his failure to cure the default(s) and of Seller's election of this remedy. Immediately upon Buyer's receipt of this second written notice, Seller shall be released from all obligations at law and equity to convey the Property to Buyer, and Buyer shall become at once a tenant-at-will of Seller. All payments which have been made by Buyer prior thereto under this contract shall, subject to then existing law and equity, be retained by Seller as liquidated and agreed damages for breach of this contract; or

        B.   Seller may bring suit and recover judgment for all delinquent installments and all reasonable costs and attorneys' fees, and the use of this remedy on one or more occasions shall not prevent Seller, at Seller's option, from resorting to this or any other available remedy in the case of subsequent default; or

        C.   Seller shall give Buyer written notice specifically stating: (1) The Buyer's default(s); (2) that Buyer shall have thirty (30) days from his receipt of such written notice within which to cure the default(s), which cure shall include payment of Seller's costs and reasonable attorney's fees; and (3) Seller's intent to elect this remedy if the Buyer does not cure the default(s) with the thirty (30) days. Should Buyer fail to cure such default(s) within the thirty (30) days, then Seller shall give to Buyer another written notice informing Buyer of his failure to cure the default(s), Seller's election of this remedy, and that the entire unpaid balance hereunder is at once due and payable. Thereupon, Seller may treat this contract as a note and mortgage, pass or tender title to Buyer subject thereto, and proceed immediately with a mortgage foreclosure in accordance with the laws of the State of Utah. Upon filing the foreclosure complaint in court, Seller shall be entitled to the immediate appointment of a receiver. The receiver may take possession of the premises, collect the rents, issue and profits therefrom and apply them to the payment of the obligation hereunder, or hold them pursuant to the order of the court. Upon entry of a judgment of foreclosure, Seller shall be entitled to possession of the premises during the period of redemption.

17.   **Time of Essence.**   It is expressly agreed that time is of the essence in this contract.

18.   **Warranties of Physical Condition.**   With respect to the physical condition of the Property, Seller warrants the following: ____
_____
_____
_____

19.   **Other Provisions.**   _____
_____
_____
_____
_____
_____
_____
_____
_____
_____

20.   **Captions.**   Section captions shall not in any way limit, modify, or alter the provisions in the Section.

21.   **Notices.**   Except as otherwise provided herein, all notices required under this contract will be effective when: (a) personally delivered or; (b) mailed certified or registered, addressed to the applicable party at the address shown in Section 1, or at such other address as may be hereinafter designated by such party by written notice to the other party.

22.   **Binding Effect.**   This contract is binding on the heirs, personal representatives, successors and assigns of the respective parties hereto.

23.   **Entire Agreement.**   This contract contains the entire agreement between the parties hereto. Any provisions hereof not enforceable under the laws of the State of Utah shall not affect the validity of any other provisions hereof. No supplement modification or amendment of this contract shall be binding on the parties hereto unless signed in writing by both parties hereto.

IN WITNESS WHEREOF, the parties have set their signatures on the day and year first above written.

BUYER: SELLER:

_____   _____

_____   _____

STATE OF UTAH
                                   ss.
COUNTY OF _____

On the _____ day of _____ , 19 _____ personally appeared before me
_____ , Seller and signer of the above instrument, who duly acknowledged to me that ____he____ executed the same.

_____
                     NOTARY PUBLIC
My Commission Expires:
_____   Residing at:

STATE OF UTAH
                                   ss.
COUNTY OF _____

On the _____ day of _____ , 19 _____ personally appeared before me
_____ , Buyer and signer of the above instrument, who duly acknowledged to me that ____he____ executed the same.

_____
                     NOTARY PUBLIC
My Commission Expires:
_____   Residing at:

All-Inclusive Trust Deed

With Assignment of Rents

THIS ALL-INCLUSIVE TRUST DEED made this _____ day of _____, 19 _____, between _____
_____ , as TRUSTOR,
whose address is _____
               (Street and Number)   (City)   (State)
_____ , as TRUSTEE,* and
_____
_____ , as BENEFICIARY,
      WITNESSETH: That Trustor CONVEYS AND WARRANTS TO TRUSTEE IN TRUST, WITH POWER OF SALE, the following described property situated in _____ County, State of Utah.

      Together with all buildings, fixtures and improvements thereon and all water rights, rights of way, easements, rents, and issues, profits, income tenements, hereditaments, privileges and appurtenances hereunto belonging, now or hereafter used or enjoyed with said property, or any part thereof, SUBJECT, HOWEVER, to the right, power and authority hereinafter given to and conferred upon Beneficiary to collect and apply such rents, issues, and profits;

      FOR THE PURPOSE OF SECURING (1) payment of the indebtedness evidenced by an All-Inclusive Promissory Note (hereinafter the "Note") of even date herewith, in the principal sum of $ _____, made by Trustor, payable to the order of Beneficiary at the times, in the manner and with interest as therein set forth, and any extensions and/or renewals or modifications thereof; (2) the performance of each agreement of Trustor herein contained; (3) the payment of such additional loans or advances as hereafter may be made to Trustor, or his successors or assigns, when evidenced by a Promissory Note or Notes reciting that they are secured by this Trust Deed; and (4) the payment of all sums expended or advanced by Beneficiary under or pursuant to the terms hereof, together with interest thereon as herein provided.

      This instrument is an All-Inclusive Trust Deed subject and subordinate to the following instruments (hereinafter "Senior Encumbrances"):

      (1) A Trust Deed/Mortgage recorded _____, as Entry No. _____, in Book _____, at Page _____ of Official Records of _____, which, if a Trust Deed secures a Promissory Note in the original principal amount of, or if a Mortgage, is in the original principal amount of _____ Dollars, ($ _____), dated _____, 19 _____, in favor of _____ Beneficiary/Mortgagee, with the Trustor/Mortgagor being _____ . If a Trust Deed, its Trustee is _____ .

      (2) A Trust Deed/Mortgage recorded _____, as Entry No. _____, in Book _____, at Page _____ of Official Records of _____, which, if a Trust Deed secures a Promissory Note in the original principal amount of, or if a Mortgage, is in the original principal amount of _____ Dollars, ($ _____), dated _____, 19 _____, in favor of _____ Beneficiary/Mortgagee, with the Trustor/Mortgagor being _____ . If a Trust Deed, its Trustee is _____ .

      The Promissory Note(s) secured by said Trust Deed(s) is (are) hereinafter referred to as the "Senior Note(s)". Nothing in this Trust Deed, the Note, or any deed in connection herewith shall be deemed to be an assumption by the Trustor of the Senior Notes or Senior Encumbrances.

*NOTE: Trustee must be a member of the Utah State Bar, a bank, building and loan association, savings and loan association, or insurance company authorized to do such business in Utah; a corporation authorized to conduct a trust business in Utah; a title insurance or abstract company authorized to do such business in Utah, or a U.S. Government Agency.

This form has been approved by the Utah Real Estate Commission.
    — ALL-INCLUSIVE TRUST DEED —   Oct. 1, 1983

rents, issues, and profits, including those past due and unpaid, and apply the same, less costs and expenses of operation and collection, including reasonable attorney's fees, upon any indebtedness secured hereby, and in such order as Beneficiary may determine.

12. The entering upon and taking possession of said property, the collection of such rents, issues, and profits, or the proceeds of fire and other insurance policies, or compensation or awards for any taking or damages of said property, and the application or release thereof as aforesaid, shall not cure or waive any default or notice of default hereunder or invalidate any act done pursuant to such notice.

13. The failure on the part of Beneficiary to promptly enforce any right hereunder shall not operate as a waiver of such right and the waiver by Beneficiary of any default shall not constitute a waiver of any other or subsequent default.

14. Time is of the essence hereof. Upon default by Trustor in the payment of any indebtedness secured hereby or in the performance of any agreement hereunder, all sums secured hereby shall immediately become due and payable at the option of Beneficiary. In the event of such default, Beneficiary may execute or cause Trustee to execute a written notice of default and of election to cause said property to be sold to satisfy the obligations hereof, and Trustee shall file such notice for record in each county wherein said property or some part of parcel thereof is situated. Beneficiary also shall deposit with Trustee, the note and all documents evidencing expenditures secured hereby.

15. After the lapse of such time as may then be required by law following the recordation of said notice of default, and notice of default and notice of sale having been given as then required by law, Trustee, without demand on Trustor, shall sell said property on the date and at the time and place designated in said notice of sale, either as a whole or in separate parcels, and in such order as it may determine (but subject to any statutory right of Trustor to direct the order in which property, if consisting of several known lots or parcels, shall be sold), at public auction to the highest bidder, the purchase price payable in lawful money of the United States at the time of sale. The person conducting the sale may, for any cause he deems expedient, postpone the sale from time to time until it shall be completed and, in every case, notice of postponement shall be given by public declaration thereof by such person at the time and place last appointed for the sale; provided, if the sale is postponed for longer than one day beyond the day designated in the notice of sale, notice thereof shall be given in the same manner as the original notice of sale. Trustee shall execute and deliver to the purchaser its Deed conveying said property so sold, but without any covenant or warranty, express or implied. The recitals in the Deed of any matters or facts shall be conclusive proof of the trustfulness thereof. Any person, including Beneficiary, may bid at the same. Trustee shall apply the proceeds of the sale to payment of (1) the costs and expenses of exercising the power of sale and of the sale, including the evidence of title procured in connection with such sale; (2) all sums expended under the terms hereof, not then repaid, with accrued interest at the rate borne by the principal balance under the Note from date of expenditure; (3) all other sums then secured hereby; and (5) the remainder, if any, to the person or persons legally entitled thereto, or the Trustee, in its discretion, may deposit the balance of such proceeds with the County Clerk of the county in which the sale took place.

16. Upon the occurrence of any default hereunder, Beneficiary shall have the option to declare all sums secured hereby immediately due and payable and foreclose this Trust Deed in the manner provided by law for the foreclosure of mortgages on real property and beneficiary shall be entitled to recover in such proceedings all costs and expenses incident thereto, including a reasonable attorney's fee in such amount as shall be fixed by the court.

17. Beneficiary may appoint a Successor Trustee at any time by filing for record in the office of the County Recorder of each county in which said property or some part hereof is situated, a substitution of Trustee. From the time the substitution is filed for record, the new Trustee shall succeed to all powers, duties, authority and title of the Trustee named herein or of any Successor Trustee. Each such substitution shall be executed and acknowledged, and notice thereof shall be given and proof thereof made, in the manner provided by law.

18. This Trust Deed shall apply to, inure to the benefit of, and bind all parties hereto, their heirs, legatees, divisees, administrators, executors, successors and assigns. All obligations of Trustor hereunder are joint and several. The term "Beneficiary" shall mean the owner and holder, including any pledgee, of the note secured hereby. In this Trust Deed, whenever the contest requires, the masculine gender includes the feminine and/or neuter, and the singular includes the plural.

19. Trustee accepts this Trust when this Trust Deed, duly executed and acknowledged, is made a public record as provided by law. Trustee is not obligated to notify any party hereto of pending sale under any other Trust Deed or of any action or proceeding in which Trustor, Beneficiary, or Trustee shall be a party, unless brought by Trustee.

20. This Trust Deed shall be construed according to the laws of the State of Utah.

21. The undersigned Trustor requests that a copy of any notice of default and of any notice of sale hereunder be mailed to him at the address hereinbefore set forth.

Signature of Trustor

_____

_____

_____

_____

TO PROTECT THE SECURITY OF THIS TRUST DEED, TRUSTOR AGREES:

1. To keep said property in good condition and repair; not to remove or demolish any building thereon, to complete or restore promptly and in good and workmanlike manner any building which may be constructed, damaged or destroyed thereon; to comply with all laws, covenants and restrictions affecting said property; not to commit or permit waste thereof; not to commit, suffer or permit any act upon said property in violation of law; to do all other acts which from the character or use of said property may be reasonably necessary, the specific enumerations herein not excluding the general; and, if the loan secured hereby or any part thereof is being obtained for the purpose of financing construction of improvements on said property, Trustor further agrees:

   (a) To commence construction promptly and to pursue same with reasonable diligence to completion in accordance with plans and specifications satisfactory to Beneficiary, and

   (b) To allow Beneficiary to inspect said property at all times during construction.

   Trustee, upon presentation to it of an affidavit signed by Beneficiary, setting forth facts showing a default by Trustor under this paragraph, is authorized to accept as true and conclusive all facts and statements therein, and to act thereon hereunder.

2. To provide and maintain insurance, of such type or types and amounts as Beneficiary may require, on the improvements now existing or hereafter erected or placed on said property. Such insurance shall be carried in companies approved by Beneficiary with loss payable clauses in favor of and in form acceptable to Beneficiary. In event of loss, Trustor shall give immediate notice to Beneficiary, who may make proof of loss, and each insurance company concerned is hereby authorized and directed to make payment for such loss directly to Beneficiary instead of to Trustor and Beneficiary jointly, and the insurance proceeds, or any part thereof, may be applied by Beneficiary, at its option, to reduction of the indebtedness hereby secured or to the restoration or repair of the property damaged.

3. To deliver to, pay for and maintain with Beneficiary until the indebtedness secured hereby is paid in full such evidence of title as Beneficiary may require, including abstracts of title or policies of title insurance and any extensions or renewals thereof or supplements thereto.

4. To appear in and defend any action or proceeding purporting to affect the security thereof, the title to said property, or the rights or powers of Beneficiary or Trustee; and should Beneficiary or Trustee elect to also appear in or defend any such action or proceeding, to pay all costs and expenses, including cost of evidence of title and attorney's fees in a reasonable sum incurred by Beneficiary or Trustee.

5. To pay all taxes, insurance and assessments of every kind or nature as and when required by the Holders of Senior Encumbrances or when otherwise due in absence of any requirements under the Senior Encumbrances.

6. Should Trustor fail to make any payment or to do any act as herein provided, then Beneficiary or Trustee, but without obligation to do so and without notice to or demand upon Trustor and without releasing Trustor from any obligation hereof, may: Make or do the same in such manner and to such extent as either may deem necessary to protect the security hereof, Beneficiary or Trustee being authorized to enter upon said property for such purposes; commence, appear in and defend any action or proceeding purporting to affect the security hereof or the rights or powers of Beneficiary or Trustee; pay, purchase, contest, or compromise any encumbrance, charge or lien which in the judgment of either appears to be prior or superior hereto; and in exercising any such powers, incur any liability, expend whatever amounts in its absolute discretion it may deem necessary therefor, including cost of evidence of title, employ counsel, and pay reasonable legal fees.

7. To pay immediately and without demand all sums expended hereunder by Beneficiary or Trustee, with interest from date of expenditure at the rate borne by the principal balance under the Note until paid, and the repayment thereof shall be secured hereby.

IT IS MUTUALLY AGREED THAT:

8. Should said property or any part thereof be taken or damaged by reason of any public improvement or condemnation proceeding, or damaged by fire, or earthquake, or in any other manner, Beneficiary shall be entitled to all compensation, awards, and other payments or relief therefor, and shall be entitled at its option to commence, appear in and prosecute in its own name, any action or proceedings, or to make any compromise or settlement, in connection with such taking or damage. All such compensation, awards, damages, rights or action and proceeds, including the proceeds of any policies of fire and other insurance affecting said property, are hereby assigned to Beneficiary, who may, after deducting therefrom all its expenses, including attorney's fees, apply the same on any indebtedness secured hereby. Trustor agrees to execute such further assignments of any compensation, award, damages, and rights of action and proceeds as Beneficiary or Trustee may require.

9. At any time and from time to time upon written request of Beneficiary, payment of its fees and presentation of this Trust Deed and the note of endorsement (in case of full reconveyance, for cancellation and retention), without affecting the liability of any persons for the payment of the indebtedness secured hereby, Trustee may (a) consent to the making of any map or plat of said property; (b) join in granting any easement or creating any restriction thereon; (c) join in any subordination or other agreement affecting this Trust Deed or the lien or charge thereof; (d) reconvey, without warranty, all or any part of said property. The grantee in any reconveyance may be described as "the person or persons entitled thereto", and the recitals therein of any matters or facts shall be conclusive proof of truthfulness thereof. Trustor agrees to pay reasonable Trustee's fees for any of the services mentioned in this paragraph.

10. As additional security, Trustor hereby assigns Beneficiary, during the continuance of these trusts, all rents, issues, royalties, profits of the property affected by this Trust Deed and of any personal property located thereon. Until Trustor shall default in the payment of any indebtedness secured hereby or in the performance of any agreement hereunder, Trustor shall have the right to collect all such rents, issues, royalties, and profits earned prior to default as they become due and payable. If Trustor shall default as aforesaid, Trustor's right to collect any of such moneys shall cease and Beneficiary shall have the right, with or without taking possession of the property affected hereby, to collect all rents, royalties, issues, and profits. Failure or discontinuance of Beneficiary at any time or from time to time to collect any such moneys shall not in any manner affect the subsequent enforcement by Beneficiary of the right, power, and authority to collect the same. Nothing contained herein, nor the exercise of the right by Beneficiary to collect, shall be, or be construed to be, an affirmation by Beneficiary of any tenancy, lease or option, nor an assumption of liability under, nor a subordination of the lien or charge of this Trust Deed to any such tenancy, lease or option.

11. Upon any default by Trustor hereunder, Beneficiary may at any time without notice, either in person, by agent, or by a receiver to be appointed by a court (Trustor hereby consenting to the appointment of Beneficiary as such receiver), and without regard to the adequacy of any security for the indebtedness hereby secured, enter upon and take possession of said property or any part thereof, in its own name sue for or otherwise collect said

(If Trustor an Individual)

STATE OF UTAH

                                    ss.

COUNTY OF _____

        On the _____ day of _____, 19 ____, personally appeared before me _____,

the signer(s) of the above instrument, who duly acknowleged to me that __he__ executed the same.

My Commission Expires:

_____

NOTARY PUBLIC

Residing at:

(If Trustor a Corporation)

STATE OF UTAH

                                    ss.

COUNTY OF _____

        On the _____ day of _____, 19 ____, personally appeared before me _____,

who being by me duly sworn, says that he is the _____ of the corporation

that executed the above and foregoing instrument and that said instrument was signed in behalf of said corporation by authority of its by-laws (or by

authority of a resolution of its board of directors) and said _____

acknowledged to me that said corporation executed the same.

My Commission Expires:

_____

NOTARY PUBLIC

Residing at:

REQUEST FOR FULL RECONVEYANCE

(To be used only when indebtedness secured hereby has been paid in full)

TO: TRUSTEE

    The undersigned is the legal owner and holder of the note and all other indebtedness secured by the within Trust Deed. Said note, together with all other indebtedness secured by said Trust Deed has been fully paid and satisfied; and you are hereby requested and directed, on payment to you of any sums owing to you under the terms of said Trust Deed, to cancel said note above mentioned, and all other evidences of indebtedness secured by said Trust Deed delivered to you herewith, together with the said Trust Deed, and to reconvey, without warranty, to the parties designated by the terms of said Trust Deed, all of the estate now held by you thereunder.

    DATED _____, 19 ____

_____

_____

Mail reconveyance to _____

ALL-INCLUSIVE PROMISSORY NOTE SECURED BY
ALL-INCLUSIVE TRUST DEED

(Installment Note, Interest Included)

$ _____   _____ , Utah

                                             _____ , 19 ____

   1.   In Installments as herein stated, for value received, I/we _____ _____,
hereinafter referred to as "Maker", promise to pay to _____,
hereinafter referred to as "Holder", or order, at _____ the sum of
_____ Dollars ($_____) with interest from
_____ on unpaid principal at the rate of _____ percent (_____%) per annum, said principal and interest being
payable as follows:

A late payment penalty of _____ percent (_____%) of any payment due shall be assessed against the Maker if said payment has not been
received by Holder within _____ (_____) days of the due date. Each payment shall be credited first to any late payments due, then to accrued
interest due and the remainder to principal.

   2.   The total principal amount of this Note includes the unpaid principal balance of any existing Promissory Note(s) ("Senior Note(s)") secured by
Trust Deed(s), or any Mortgages. Such Trust Deeds and Mortgage(s) are hereinafter collectively referred to as "Senior Encumbrance(s)". The Senior
Note(s) and/or Mortgage(s) is/are more particularly described as follows:

   A.   A Promissory Note/Mortgage in an original principal amount of _____
_____ Dollars ($_____) dated _____ , 19_____ in favor of
_____ as Holder/Mortgagee, with the Maker/Mortgagor
being _____ .
There is an unpaid principal balance of $_____ as of _____ , 19 _____ bearing interest at the rate of
_____ percent (_____%) per annum payable $ _____ (principal and interest) per month. The monthly payment
☐ includes taxes ☐ does not include taxes.

   B.   (If applicable:)   A Promissory Note/Mortgage in an original principal amount of _____
_____ Dollars ($_____) dated _____ , 19_____ in favor of
_____ as Holder/Mortgagee, with the Maker/Mortgagor
being _____ .
There is an unpaid principal balance of $_____ as of _____ , 19 _____ bearing interest at the rate of
_____ percent (_____%) per annum payable $ _____ (principal and interest) per month. The monthly payment
☐ includes taxes ☐ does not include taxes.

   C.   (If applicable:)   A Promissory Note/Mortgage in an original principal amount of _____
_____ Dollars ($_____) dated _____ , 19_____ in favor of
_____ as Holder/Mortgagee, with the Maker/Mortgagor
being _____ .
There is an unpaid principal balance of $_____ as of _____ , 19 _____ bearing interest at the rate of
_____ percent (_____%) per annum payable $ _____ (principal and interest) per month. The monthly payment
☐ includes taxes ☐ does not include taxes.

   3.   Maker, at his option at any time, may prepay the amounts required herein, provided, however:

   A.   Maker shall designate at the time the prepayment is made whether the prepayment shall be credited to unpaid principal or in prepayment
of future installments due under this Note; and

   B.   In the event that Holder is required under the terms of this Note or the All-Inclusive Trust Deed securing this Note, to make prepayments
on the Senior Note(s) as a direct result of any prepayment(s) on this Note by Maker, and Holder thereby incurs a prepayment penalty under the Senior
Note(s), then in such event, Maker agrees to pay to Holder, on demand, the full amount of such prepayment penalty. Any prepayment penalties so paid
by Maker shall not reduce the unpaid balance of this Note.

This form has been approved by the Utah Real Estate Commission.   October 1, 1983

4.   When all the sums payable pursuant to the terms of this Note and the All-Inclusive Deed of Trust securing this Note have been paid in full, Holder shall: (1) immediately pay all remaining sums to be paid under the terms of the Senior Note(s) and Senior Encumbrance(s), and (2) surrender this Note to Maker marked paid in full and execute and deliver to the Trustee a Request for Full Reconveyance of the All-Inclusive Trust Deed securing this Note.

5.   Provided Maker is not in default under any terms of the Note or the All-Inclusive Deed of Trust securing this Note, Holder shall pay when due all installments required under the terms of the Senior Note(s) and Senior Encumbrance(s). In the event of any default by Maker under any terms of this Note or the All-Inclusive Trust Deed securing this Note, Holder's obligation to make payments on the Senior Note(s) shall be deferred until any such default is cured. All penalties, charges and other expenses incurred under the Senior Note(s) and the Senior Encumbrance(s) as a result of any such default by Maker shall be added to the principal amount of this Note and shall be immediately payable by Maker to Holder. Should Holder default in making any payment(s) on the Senior Note(s) as required herein, Maker may make said payment(s) directly to the Holder(s) of such Senior Note(s); any and all payments so made by Maker shall be credited to this Note.

6.   When all sums due pursuant to the terms of this Note and the All-Inclusive Trust Deed securing this Note, at any time, is equal to or less than the unpaid balance of principal and interest then due under the terms of the Senior Note(s), then:

A.   Upon (i) assumption by Maker of the Senior Note(s) and (ii) release of Holder from all liabilities and obligations on the Senior Note(s) and Senior Encumbrance(s), Maker, at his option, may request and shall receive from Holder, cancellation and delivery of this Note, and Holder shall execute and deliver to the Trustee a Request for Full Reconveyance of the All-Inclusive Trust Deed securing this Note; or

B.   Even in the absence of assumption and release under sub-section A. above, Holder, at his option, may cancel this Note and deliver same to Maker and execute and deliver to Trustee a Request for Full Reconveyance of the All-Inclusive Trust Deed securing this Note; or

C.   In the event neither Holder nor Maker exercises the options provided in A. and B. of this section, and this Note and the All-Inclusive Trust Deed securing this Note therefore remain in effect, then the payments and interest rate shown in Section 1. of this Note, to the extent they differ from the Senior Note(s) shall immediately and automatically be adjusted to equal the payments and interest rate then required under the Senior Note(s), and Maker, in addition to such adjusted payments, shall also pay a monthly servicing fee to Holder of an amount equal to _____ percent (_____%) of such adjusted monthly payments.

7.   Holder shall have no further obligation under the terms of this Note or the All-Inclusive Trust Deed securing this Note, after: (1) foreclosure by Holder or his Trustee of the All-Inclusive Deed of Trust securing this Note, or (2) delivery by Holder to Trustee of a Request for Reconveyance of the All-Inclusive Trust Deed securing this Note.

8.   In the event the Holder(s) of the Senior Note(s) is entitled to any remedy pursuant to any due on sale, non-alienation, or non-assumption provision as a result of the execution of this Note and/or any document(s) related hereto, the entire unpaid balance of this Note, without futher notice, shall become immediately due and payable thirty days following written notice to the Maker of this Note of the intent of the Holder(s) of the Senior Note(s) to exercise any such remedy.

9.   In the event that any payment under this Note is not made, or any obligation provided to be satisfied or performed under this Note or the All-Inclusive Trust Deed securing this Note is not satisfied or performed at the time and in the manner required, Holder, at his option and without notice or demand, may declare the entire principal balance, all amounts of accrued interest and all other amonts then due under the terms of this Note and the All-Inclusive Trust Deed securing this Note immediately due and payable.

10.   In the event that any payment under this Note is not made, or any obligation provided to be satisfied or performed under this Note or the All-Inclusive Trust Deed securing this Note is not satisfied or performed at the time and in the manner required, the defaulting party shall pay any and all costs and expenses (regardless of the particular nature thereof and whether or not incurred in connection with the exercise of the power of sale provided for in the All-Inclusive Trust Deed securing this Note) which may be incurred by the Maker or Holder hereof in connection with the enforcement of any rights under this Promissory Note, including, without limitation, court costs and reasonable attorney's fees.

11.   The Maker and endorser hereof waive presentment for payment, protest, demand, notice of protest, notice of dishonor and notice of nonpayment and expressly agree that this Note or any payment hereunder may be extended from time to time by the Holder hereof without in any way affecting the liability of such parties. No course of dealing between the Maker and Holder in exercising any rights hereunder, shall operate as a waiver of rights of Holder.

12.   This Note shall inure to the benefit of and shall be binding upon respective successors and assigns of the Maker and Holder.

13.   This Note shall be construed in accordance with the laws of the State of Utah.

14.   In this Note, whenever the context requires, the masculine gender includes the feminine and/or neuter, and the singular number includes the plural.

15.   This Note is secured by an All-Inclusive Trust Deed of even date herewith.

_____   _____
MAKER   MAKER

_____   _____
MAKER   MAKER

The undersigned hereby accept(s) the foregoing All-Inclusive Promissory Note and agree(s) to perform each and all of the terms thereof on the part of the Holder to be performed.

Executed as of the date and place first above written.

_____   _____
HOLDER   HOLDER

_____   _____
HOLDER   HOLDER

Page ____ of _____

ADDENDUM NO.
TO
REAL ESTATE PURCHASE CONTRACT

THIS IS AN [ ] ADDENDUM [ ] COUNTEROFFER to that REAL ESTATE PURCHASE CONTRACT (the "REPC") with an Offer Reference Date of _____, including all prior addenda and counteroffers, between _____ as Buyer, and _____ as Seller, regarding the Property located at _____. The following terms are hereby incorporated as part of the REPC:

_____

_____

_____

_____

_____

_____

_____

_____

_____

_____

_____

_____

_____

BUYER AND SELLER AGREE THAT THE CONTRACT DEADLINES REFERENCED IN SECTION 24 OF THE REPC (CHECK APPLICABLE BOX): [ ] REMAIN UNCHANGED [ ] ARE CHANGED AS FOLLOWS:_____
_____

To the extent the terms of this ADDENDUM modify or conflict with any provisions of the REPC, including all prior addenda and counteroffers, these terms shall control. All other terms of the REPC, including all prior addenda and counteroffers, not modified by this ADDENDUM shall remain the same. **[ ] Seller [ ] Buyer** shall have until _____ **[ ] AM [ ] PM** Mountain Time on_____(Date), to accept the terms of this ADDENDUM in accordance with the provisions of Section 23 of the REPC. Unless so accepted, the offer as set forth in this ADDENDUM shall lapse.

_____   _____
[ ] Buyer [ ] Seller Signature   (Date)   (Time)   [ ] Buyer [ ] Seller Signature   (Date)   (Time)

ACCEPTANCE/COUNTEROFFER/REJECTION
CHECK ONE:
[ ] ACCEPTANCE: [ ] Seller [ ] Buyer hereby accepts the terms of this ADDENDUM.

[ ] COUNTEROFFER: [ ] Seller [ ] Buyer presents as a counteroffer the terms of attached ADDENDUM NO. ____.

_____   _____
(Signature)   (Date)   (Time)   (Signature)   (Date)   (Time)

[ ] REJECTION: [ ] Seller [ ] Buyer rejects the foregoing ADDENDUM.

_____   _____
(Signature)   (Date)   (Time)   (Signature)   (Date)   (Time)

THIS FORM APPROVED BY THE UTAH REAL ESTATE COMMISSION AND THE OFFICE OF THE UTAH ATTORNEY GENERAL, EFFECTIVE AUGUST 5, 2003. IT REPLACES AND SUPERSEDES ALL PREVIOUSLY APPROVED VERSIONS OF THIS FORM.

SELLER FINANCING ADDENDUM
TO
REAL ESTATE PURCHASE CONTRACT

THIS SELLER FINANCING ADDENDUM is made a part of that REAL ESTATE PURCHASE CONTRACT (the "REPC") with an Offer Reference Date of _____, between _____ as Buyer, and _____ as Seller, regarding the Property located at _____. The terms of this ADDENDUM are hereby incorporated as part of the REPC.

1. CREDIT DOCUMENTS. Seller's extension of credit to Buyer shall be evidenced by: [ ] **Note and Deed of Trust** [ ] **Note and All-Inclusive Deed of Trust** [ ] **Other:** _____

2. CREDIT TERMS. The terms of the credit documents referred to in Section 1 above are as follows: $_____ principal amount of the note (the "Note"); interest at _____ % per annum; payable at approximately $_____ per _____. The entire unpaid balance of principal plus accrued interest is due in _____ months from date of the Note. First payment due _____. Additional principal payments, balloon payments or other terms as follows:
_____
_____
_____

The credit documents referenced in Section 1 of this ADDENDUM will contain a due-on-sale clause in favor of Seller. Seller agrees to provide to Buyer at **Settlement**: (a) an amortization schedule based on the above terms; (b) a written disclosure of the total interest Buyer will pay to maturity of the Note; and (c) the annual percentage rate on the Note based on loan closing costs.

3. TAXES AND ASSESSMENTS. Buyer shall also be responsible for: (a) property taxes; (b) homeowners association dues; (c) special assessments; and (d) hazard insurance premiums on the Property. These specific obligations will be paid: [ ] **directly to Seller/Escrow Agent on a monthly basis** [ ] **directly to the applicable county treasurer, association, and insurance company** as required by those entities.

4. PAYMENT. Buyer's payments under Section 2 above will be made to: [ ] **Seller** [ ] **an Escrow Agent**. If an Escrow Agent, _____ will act as Escrow Agent and will be responsible for disbursing payments on any underlying mortgage or deed of trust (the "underlying mortgage") and to the Seller. Cost of setting up and maintaining the escrow account shall be paid by: [ ] **Buyer** [ ] **Seller** [ ] **split evenly between the parties**.

5. LATE PAYMENT/PREPAYMENT. Any payment not made within _____ days after it is due is subject to a late charge of $_____ or _____ % of the installment due, whichever is greater. Amounts in default shall bear interest at a rate of ___ % per annum. All or part of the principal balance on the Note may be paid prior to maturity without penalty.

6. DUE-ON-SALE. As part of the Seller Disclosures referenced in Section 7 of the REPC, Seller shall provide to Buyer a copy of the underlying mortgage, the note secured thereby, and the amortization schedule. Buyer=s obligation to purchase under this Contract is conditioned upon Buyer=s approval of the content of those documents, in accordance with Section 8 of the REPC. If the holder of the underlying mortgage calls the loan due as a result of this transaction, Buyer agrees to discharge the underlying loan as required by the mortgage lender. In such event, Seller=s remaining equity shall be paid as provided in the credit documents.

7. BUYER DISCLOSURES. Buyer has provided to Seller, as **a required** part of this ADDENDUM, the attached Buyer Financial Information Sheet. Buyer may use the Buyer Financial Information Sheet approved by the Real Estate Commission and the Attorney General=s Office, or may provide comparable written information in a different format, together with such additional information as Seller may reasonably require. Buyer [ ] **WILL** [ ] **WILL NOT** provide Seller with copies of IRS returns for the two preceding tax years. Buyer acknowledges that Seller may contact Buyer's current employer for verification of employment as represented by Buyer in the Buyer Financial Information Sheet.

8. SELLER APPROVAL. By the Seller Disclosure Deadline referenced in Section 24(a) of the REPC, Buyer shall provide to Seller, at Buyer's expense, a current credit report on Buyer from a consumer credit reporting agency. Seller may use the credit report and the information referenced in Section 7 of this Addendum ("Buyer Disclosures") to review and evaluate the credit-worthiness of Buyer ("Seller's Review").

8.1 Seller Review. If Seller determines, in Seller's sole discretion, that the results of the Seller's Review are unacceptable, Seller may either: (a) no later than the Due Diligence Deadline referenced in Section 24(b) of the REPC, cancel the REPC by providing written notice to Buyer, whereupon the Earnest Money Deposit shall be released to Buyer without the requirement of further written authorization from Seller; or (b) no later than the Due Diligence Deadline referenced in Section 24(b), resolve in writing with Buyer any objections Seller has arising from Seller's Review.

8.2 Failure to Cancel or Resolve Objections. If Seller fails to cancel the REPC or resolve in writing any objections Seller has arising from Seller's Review, as provided in Section 8.1 of this ADDENDUM, Seller shall be deemed to have waived the Seller=s Review.

9. TITLE INSURANCE. Buyer [ ] SHALL [ ] SHALL NOT provide to Seller a lender=s policy of title insurance in the amount of the indebtedness to the Seller, and shall pay for such policy at Settlement.

10. DISCLOSURE OF TAX IDENTIFICATION NUMBERS. By no later than Settlement, Buyer and Seller shall disclose to each other their respective Social Security Numbers or other applicable tax identification numbers so that they may comply with federal laws on reporting mortgage interest in filings with the Internal Revenue Service.

To the extent the terms of this ADDENDUM modify or conflict with any provisions of the REPC, including all prior addenda and counteroffers, these terms shall control. All other terms of the REPC, including all prior addenda and counteroffers, not modified by this ADDENDUM shall remain the same. [ ] Seller [ ] Buyer shall have until _____ [ ] AM [ ] PM Mountain Time on _____(Date), to accept the terms of this SELLER FINANCING ADDENDUM in accordance with Section 23 of the REPC. Unless so accepted, the offer as set forth in this SELLER FINANCING ADDENDUM shall lapse.

_____
[ ] Buyer [ ] Seller Signature   (Date) (Time)   Social Security Number

_____
[ ] Buyer [ ] Seller Signature   (Date) (Time)   Social Security Number

ACCEPTANCE/COUNTEROFFER/REJECTION
CHECK ONE:

[ ]ACCEPTANCE: [ ] Seller [ ] Buyer hereby accepts these terms.

[ ]COUNTEROFFER: [ ] Seller [ ] Buyer presents as a counteroffer the terms set forth on the attached ADDENDUM NO. _____.

[ ]REJECTION: [ ] Seller [ ] Buyer rejects the foregoing SELLER FINANCING ADDENDUM.

_____
(Signature)   (Date) (Time)   (Signature)   (Date) (Time)

_____
(Signature)   (Date) (Time)   (Signature)   (Date) (Time)

THIS FORM APPROVED BY THE UTAH REAL ESTATE COMMISSION AND THE OFFICE OF THE UTAH ATTORNEY GENERAL, EFFECTIVE AUGUST 27, 2008. AS OF JANUARY 1, 2009, IT WILL REPLACE AND SUPERSEDE THE PREVIOUSLY APPROVED VERSION OF THIS FORM.

Page 2 of 2 pages   Buyer's Initials_____ Date_____ Seller's Initials_____ Date_____

BUYER FINANCIAL INFORMATION SHEET

(If there is more than one buyer, a separate Buyer Financial
Information Sheet shall be completed for each.)

INFORMATION ABOUT BUYER

Last Name	First Name	Initial	Sr,Jr,II	Date of Birth Mo. Day Year	Social Security No.
Home Address	Street	City	State	Zip Code	How Long? Rent Own	Home Phone
Previous Address	Street	City	State	Zip Code	How Long?	No. of Dependents
Name and address of nearest relative not living with you				Relationship	Home Phone
Name/address of employer	Position held	Gross mo. salary	How long with firm?	Business Phone

OTHER INCOME: You need not disclose alimony, child support or separate maintenance payments unless you wish to use such income to establish your creditworthiness.

Other monthly income $_____
Source: _____

Name of your bank, credit union or savings & loan:
_____
Checking No._____ Balance_____
Savings No._____ Balance_____

ASSETS (What you own)

Description	If co-owned, show name of co-owner	Value
Home: Own Rent		$
Other Real Estate		
Car		
Furniture		
Other Assets (Stocks, Bonds, Insurance, etc.)		
Total Assets		$

DEBTS (What you owe)

List ALL debts, rents and lease payments and to whom they are payable (name and address)*	Present Balance	Monthly Payment
	$	$
Alimony, Child Support or Maintenance Obligations		
Medical Bills		
Total Liabilities	$	$

* List all lines of credit and credit cards whether balance is owing or not.
If additional space is required for what you owe, attach separate form.

YES	NO	
☐	☐	1. Are any of your debts past due?
☐	☐	2. Do you have any debts under a name other than the one used on this loan application?
☐	☐	3. Have you ever had any auto, furniture or other property repossessed?
☐	☐	4. Are you a cosigner or guarantor on any debts not listed above?
☐	☐	5. Have you filed bankruptcy within the last seven years?
☐	☐	6. Do you have any judgments against you which have not been fully paid and satisfied?

Everything I have stated in this form is correct to the best of my knowledge. I understand that you will retain this form whether or not it is approved. You are authorized to check my credit and employment history. I have read and understood this form and agree to promptly provide you with any additional information you may reasonably require to determine my creditworthiness.

_____   _____
Buyer's Signature   Date

THIS FORM APPROVED BY THE UTAH REAL ESTATE COMMISSION AND THE OFFICE OF THE UTAH ATTORNEY GENERAL, EFFECTIVE JUNE 12, 1996. IT REPLACES AND SUPERSEDES ANY PREVIOUSLY APPROVED VERSIONS OF THIS FORM.

FHA/VA LOAN ADDENDUM
TO
REAL ESTATE PURCHASE CONTRACT

THIS IS AN ADDENDUM to that REAL ESTATE PURCHASE CONTRACT (the "REPC" with an Offer Reference Date of _____, 20 _____, including all prior addenda and counteroffers, between _____ _____ as Buyer, and _____ as Seller, regarding the Property located at _____. The following terms are hereby incorporated as part of the REPC. All references to FHA/VA shall mean the Federal Housing Administration/Department of Veterans Affairs. **(CHECK APPLICABLE BOXES)**

1.   Buyer **[   ] DOES [   ] DOES NOT** intend to occupy the Property as his/her residence.

2.   Buyer shall not be obligated to complete the purchase of the Property or incur any penalty or forfeiture of the Earnest Money Deposit or other down payment, or otherwise be obligated to purchase the Property, if: (a) for a VA loan, the Purchase Price exceeds the reasonable value of the Property established by the VA Certificate of Reasonable Value or VA appraisal; or (b) for an FHA loan, the Purchase Price exceeds the appraised value of the Property (excluding closing costs) established by the FHA appraisal. Buyer shall, however, have the right to complete the sale without regard to the amount of the appraised valuation made by the applicable FHA or the VA. The appraised valuation is used to determine the maximum loan that FHA will insure or VA will guarantee. Neither FHA nor the VA warrants the value or condition of the Property. Buyer should satisfy himself/herself that the price and condition of the Property are acceptable. Buyer acknowledges that an FHA/VA appraisal does not constitute a property inspection.

3.   Seller shall make any and all appraisal required repairs, provided that the cost does not exceed $_____.

4.   If required by applicable FHA or VA rules, Seller shall furnish Buyer with a current Pest Control Report showing the Property to be free and clear from termite infestation. In the event of termite infestation, Seller shall eradicate the same and repair any damage at Seller's expense, provided that the cost does not exceed $_____.

5.   There are certain costs associated with the granting of a mortgage loan, some of which FHA/VA will not allow the Buyer to pay. **(Check applicable box):**

       5.1   **[   ]** Seller shall contribute at settlement an amount toward payment of loan discount points and other loan and closing related costs ("Loan Costs"). The amount of Seller's contribution shall be $_____. Such contribution shall first be applied to Loan Costs that FHA/VA will not permit Buyer to pay, and any remainder shall be allocated at Buyer's discretion toward remaining Loan Costs. Seller shall have no further obligation toward Loan Costs. If the amount of Seller's contribution exceeds the amount of actual Loan Costs, then such excess shall be returned to Seller. Seller's agreement to contribute toward payment of Loan Costs shall not modify Seller's obligations under Section 3 of the REPC.

       5.2   **[   ]** Seller shall not contribute any amount toward Loan Costs.

6.   [APPLIES TO FHA ONLY] The undersigned hereby certify that the terms of the REPC are true to the best of our knowledge and belief, and that any other agreement entered into by any of the parties has been fully disclosed and is attached to the REPC.

7.   If any provision in the REPC or this ADDENDUM is inconsistent with any currently applicable law governing FHA/VA loan transactions, then to the extent of such inconsistency, that law shall govern.

Page 1 of 2 pages Buyer's Initials_____ Date_____ Seller's Initials_____ Date_____

ASSUMPTION ADDENDUM
TO
REAL ESTATE PURCHASE CONTRACT

THIS IS AN ADDENDUM to that REAL ESTATE PURCHASE CONTRACT (the "REPC") with an Offer Reference Date of _____, including all prior addenda and counteroffers, between _____ ___ as Buyer, and _____ as Seller, regarding the Property located at _____. The following terms are hereby incorporated as part of the REPC. **(CHECK APPLICABLE BOXES)**

1. Assumption of Existing Loan. Except as may be provided in Section 2 of this Assumption Addendum, Buyer shall assume and pay an existing loan (the "Existing Loan") in the approximate amount of $_____. The Existing Loan is presently payable at **$_____** per month including: **[ ] principal and interest (presently at _____ % per annum); [ ] real estate taxes; [ ] property insurance premium; [ ] mortgage insurance premium**. Seller agrees to provide to Buyer (as an additional Seller Disclosure under Section 7 of the REPC) copies of any notes and trust deeds to be assumed by Buyer. Seller represents that the Existing Loan is assumable. Buyer agrees to make application to the Lender to assume the Existing Loan, if required.

2. Assumption Fees and Other Charges by Lender. Buyer agrees to pay any assumption and transfer fees charged by the Lender, as long as the total of these fees does not exceed _____ % of the Existing Loan balance. Buyer also agrees to pay any interest rate increase demanded by the Lender as long as this does not make the new interest rate on the Existing Loan exceed _____ %. If such fees and interest rate increases exceed these amounts, then the Buyer shall have no obligation to assume the Existing Loan or purchase the Property.

3. Release of Liability. The sale **[ ] IS [ ] IS NOT** conditioned on Seller being released from liability on the Existing Loan.

4. Difference in Loan Balance. Any net differences between the approximate balance owed on the Existing Loan as shown above and the actual balance on the Existing Loan at Settlement shall be adjusted in **[ ] Cash [ ] Other (specify)**

_____

5. Reserve Account. Buyer agrees to purchase at Settlement any reserve account balance held by the Lender.

To the extent the terms of this ADDENDUM modify or conflict with any provisions of the REPC, including all prior addenda and counteroffers, these terms shall control. All other terms of the REPC, including all prior addenda and counteroffers, not modified by this ADDENDUM shall remain the same. **[ ] Seller [ ] Buyer** shall have until _____ **[ ] AM [ ] PM** Mountain Time on_____ (Date), to accept the terms of this ASSUMPTION ADDENDUM in accordance with the provisions of Section 23 of the REPC. Unless so accepted, the offer as set forth in this ASSUMPTION ADDENDUM shall lapse.

_____

[ ] Buyer [ ] Seller Signature   (Date) (Time)   [ ] Buyer [ ] Seller Signature   (Date) (Time)

ACCEPTANCE/COUNTEROFFER/REJECTION

CHECK ONE:

[ ]   ACCEPTANCE: [ ] Seller [ ] Buyer hereby accepts the terms of this ASSUMPTION ADDENDUM.

[ ]   COUNTEROFFER: [ ] Seller [ ] Buyer presents as a counteroffer the terms of attached ADDENDUM NO. ___.

_____

(Signature)   (Date) (Time)   (Signature)   (Date) (Time)

[ ]   REJECTION: [ ] Seller [ ] Buyer rejects the foregoing ASSUMPTION ADDENDUM.

_____

(Signature)   (Date) (Time)   (Signature)   (Date) (Time)

THIS FORM APPROVED BY THE UTAH REAL ESTATE COMMISSION AND THE OFFICE OF THE UTAH ATTORNEY GENERAL, EFFECTIVE AUGUST 17, 1998. IT REPLACES AND SUPERSEDES ALL PREVIOUSLY APPROVED VERSIONS OF THIS FORM.

LEAD-BASED PAINT ADDENDUM TO REAL ESTATE PURCHASE CONTRACT

THIS IS AN ADDENDUM to that REAL ESTATE PURCHASE CONTRACT (the "REPC") with an Offer Reference Date of _____, including all prior addenda and counteroffers, between _____ _____ as Buyer, and _____ as Seller, regarding the Property located at _____. The following terms are hereby incorporated as part of the REPC.

1. OPPORTUNITY TO CONDUCT A RISK ASSESSMENT OR INSPECTION. (Check applicable boxes)

1.1 Buyer's obligation to purchase the Property is conditioned upon Buyer's approval of a risk assessment or inspection of the Property for the presence of lead-based paint and/or lead-based paint hazards.

1.2 The risk assessment or inspection ("Risk Assessment") of the Property shall be paid for by Buyer and shall be conducted by individuals or entities of Buyer's choice. Seller shall cooperate in making the Property available for the Risk Assessment. The deadline for Buyer to complete and review the Risk Assessment ("Risk Assessment Deadline") shall be: **(Check one box)**

[ ] ten calendar days after Acceptance   **OR**   [ ] _____ calendar days after Acceptance.

1.3 If the results of the Risk Assessment are not acceptable to Buyer, Buyer may either (a) provide written objections to Seller as provided in Section 1.4 of this ADDENDUM; or (b) immediately cancel the REPC by providing written notice of cancellation to Seller by the Risk Assessment Deadline referenced in Section 1.2 above, together with a copy of the Risk Assessment report. The Brokerage, upon receipt of a copy of Buyer's written notice of cancellation, shall return the Earnest Money Deposit to Buyer.

1.4 If Buyer does not immediately cancel the REPC as provided above, Buyer may, by the Risk Assessment Deadline referenced in Section 1.2 above, provide Seller with written objections and a copy of the Risk Assessment report. Buyer and Seller shall have seven calendar days after Seller's receipt of the objections (the "Response Period") in which to agree in writing upon a manner of resolving Buyer's objections. Seller may, but shall not be required to, resolve Buyer's objections. If Buyer and Seller have not agreed in writing upon the manner of resolving Buyer's objections, Buyer may cancel the REPC by providing written notice to Seller no later than three calendar days after expiration of the Response Period. The Brokerage, upon receipt of a copy of Buyer's written notice of cancellation, shall return the Earnest Money Deposit to Buyer.

1.5 If Buyer does not deliver a written objection to Seller regarding the results of the Risk Assessment as provided in Section 1.4 above, or cancel the REPC as provided in Sections 1.3 or 1.4 above, any objections to the results of the Risk Assessment shall be deemed waived by Buyer and Buyer shall take the Property "as is" with regard to any lead-based paint or lead-based paint hazards that may be present in the Property.

To the extent the terms of this ADDENDUM modify or conflict with any provisions of the REPC, including all prior addenda and counteroffers, these terms shall control. All other terms of the REPC, including all prior addenda and counteroffers, not modified by this ADDENDUM shall remain the same. [ ] **Seller** [ ] **Buyer** shall have until _____ [ ] AM [ ] PM Mountain Time on_____(Date), to accept the terms of this ADDENDUM in accordance with the provisions of Section 23 of the REPC. Unless so accepted, the offer as set forth in this ADDENDUM shall lapse.

_____   _____
[ ] Buyer [ ] Seller Signature   (Date) (Time)   [ ] Buyer [ ] Seller Signature   (Date) (Time)

ACCEPTANCE/COUNTEROFFER/REJECTION

CHECK ONE:

[ ]   **ACCEPTANCE:** [ ] **Seller** [ ] **Buyer** hereby accepts the terms of this ADDENDUM.

[ ]   **COUNTEROFFER:** [ ] **Seller** [ ] **Buyer** presents as a counteroffer the terms of attached ADDENDUM NO. ___.

_____   _____
(Signature)   (Date) (Time)   (Signature)   (Date) (Time)

[ ]   **REJECTION:** [ ] **Seller** [ ] **Buyer** rejects the foregoing ADDENDUM.

_____   _____
(Signature)   (Date) (Time)   (Signature)   (Date) (Time)

THIS FORM APPROVED BY THE UTAH REAL ESTATE COMMISSION AND THE OFFICE OF THE UTAH ATTORNEY GENERAL, EFFECTIVE AUGUST 17, 1998. IT REPLACES AND SUPERSEDES ALL PREVIOUSLY APPROVED VERSIONS OF THIS FORM.

DISCLOSURE AND ACKNOWLEDGMENT REGARDING
LEAD-BASED PAINT AND/OR LEAD-BASED PAINT HAZARDS

THIS IS A DISCLOSURE AND ACKNOWLEDGMENT concerning Property (the "Property") located at _____
_____. This document contains certain provisions required by federal law. If Buyer and Seller enter into a contract for the purchase of the Property (a "REPC"), this document shall be attached to that contract and made a part thereof.

1. LEAD WARNING STATEMENT. *Every purchaser of any interest in residential real property on which a residential dwelling was built prior to 1978 is notified that such property may present exposure to lead from lead-based paint that may place young children at risk of developing lead poisoning. Lead poisoning in young children may produce permanent neurological damage, including learning disabilities, reduced intelligence quotient, behavioral problems, and impaired memory. Lead poisoning also poses a particular risk to pregnant women. The seller of any interest in residential real property is required to provide the buyer with any information on lead-based paint hazards from risk assessments or inspections in the seller's possession and notify the buyer of any known lead-based paint hazards. A risk assessment or inspection for possible lead-based paint hazards is recommended prior to purchase.*

2. SELLER'S DISCLOSURE AND ACKNOWLEDGMENT. (Initial applicable boxes)
    (a) Presence of lead-based paint and/or lead-based paint hazards (initial one box only):
        (i) [   ] Known lead-based paint and/or lead-based paint hazards are present in the Property (explain):
        _____
        (ii) [   ] Seller has no knowledge of lead-based paint and/or lead-based paint hazards in the Property.
    (b) Records and reports available to Seller (initial one box only):
        (i) [   ] Seller has provided Buyer with all available records and reports pertaining to lead-based paint and/or lead-based hazards in the Property (list documents):
        _____
        (ii) [   ] Seller has no reports or records pertaining to lead-based paint and/or lead-based paint hazards in the Property.
    (c) Seller understands that under federal law, if Seller has not yet made the disclosures in Sections 2(a) and 2(b) of this document, or Buyer has not yet been provided with an EPA approved lead hazard information pamphlet, Seller may not accept an offer by Buyer to purchase the property until after those steps have been completed and Buyer has been given an opportunity to review that information and amend the offer.
    (d) Seller understands that if Buyer initials the box in Section 3(d)(i) of this document, the REPC must include the Lead-Based Paint Addendum.

3. BUYER'S ACKNOWLEDGMENT. (Initial)
    (a) [   ] Buyer has received copies of any information listed in Sections 2(a) and 2(b) above.
    (b) [   ] Buyer has received the pamphlet *Protect Your Family from Lead in Your Home* or an equivalent lead hazard information pamphlet approved by the federal Environmental Protection Agency.
    (c) [   ] Buyer has read the Lead Warning Statement in Section 1 above and understands its contents.
    (d) Buyer has **(initial one box only)**:
        (i) [   ] a 10-day opportunity (or mutually agreed upon period) to conduct a risk assessment or inspection for the presence of lead-based paint and/or lead-based paint hazards. **If this box is initialed, the REPC must include the Lead-Based Paint Addendum; OR**
        (ii) [   ] by initialing this box, waived the opportunity to conduct a risk assessment or inspection for the presence of lead-based paint and/or lead-based paint hazards.

4. AGENT'S ACKNOWLEDGMENT. (Initial)
    [   ] Agent has informed Seller of Seller's obligations under 42 U.S.C. 4852d and is aware of his/her responsibility to ensure compliance.

5. CERTIFICATION OF ACCURACY. (Buyer, Seller and Agent(s) must sign)
    The following parties have reviewed the information above and certify, to the best of their knowledge, that the information they have each respectively provided is true and accurate.

Seller Signature	Date	Time	Seller Signature	Date	Time
Buyer Signature	Date	Time	Buyer Signature	Date	Time
Agent Signature	Date	Time	Agent Signature	Date	Time

THIS FORM APPROVED BY THE UTAH REAL ESTATE COMMISSION AND THE OFFICE OF THE UTAH ATTORNEY GENERAL, EFFECTIVE SEPTEMBER 5, 1996.

Page _____ of _____

DEPOSIT OF EARNEST MONEY WITH
TITLE INSURANCE COMPANY ADDENDUM
TO
REAL ESTATE PURCHASE CONTRACT

THIS IS AN [ ] ADDENDUM [ ] COUNTEROFFER to that REAL ESTATE PURCHASE CONTRACT (the "REPC") with an Offer Reference Date of _____, including all prior addenda and counteroffers, between _____ as Buyer, and _____ as Seller, regarding the Property located at _____. The following terms are hereby incorporated as part of the REPC:

1. The REPC is amended as follows: Buyer and Seller agree that the Earnest Money Deposit, or Deposits, will be held with a Title Insurance Company instead of deposited in the Buyer's Brokerage Trust Account. The Title Insurance Company is _____located at: _____ _____ phone number_____ and email _____.

ATTENTION: Buyer and Seller are advised that the Title Insurance Company may require, through separate written instructions, that **BOTH** the Buyer and Seller mutually authorize disbursement of the Earnest Money Deposit, even if the REPC states that no additional written authorization is required, which may result in additional delays and costs for either party to receive the Earnest Money Deposits

Buyer and Seller acknowledge that the Utah Division of Real Estate has no authority over the Title Insurance Company's release or disbursement of the Earnest Money Deposit.

To the extent the terms of this ADDENDUM modify or conflict with any provisions of the REPC, including all prior addenda and counteroffers, these terms shall control. All other terms of the REPC, including all prior addenda and counteroffers, not modified by this ADDENDUM shall remain the same. **[ ] Seller [ ] Buyer** shall have until _____ **[ ] AM [ ] PM** Mountain Time on_____(Date), to accept the terms of this ADDENDUM in accordance with the provisions of Section 23 of the REPC. Unless so accepted, the offer as set forth in this ADDENDUM shall lapse.

_____   _____
[ ] Buyer [ ] Seller Signature   (Date)   (Time)   [ ] Buyer [ ] Seller Signature   (Date)   (Time)

ACCEPTANCE/COUNTEROFFER/REJECTION

CHECK ONE:

[ ] ACCEPTANCE: [ ] Seller [ ] Buyer hereby accepts the terms of this ADDENDUM.

[ ] COUNTEROFFER: [ ] Seller [ ] Buyer presents as a counteroffer the terms of attached ADDENDUM NO. ____.

[ ] REJECTION: [ ] Seller [ ] Buyer rejects the foregoing ADDENDUM.

_____   _____
(Signature)   (Date)   (Time)   (Signature)   (Date)   (Time)

_____   _____
(Signature)   (Date)   (Time)   (Signature)   (Date)   (Time)

THIS FORM APPROVED BY THE UTAH REAL ESTATE COMMISSION AND THE OFFICE OF THE UTAH ATTORNEY GENERAL, EFFECTIVE JANUARY 1, 2018

The following forms are provided as illustrations of agency forms and addenda that comply with Utah law. These forms have been prepared by the legal team representing the Utah Association of Realtors®. They are used here by permission. Outside this educational setting, they are only available for use by members of the Utah Association of Realtors®.

UAR® Agency and Addenda Forms

 Utah Association of REALTORS®

**EXCLUSIVE RIGHT TO SELL LISTING AGREEMENT &
AGENCY DISCLOSURE**

 EQUAL HOUSING OPPORTUNITY

(PART A)
THIS IS A LEGALLY BINDING CONTRACT. – READ CAREFULLY BEFORE SIGNING.
DESIGNATED AGENCY BROKERAGE

THIS AGREEMENT is entered into effective the _____ day of _____, _____, by and between _____ (the "Company") and _____ (the "Seller").

1. TERM OF LISTING. The Seller hereby grants to the Company, including _____ (the "Seller's Agent") as the authorized agent for the Company, for the period of _____ months starting on the date listed above, and ending at 5:00 P.M. (MST) on the _____ day of _____, _____ (the "Listing Period"), the Exclusive Right to Sell, Lease, or Exchange real property owned by the Seller, described as: _____ (the "Property"), at the listing price and terms stated on the attached property data form (the "Data Form"), or at such other price and terms to which the Seller may agree in writing.

2. BROKERAGE FEE. If, during the Listing Period, the Company, the Seller's Agent, the Seller, another real estate agent, or anyone else locates a party who is ready, willing and able to buy, lease, or exchange (collectively "acquire") the Property, or any part thereof, at the listing price and terms stated on the Data Form, or any other price and terms to which the Seller may agree in writing, the Seller agrees to pay to the Company a brokerage fee in the amount of $_____ or _____% of such acquisition price. The brokerage fee, unless otherwise agreed in writing by the Seller and the Company, shall be due and payable from the Seller's proceeds on: (a) if a purchase, the date of recording of the closing documents for the acquisition of the Property; (b) if a lease, the effective date of the lease; or (c) if an option, the date the option agreement is signed. If within the Listing Period, or any extension of the Listing Period, the Property is withdrawn from sale, transferred, conveyed, leased, rented, or made unmarketable by a voluntary act of Seller, without the written consent of the Company; or if the sale is prevented by default of the Seller, the brokerage fee shall be immediately due and payable to the Company. The Company is authorized to share the brokerage fee with another brokerage participating in any transaction arising out of this Listing Agreement.

3. PROTECTION PERIOD. If within _____ months after the termination or expiration of this Listing Agreement, the Property is acquired by any party to whom the Property was offered or shown by the Company, the Seller's Agent, the Seller, or another real estate agent during the Listing Period, or any extension of the Listing Period, the Seller agrees to pay to the Company the brokerage fee stated in Section 2, unless the Seller is obligated to pay a brokerage fee on such acquisition to another brokerage based on another valid listing agreement entered into after the expiration or termination date of this Listing Agreement.

4. SELLER WARRANTIES/DISCLOSURES. The Seller warrants to the Company that the individuals or entity listed above as the "Seller" represents all of the record owners of the Property. The Seller warrants that it has marketable title and an established right to sell, lease, or exchange the Property. The Seller agrees to execute the necessary documents of conveyance. The Seller agrees to furnish buyer with good and marketable title, and to pay at Settlement, for a standard coverage owner's policy of title insurance for the buyer in the amount of the purchase price. The Seller agrees to fully inform the Seller's Agent regarding the Seller's knowledge of the condition of the Property. Upon signing of this Listing Agreement, the Seller agrees to personally complete and sign a Seller's Property Condition Disclosure form. The Seller agrees to indemnify and hold harmless the Seller's Agent and the Company against any claims that may arise from: (i) the Seller providing incorrect or inaccurate information regarding the Property; (ii) the Seller failing to disclose material information regarding the Property, including, but not limited to, the condition of all appliances; the condition of heating, plumbing, and electrical fixtures and equipment; sewer problems; moisture or other problems in the roof or foundation; the availability and location of utilities; and the location of property lines; and (iii) any injuries resulting from any unsafe conditions within the Property.

5. AGENCY RELATIONSHIPS. By signing this Listing Agreement, the Seller designates the Seller's Agent and the Principal/Branch Broker for the Company (the "Broker"), as agents for the Seller to locate a buyer for the Property. The Seller authorizes the Seller's Agent or the Broker to appoint another agent in the Company to also represent the Seller in the event the Seller's Agent or the Broker will be unavailable to service the Property. As agents for the Seller, they have fiduciary duties to the Seller that include loyalty, full disclosure, confidentiality, and reasonable care. The Seller understands, however, that the Seller's Agent and the Broker may now, or in the future, be agents for a buyer who may wish to negotiate a purchase of the Property. Then the Seller's Agent and the Broker would be acting as Limited Agents – representing both the Seller and buyer at the same time. A Limited Agent has fiduciary duties to both the Seller and the buyer. However, those duties are "limited" because the agent cannot provide to both parties undivided loyalty, full confidentiality and full disclosure of all information known to the agent. For this reason, the Limited Agent is bound by a further duty of neutrality. Being neutral, the Limited Agent may not disclose to either party information likely to weaken the bargaining position of the other – for example, the highest price the buyer will offer, or the lowest price the Seller will accept. THE SELLER IS ADVISED THAT NEITHER THE SELLER NOR THE BUYER IS REQUIRED TO ACCEPT A LIMITED AGENCY SITUATION IN THE COMPANY, AND EACH PARTY IS ENTITLED TO BE REPRESENTED BY ITS OWN AGENT. If Limited Agency is agreed to below; (a) the Seller authorizes the Seller's Agent and the Broker to represent both the Buyer and the Seller as Limited Agents when the Seller's Agent and the Broker also represent the Buyer of the Property that the Seller owns; (b) the Seller further agrees that when another agent in the Company represents the Buyer, that agent will exclusively represent the Buyer, the Seller's Agent will exclusively represent the Seller, and the Broker will act as a Limited

Page 1 of 3   [   ] [   ] Seller's Initials   Date_____   UAR FORM 8

Broker. **IN EITHER EVENT, IF LIMITED AGENCY IS AGREED TO BELOW, THE BUYER AND THE SELLER WILL BE REQUIRED TO SIGN A SEPARATE LIMITED AGENCY CONSENT AGREEMENT AT THE TIME THE LIMITED AGENCY SITUATION ARISES.   INITIAL APPLICABLE BOX: [   ] I AGREE TO LIMITED AGENCY; OR [   ] I DO NOT AGREE TO LIMITED AGENCY.**

6. PROFESSIONAL ADVICE. The Company and the Seller's Agent are trained in the marketing of real estate. Neither the Company nor its agents are trained or licensed to provide the Seller or any prospective buyer with legal or tax advice, or with technical advice regarding the physical condition of the Property. SELLER IS ADVISED NOT TO RELY ON THE COMPANY, OR ON ANY AGENTS OF THE COMPANY, FOR A DETERMINATION REGARDING THE PHYSICAL OR LEGAL CONDITION OF THE PROPERTY. If the Seller desires advice regarding: (i) past or present compliance with zoning and building code requirements; (ii) legal or tax matters; (iii) the physical condition of the Property; (iv) this Listing Agreement; or (v) any transaction for the acquisition of the Property, the Seller's Agent and the Company STRONGLY RECOMMEND THAT THE SELLER OBTAIN SUCH INDEPENDENT ADVICE. IF THE SELLER FAILS TO DO SO, THE SELLER IS ACTING CONTRARY TO THE ADVICE OF THE COMPANY.

7. DISPUTE RESOLUTION. The parties agree that any dispute, arising prior to or after a closing, related to this Listing Agreement shall first be submitted to mediation through a mediation provider mutually agreed upon by the Seller and the Company. If the parties cannot agree upon a mediation provider, the dispute shall be submitted to the American Arbitration Association. Each party agrees to bear its own costs of mediation. If mediation fails, the other remedies available under this Listing Agreement shall apply.

8. ATTORNEY FEES. Except as provided in Section 7, in case of the employment of an attorney in any matter arising out of this Listing Agreement, the prevailing party shall be entitled to receive from the other party all costs and attorney fees, whether the matter is resolved through court action or otherwise. If, through no fault of the Company, any litigation arises out of the Seller's employment of the Company under this Listing Agreement (whether before or after a closing), the Seller agrees to indemnify the Company and the Seller's Agent from all costs and attorney fees incurred by the Company and/or the Seller's Agent in pursuing and/or defending such action.

9. SELLER AUTHORIZATIONS. Seller authorizes the Company and/or Seller's Agent as follows **(check applicable boxes)**: [ ] Advertise the Property through each MLS in which the Company participates, advertise via the internet, and disclose to the MLS after Closing, the final terms and sales price, consistent with the requirements of the MLS; [ ] Communicate with Seller for the purpose of soliciting real estate–related goods and services during and after the term of this Listing Agreement, at the following numbers or email address: _____ hm: _____ wk: _____ cell: _____ fax: _____; [ ] Obtain financial information from any mortgagee or other party holding a lien or interest on the Property; [ ] Have keys to the Property; [ ] Have a key–box installed on the Property; [ ] Hold Open–Houses at the Property; [ ] Place a for sale sign(s) on the Property (i.e., the only for sale sign(s) on the Property shall be that of the Company); [ ] Order a Preliminary Title Report; on the Property, [ ] In any transaction for the acquisition of the Property, Seller agrees that the Earnest Money Deposit may be placed in an interest–bearing trust account with interest paid to the Utah Association of Realtors Housing Opportunity Fund (UARHOF) to assist in creating affordable housing throughout the state; [ ] Order a Home Warranty Plan. Seller acknowledges that the Company has discussed with Seller the safeguarding of personal property and valuables located within the Property. Seller acknowledges that the Company is not an insurer against the loss of or damage to personal property. Seller agrees to hold the Company harmless from any loss or damage that might result from any authorizations given in this Section 9. [   ] **Seller's Initials**

10. ATTACHMENT. The Data Form is incorporated into this Listing Agreement by this reference. In addition to the Data Form, there [ ] ARE [ ] ARE NOT additional terms contained in an Addendum attached to this Listing Agreement. If an Addendum is attached, the terms of that Addendum are incorporated into this Listing Agreement by this reference.

11. EQUAL HOUSING OPPORTUNITY. The Seller and the Company shall comply with Federal, State, and local fair housing laws.

12. FAXES. Facsimile (fax) transmission of a signed copy of this Listing Agreement, and retransmission of a signed fax, shall be the same as delivery of an original. If this transaction involves multiple owners this Listing Agreement may be executed in counterparts.

13. ENTIRE AGREEMENT. This Listing Agreement, including the Seller's Property Condition Disclosure form and the Data Form, contain the entire agreement between the parties relating to the subject matter of this Listing Agreement. This Listing Agreement may not be modified or amended except in writing signed by the parties hereto.

THE UNDERSIGNED Seller does hereby agree to the terms of this Listing Agreement.

_____   _____   _____
(Seller's Signature)   (Address/Phone)   (Date)

_____   _____   _____
(Seller's Signature)   (Address/Phone)   (Date)

ACCEPTED BY The Company

By: _____ _____   By: _____ _____
    (Authorized Seller's Agent)   (Date)   (Principal/Branch Broker)   (Date)
                                                     Paul Naylor

This form is COPYRIGHTED by the UTAH ASSOCIATION OF REALTORS ® for use solely by its members. Any unauthorized use, modification, copying or distribution without written consent is prohibited. NO REPRESENTATION IS MADE AS TO THE LEGAL VALIDITY OR ADEQUACY OF ANY PROVISION OF THIS FORM IN ANY SPECIFIC TRANSACTION. IF YOU DESIRE SPECIFIC LEGAL OR TAX ADVICE, CONSULT AN APPROPRIATE PROFESSIONAL.

COPYRIGHT © UTAH ASSOCIATION OF REALTORS ® – 1995 – REVISED 4.11.06 – ALL RIGHTS RESERVED

 Utah Association of REALTORS®

EXCLUSIVE BUYER–BROKER AGREEMENT & AGENCY DISCLOSURE
THIS IS A LEGALLY BINDING CONTRACT. – READ CAREFULLY BEFORE SIGNING.
DESIGNATED AGENCY BROKERAGE

 EQUAL HOUSING OPPORTUNITY

THIS EXCLUSIVE BUYER–BROKER AGREEMENT is entered into on this _____ day of _____, _____, by and between _____ (the "Company") and _____ ("Buyer")

1. TERM OF AGREEMENT. The Buyer hereby retains the Company, including _____ (the "Buyer's Agent") as the authorized agent for the Company, starting on the date listed above, and ending at 5:00 P.M. (MST) on the _____ day of _____, _____, or the closing of the acquisition of a property, which ever occurs first (the "Initial Term"), to act as the **EXCLUSIVE** Buyer's Agent in locating and/or negotiating for the acquisition of a property in _____ County, Utah. During the Initial Term of this Exclusive Buyer–Broker Agreement, and any extensions thereof, the Buyer agrees not to enter into another buyer–broker agreement with another real estate agent or brokerage.

2. BROKERAGE FEE. If, during the Initial Term, or any extension of the Initial Term, the Buyer, or any other person acting in the Buyer's behalf, acquires an interest in any real property, the Buyer agrees to pay to the Company a brokerage fee in the amount of $_____ or _____% of the acquisition price of the property. If the property acquired by the Buyer is listed with a brokerage, the selling commission paid to the Company by the listing brokerage shall satisfy the Buyer's obligation for the brokerage fee shown above provided that the brokerage fee is not less than the amount shown above. If the brokerage fee is less than the amount shown above, Buyer will pay the difference at closing. If the property is not listed with a brokerage, in the absence of a commission agreement with the owner of the selected property, the brokerage fee shown above shall be paid by the Buyer. Unless otherwise agreed to in writing by the Buyer and the Company, the brokerage fee shown above shall be due and payable on: (a) if a purchase, the date of recording of the closing documents; (b) if a lease, the effective date of the lease, or (c) if an option, the date the option agreement is signed. If the transaction is prevented by default of Buyer, the compensation shall be immediately payable to the Company.

3. PROTECTION PERIOD. If within _____ months after the termination or expiration of this Exclusive Buyer–Broker Agreement, Buyer or any person acting on the Buyer's behalf, enters into an agreement to purchase, exchange for, obtain an option on, or lease any property located for Buyer by Buyer's Agent or the Company, or on which Buyer's Agent negotiates in Buyer's behalf during the Initial Term, Buyer agrees to pay to the Company the brokerage fee referenced in Section 2.

4. BUYER REPRESENTATIONS/DISCLOSURES. THE BUYER WARRANTS THAT THE BUYER HAS NOT ENTERED INTO ANY OTHER BUYER–BROKER AGREEMENT WITH ANY OTHER BROKERAGE THAT IS STILL IN FORCE AND EFFECT. The Buyer will: (a) in all communications with other real estate agents, notify the agents in advance that the Buyer has entered into this Exclusive Buyer–Broker Agreement with the Company; (b) furnish the Buyer's Agent with relevant personal and financial information to facilitate the Buyer's ability to acquire a property; (c) exercise care and diligence in evaluating the physical and legal condition of the property selected by the Buyer; (d) hold harmless the Company and the Buyer's Agent against any claims as the result of any injuries incurred while inspecting any property; (e) upon signing of this Exclusive Buyer–Broker Agreement, personally review and sign the Buyer Due Diligence Checklist form; and (f) disclose to the Buyer's Agent all properties in which the Buyer, as of the date of this Exclusive Buyer–Broker Agreement, is either negotiating to acquire or has a present interest in acquiring.

5. AGENCY RELATIONSHIPS. By signing this Exclusive Buyer–Broker Agreement, the Buyer designates the Buyer's Agent and the Principal/Branch Broker for the Company (the "Broker"), as agents for the Buyer to locate properties for the Buyer's consideration and review. The Buyer authorizes the Buyer's Agent or the Broker to appoint another agent in the Company to also represent the Buyer in the event the Buyer's Agent or the Broker will be unavailable to service the Buyer. As agents for the Buyer, the Buyer's Agent and the Broker have fiduciary duties to the Buyer that include loyalty, full disclosure, confidentiality, and reasonable care. The Buyer understands, however, that the Buyer's Agent and the Broker may now, or in the future, be agents for a Seller who may have a property that the Buyer may wish to acquire. Then the Buyer's Agent and the Broker would be acting as Limited Agents – representing both the Buyer and seller at the same time. A Limited Agent has fiduciary duties to both the Buyer and the seller. However, those duties are "limited" because the agent cannot provide to both parties undivided loyalty, full confidentiality and full disclosure of all information known to the agent. For this reason, the Limited Agent is bound by a further duty of neutrality. Being neutral, the Limited Agent may not disclose to either party information likely to weaken the bargaining position of the other – for example, the highest price the Buyer will offer, or the lowest price the seller will accept. THE BUYER IS ADVISED THAT NEITHER THE BUYER NOR THE SELLER IS REQUIRED TO ACCEPT A LIMITED AGENCY SITUATION IN THE COMPANY, AND EACH PARTY IS ENTITLED TO BE REPRESENTED BY ITS OWN AGENT. If Limited Agency is agreed to below; (a) the Buyer authorizes the Buyer's Agent and the Broker to represent both the Buyer and the Seller as Limited Agents when the Buyer's Agent and the Broker also represent the Seller of the Property the Buyer desires to acquire; (b) the Buyer further agrees that when another agent in the Company represents the Seller, that agent will exclusively represent the Seller, the Buyer's Agent will exclusively represent the Buyer, and the Broker will act as Limited Broker. **IN EITHER EVENT, IF LIMITED AGENCY IS AGREED TO BELOW, THE BUYER AND THE SELLER WILL BE REQUIRED TO SIGN A SEPARATE LIMITED AGENCY CONSENT AGREEMENT AT THE TIME THE LIMITED AGENCY SITUATION ARISES. INITIAL APPLICABLE BOX: [   ] I AGREE TO LIMITED AGENCY; OR [   ] I DO NOT AGREE TO LIMITED AGENCY.**

Page 1 of 2   [   ] [   ] Buyer's Initials Date_____

6. PROFESSIONAL ADVICE. The Company and the Buyer's agent are trained in the marketing of real estate. Neither the Company nor the Buyer's Agent are trained or licensed to provide the Buyer with professional advice regarding the physical condition of any property or regarding legal or tax matters. BUYER IS ADVISED NOT TO RELY ON THE COMPANY, OR ON ANY AGENTS OF THE COMPANY, FOR A DETERMINATION REGARDING THE PHYSICAL OR LEGAL CONDITION OF THE PROPERTY, including, but not limited to: past or present compliance with zoning and building code requirements; the condition of any appliances; the condition of heating/cooling, plumbing, and electrical fixtures and equipment; sewer problems; moisture or other problems in the roof or foundation; the availability and location of utilities; the location of property lines; and the exact square footage or acreage of the property. AS PART OF ANY WRITTEN OFFER TO PURCHASE A PROPERTY, THE COMPANY STRONGLY RECOMMENDS THAT THE BUYER ENGAGE THE SERVICES OF APPROPRIATE PROFESSIONALS TO CONDUCT INSPECTIONS, INVESTIGATIONS, TESTS, SURVEYS, AND OTHER EVALUATIONS OF THE PROPERTY AT THE BUYER'S EXPENSE. IF THE BUYER FAILS TO DO SO, THE BUYER IS ACTING CONTRARY TO THE ADVICE OF THE COMPANY.

7. DISPUTE RESOLUTION. The parties agree that any dispute related to this Exclusive Buyer–Broker Agreement, arising prior to or after the acquisition of a property, shall first be submitted to mediation through a mediation provider mutually agreed upon by the Buyer and the Company. If the parties cannot agree upon a mediation provider, the dispute shall be submitted to the American Arbitration Association. Each party agrees to bear its own costs of mediation. If mediation fails, the other remedies available under this Exclusive Buyer–Broker Agreement shall apply.

8. ATTORNEY FEES. Except as provided in Section 7, in case of the employment of an attorney in any matter arising out of this Exclusive Buyer–Broker Agreement, the prevailing party shall be entitled to receive from the other party all costs and attorney fees, whether the matter is resolved through court action or otherwise. If, through no fault of the Company, any litigation arises out of the Buyer's employment of the Company under this Exclusive Buyer–Broker Agreement (whether before or after the acquisition of a property), the Buyer agrees to indemnify the Company and the Buyer's Agent from all costs and attorney fees incurred by the Company and/or the Buyer's Agent in pursuing and/or defending such action.

9. BUYER AUTHORIZATIONS. Buyer authorizes the Company and/or Buyer's Agent to disclose after closing to each MLS in which the Company participates (consistent with the requirements of each such MLS), the final terms and sales price of the property acquired by Buyer under the terms of this Agreement. Buyer also authorizes the Company and/or Buyer's Agent to communicate with Buyer for the purpose of soliciting real estate related goods and services during and after the term of this Buyer–Broker Agreement, at the following numbers: (hm) _____ (wk) _____ (cell) _____ (fax) _____ and/or (email) _____. In any transaction for the acquisition of a property, Buyer agrees that the Earnest Money Deposit may be placed in an interest–bearing trust account with interest paid to the Utah Association of Realtors® Housing Opportunity Fund (UARHOF) to assist in creating affordable housing throughout the state.

10. ATTACHMENT. There [ ] ARE [ ] ARE NOT additional terms contained in an Addendum attached to this Exclusive Buyer–Broker Agreement. If an Addendum is attached, the terms of that Addendum are incorporated into this Exclusive Buyer–Broker Agreement by this reference.

11. EQUAL HOUSING OPPORTUNITY. The Buyer and the Company will comply with Federal, State, and local fair housing laws.

12. FAXES. Facsimile (fax) transmission of a signed copy of this Exclusive Buyer–Broker Agreement, and retransmission of a signed fax, shall be the same as delivery of an original. If this transaction involves multiple Buyers, this Exclusive Buyer–Broker Agreement may be executed in counterparts.

13. ENTIRE AGREEMENT. This Exclusive Buyer–Broker Agreement, including the Buyer Due Diligence Checklist form, contains the entire agreement between the parties relating to the subject matter of this Exclusive Buyer–Broker Agreement. This Exclusive Buyer–Broker Agreement shall not be modified or amended except in writing signed by the parties hereto.

THE UNDERSIGNED Buyer does hereby accept the terms of this Exclusive Buyer–Broker Agreement.

_____ _____ _____
(Buyer's Signature)   (Address/Phone)   (Date)

_____ _____ _____
(Buyer's Signature)   (Address/Phone)   (Date)

The Company

By: _____ _____   By: _____ _____
(Buyer's Agent)   (Date)   (Principal/Branch Broker) (Date)
          Paul Naylor

This form is COPYRIGHTED by the UTAH ASSOCIATION OF REALTORS® for use solely by its members. Any unauthorized use, modification, copying or distribution without written consent is prohibited. NO REPRESENTATION IS MADE AS TO THE LEGAL VALIDITY OR ADEQUACY OF ANY PROVISION OF THIS FORM IN ANY SPECIFIC TRANSACTION. IF YOU DESIRE SPECIFIC LEGAL OR TAX ADVICE, CONSULT AN APPROPRIATE PROFESSIONAL.

COPYRIGHT© UTAH ASSOCIATION OF REALTORS® – 1995 – REVISED 11.08.05 – ALL RIGHTS RESERVED   UAR FORM 6

Page 2 of 2 [   ] [   ] Buyer's Initials Date_____

LIMITED AGENCY CONSENT AGREEMENT

Utah Association of REALTORS®
REALTOR®

This is a legally binding contract. If not understood, consult an attorney.

Name of Buyer(s): _____   Name of Seller(s): _____

Agent representing Buyer: _____   Agent representing Seller: _____

Name of Brokerage: Stone River Realty LLC (the "Company").

The Buyer and the Seller are both presently using the services of the Company in a possible real estate transaction involving real property located at: _____ (referred to below as the "Property").

AS THE BUYER AND THE SELLER PROCEED WITH THIS TRANSACTION IT IS IMPORTANT THAT THEY EACH UNDERSTAND THEIR PROFESSIONAL RELATIONSHIP WITH THE REAL ESTATE AGENT(S) AND WITH THE COMPANY. WHAT FOLLOWS IS A BRIEF BUT VERY IMPORTANT EXPLANATION OF THE NATURE OF AGENCY RELATIONSHIPS BETWEEN THE BUYER, THE SELLER, THE COMPANY, AND THE REAL ESTATE AGENTS WORKING IN THIS TRANSACTION.

1. **Principal or Branch Broker.** Every real estate agent must affiliate with a real estate broker. The broker is referred to as a Principal Broker or a Branch Broker (if the brokerage has a branch office). The broker is responsible for operation of the brokerage and for the professional conduct of all agents.

2. **Right of Agents to Represent Seller and/or Buyer.** An agent may represent, through the brokerage, a seller who wants to sell property or a buyer who wants to buy property. On occasion, an agent will represent both seller and buyer in the same transaction. When an agent represents a seller, the agent is a "Seller's Agent"; when representing a buyer, the agent is a "Buyer's Agent"; and when representing both seller and buyer, the agent is a "Limited Agent".

3. **Seller's Agent** A Seller's Agent works to assist the seller in locating a buyer and in negotiating a transaction suitable to the seller's specific needs. A Seller's Agent has fuduciary duties to the seller which include loyalty, full disclosure, confidentiality, diligence, obedience, reasonable care, and holding safe monies entrusted to the agent.

4. **Buyer's Agent.** A Buyer's Agent works to assist the buyer in locating and negotiating the acquisition of a property suitable to that buyer's specific needs. A Buyer's Agent has the same fiduciary duties to the buyer that the Seller's Agent has to the Seller.

5. **Limited Agent.** A Limited Agent represents both seller and buyer in the same transaction and works to assist in negotiating a mutually acceptable transaction. A Limited Agent has fiduciary duties to both seller and buyer. However, those duties are "limited" because the agent cannot provide to both parties undivided loyalty, full confidentiality and full disclosure of all information known to the agent. For this reason, a Limited Agent must remain neutral in the representation of a seller and buyer, and may not disclose to either party information likely to weaken the bargaining position of the other; such as, the highest price the buyer will pay or the lowest price the seller will accept. A Limited Agent must, however, disclose to both parties material information known to the Limited Agent regarding a defect in the Property and/or the ability of each party to fulfill agreed upon obligations, and must disclose information given to the Limited Agent in confidence, by either party, if the failure to disclose would be a material misrepresentation regarding the Property.

6. **In—House Sale.** If the buyer and the seller are both represented by one or more agents in the same brokerage, that transaction is commonly referred to as an "In—House Sale". Consequently, most In—House Sales involve limited agency because seller and buyer are represented by the same brokerage.

7. **Conflicts with the In—House Sale.** There are conflicts associated with an In—House Sale; for example, agents affiliated with the same brokerage discuss with each other the needs of their respective buyers or sellers. Such discussions could inadvertently compromise the confidentiality of information provided to those agents. For that reason, the Company has policies designed to protect the confidentiality of discussions between agents and access to confidential client and transaction files.

8. **Authorization for Limited Agency.** The Seller and Buyer are advised that they are not required to accept a limited agency situation in the Company and that Buyer and Seller are each entitled to be represented by their own agent. However, it is the business practice of the Company to participate in In—House Sales. By signing this agreement, Buyer and Seller consent to a limited agency within the Company as provided below: (Initial applicable box)

[   ] A. **One Agent.** The Buyer and the Seller consent to _____ (name of Agent); and the Principal/Branch Broker representing both the Buyer and the Seller as a Limited Agent as described above.

[   ] B. **Two Agents.** The Buyer and the Seller consent to _____ (Seller's Agent); continuing to represent the Seller; and _____ (Buyer's Agent); continuing to represent the Buyer; and the Principal/Branch Broker acting as a Limited Agent as described above.

[   ] C. **All Agents.** The Buyer and the Seller consent to all agents in the Company, including the Principal/Branch Broker, representing both the Seller and the Buyer as Limited Agents.

Page 1 of 2   Seller's Initials_____   Buyer's Initials_____

Buyer	Date	Seller	Date

Buyer	Date	Seller	Date

The Company by:_____

(Authorized Agent)   Date

This form is COPYRIGHTED by the UTAH ASSOCIATION OF REALTORS® for use solely by its members. Any unauthorized use, modification, copying or distribution without written consent is prohibited. NO REPRESENTATION IS MADE AS TO THE LEGAL VALIDITY OR ADEQUACY OF ANY PROVISION OF THIS FORM IN ANY SPECIFIC TRANSACTION. IF YOU DESIRE SPECIFIC LEGAL OR TAX ADVICE, CONSULT AN APPROPRIATE PROFESSIONAL.

COPYRIGHT © UTAH ASSOCIATION OF REALTORS® – REVISED 10.98 – ALL RIGHTS RESERVED   UAR FORM 7

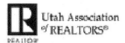

Utah Association
of REALTORS®

FOR SALE BY OWNER COMMISSION AGREEMENT & AGENCY DISCLOSURE

This is a legally binding contract. If you desire legal or tax advice, consult your attorney or tax advisor.

1. THIS COMMISSION AGREEMENT is entered into on this _____ day of _____, _____, between Stone River Realty LLC (the "Company"), including Paul Naylor (the "Agent") as the authorized agent for the Company, and _____ (the "Seller") for real property owned by Seller described as follows: _____ (the "Property").

2. BROKERAGE FEE. The Seller agrees to pay the Company, irrespective of agency relationship(s), as compensation for services, a Brokerage Fee in the amount of $_____ or _____% of the acquisition price of the Property, if the Seller accepts an offer from _____ (the "Buyer"), or anyone acting on the Buyer's behalf, to purchase or exchange the Property. The Seller agrees that the Brokerage Fee shall be due and payable, from the proceeds of the Seller, on the date of recording of closing documents for the purchase or exchange of the Property by the Buyer or anyone acting on the Buyer's behalf. If the sale or exchange is prevented by default of the Seller, the Brokerage Fee shall immediately be due and payable to the Company.

3. PROTECTION PERIOD. If within _____ months after this Commission Agreement is entered into, the Property is acquired by the Buyer, or anyone acting on the Buyer's behalf, the Seller agrees to pay the Company the Brokerage Fee stated in Section 2. The Seller agrees to exempt the Buyer upon entering into a valid listing agreement with another brokerage.

4. SELLER WARRANTIES/DISCLOSURES. The Seller warrants that the individuals or entity listed above as the "Seller" represents all of the record owners of the Property. The Seller warrants that it has marketable title and an established right to sell, lease, or exchange the Property. The Seller agrees to execute the necessary documents of conveyance. The Seller agrees to furnish buyer with good and marketable title, and to pay at Settlement, for a standard coverage owner's policy of title insurance for the buyer in the amount of the purchase price. The Seller agrees to fully inform the Agent regarding the Seller's knowledge of the condition of the Property. The Seller agrees to personally complete and sign a Seller's Property Condition Disclosure form.

5. AGENCY RELATIONSHIPS. By signing this Commission Agreement, the Seller acknowledges and agrees that the Agent and the Principal/Branch Broker for the Company (the "Broker") are representing the Buyer. As the Buyer's Agent, they will act consistent with their fiduciary duties to the Buyer of loyalty, full disclosure, confidentiality, and reasonable care. The Seller acknowledges that the Company and the Agent have advised the Seller that the Seller is entitled to be represented by a real estate agent that will represent the Seller exclusively. The Seller has however, elected not to be represented by a real estate agent in this transaction. The Seller further acknowledges and agrees that all actions of the Company and the Agent, even those that assist the Seller in performing or completing any of the Seller's contractual or legal obligations, are intended for the benefit of the Buyer exclusively. This Commission Agreement does not require the Company or the Agent to solicit offers on the Property from the Buyer, nor does it authorize the Company or the Agent to solicit offers from any other person or entity.

6. PROFESSIONAL ADVICE. The Company and the Agent are trained in the marketing of real estate. Neither the Company, nor the Agent are trained to provide the Seller or any prospective buyer with legal or tax advice, or with technical advice regarding the physical condition of the Property. If the Seller desires advice regarding: (i) past or present compliance with zoning and building code requirements; (ii) legal or tax matters; (iii) the physical condition of the Property; (iv) this Commission Agreement; or (v) any transaction for the acquisition of the Property, the Agent and the Company STRONGLY RECOMMEND THAT THE SELLER OBTAIN SUCH INDEPENDENT ADVICE. IF THE SELLER FAILS TO DO SO, THE SELLER IS ACTING CONTRARY TO THE ADVICE OF THE COMPANY.

7. DISPUTE RESOLUTION. The parties agree that any dispute, arising prior to or after a closing related to this Commission Agreement, shall first be submitted to mediation through a mediation provider mutually agreed upon by the parties. If the parties cannot agree upon a mediation provider, the dispute shall be submitted to the American Arbitration Association. Each party agrees to bear its own costs of mediation. If mediation fails, the other procedures and remedies available under this Agreement shall apply.

8. ATTORNEY FEES. Except as provided in Section 7, in any action or proceeding arising out of this Commission Agreement involving the Seller and/or the Company, the prevailing party shall be entitled to reasonable attorney fees and costs.

9. SELLER AUTHORIZATIONS. The Company is authorized to disclose after closing the final terms and sales price of the Property to the following Multiple Listing Service: Wasatch Front Regional MLS

10. ATTACHMENT. There [ ] ARE [ ] ARE NOT additional terms to this Commission Agreement. If "yes", see Addendum _____, incorporated into this Commission Agreement by this reference.

11. EQUAL HOUSING OPPORTUNITY. Seller and the Company agree to comply with Federal, State, and local fair housing laws.

Page 1 of 2

12. FAXES. Facsimile (fax) transmission of a signed copy of this Commission Agreement, and retransmission of a signed fax, shall be the same as delivery of an original. If this transaction involves multiple owners this Commission Agreement may be executed in counterparts.

13. ENTIRE AGREEMENT. This Commission Agreement, including the Seller's Property Condition Disclosure form, contain the entire agreement between the parties relating to the subject matter of this Commission Agreement. This Commission Agreement may not be modified or amended except in writing signed by the parties hereto.

THE UNDERSIGNED do hereby agree to the terms of this Commission Agreement as of the date first above written.

_____   _____
(Seller's Signature)   (Seller's Signature)

The Company

By:_____   By:_____
   (Authorized Agent)   (Principal/Branch Broker)
   Paul Naylor   Paul Naylor

This form is COPYRIGHTED by the UTAH ASSOCIATION OF REALTORS ® for use solely by its members. Any unauthorized use, modification, copying or distribution without written consent is prohibited. NO REPRESENTATION IS MADE AS TO THE LEGAL VALIDITY OR ADEQUACY OF ANY PROVISION OF THIS FORM IN ANY SPECIFIC TRANSACTION. IF YOU DESIRE SPECIFIC LEGAL OR TAX ADVICE, CONSULT AN APPROPRIATE PROFESSIONAL.

COPYRIGHT © UTAH ASSOCIATION OF REALTORS ® – 2000 – REVISED 7.8.04 – ALL RIGHTS RESERVED   UAR FORM 8B

 Utah Association
of REALTORS®

SUBJECT TO SALE OF BUYER'S PROPERTY
ADDENDUM NO. ___
TO
REAL ESTATE PURCHASE CONTRACT

THIS IS AN [ ] ADDENDUM [ ] COUNTEROFFER to that REAL ESTATE PURCHASE CONTRACT (the "REPC") with an Offer Reference Date of _____, including all prior addenda and counteroffers, between _____ as Buyer, and _____ as Seller, regarding the Property located at _____. The terms of this Addendum are hereby incorporated as part of the REPC, and to the extent the terms of this Addendum modify or conflict with any provisions of the REPC, including all prior addenda and counteroffers, these terms shall control.

1. SUBJECT TO SALE CONDITION. Buyer's obligation to purchase the Property IS CONDITIONED upon the closing of the sale of Buyer's property located at: _____ ("Buyer's Property") by 5:00 P.M. (Mountain Time) on the _____ ("Buyer's Closing Deadline"). If the closing of the sale of Buyer's Property does not occur by the Buyer's Closing Deadline, Buyer may, within four (4) days after the Buyer's Closing Deadline, cancel the REPC by providing written notice to Seller. In the event of such cancellation, the Earnest Money Deposit shall be released to Buyer. This condition is referred to below as the "Subject to Sale Condition".

2. BUYER'S DISCLOSURE. Buyer's Property [ ] IS [ ] IS NOT currently listed for sale through a real estate brokerage. If listed, the names of the Seller's agent and Seller's brokerage are as follows: _____

3. ADDITIONAL TERMS (Check Applicable Box). If neither box is checked below, this section 3 shall not apply.

A. [ ] Buyer's Property IS currently under contract with a purchaser (a "3rd Party Contract").

(1) The Settlement Deadline in the 3rd Party Contract is the _____. That Settlement Deadline MAY NOT be extended without the prior written consent of Seller.

(2) If the 3rd Party Contract is cancelled, Buyer shall provide Seller with written notice no later than four (4) days after such cancellation. In such event, Buyer or Seller may cancel the REPC by providing written notice to the other party no later than four (4) days after receipt of such notice; whereupon the Earnest Money Deposit shall be returned to Buyer without the requirement of further written authorization from Seller.

B. [ ] Buyer's Property IS NOT currently under contract with a purchaser.

(1) Buyer shall have until the _____ to enter into a 3rd Party Contract with a purchaser (the "3rd Party Contract Deadline"). If Buyer has not entered into a 3rd Party Contract by that deadline, Seller or Buyer may cancel the REPC by providing written notice to the other party no later than four (4) days after the 3rd Party Contract Deadline; whereupon the Earnest Money Deposit shall be returned to Buyer without the requirement of further written authorization from Seller.

(2) If Buyer enters into a 3rd Party Contract by the 3rd Party Contract Deadline, the Settlement Deadline in that contract shall be no later than four (4) days prior to the Settlement Deadline contained in the REPC and MAY NOT be extended without the prior written consent of Seller.

(3) If the 3rd Party Contract is cancelled, Buyer agrees to provide Seller with written notice no later than four (4) days after such cancellation. In such event, Buyer or Seller may cancel the REPC by providing written notice to the other party no later than four (4) days after receipt of such notice; whereupon the Earnest Money Deposit shall be returned to Buyer without the requirement of further written authorization from Seller.

ALL OTHER TERMS of the REPC, including all prior addenda and counteroffers, not modified by this ADDENDUM shall remain the same. [ ] Seller [ ] Buyer shall have until __:__ [ ] AM [ ] PM Mountain Time on _____ (Date), to accept the terms of this ADDENDUM in accordance with the provisions of Section 23 of the REPC. Unless so accepted, the offer as set forth in this ADDENDUM shall lapse.

[ ] Buyer [ ] Seller Signature	(Date)	(Time)	[ ] Buyer [ ] Seller Signature	(Date)	(Time)

ACCEPTANCE/COUNTEROFFER/REJECTION

CHECK ONE:

[ ] ACCEPTANCE: [ ] Seller [ ] Buyer hereby accepts the terms of this ADDENDUM.

[ ] COUNTEROFFER: [ ] Seller [ ] Buyer presents as a counteroffer the terms of attached ADDENDUM NO. ___.

[ ] REJECTION: [ ] Seller [ ] Buyer rejects the foregoing ADDENDUM.

(Signature)	(Date)	(Time)	(Signature)	(Date)	(Time)

This form is COPYRIGHTED by the UTAH ASSOCIATION OF REALTORS® for use solely by its members. Any unauthorized use, modification, copying or distribution without written consent is prohibited. NO REPRESENTATION IS MADE AS TO THE LEGAL VALIDITY OR ADEQUACY OF ANY PROVISION OF THIS FORM IN ANY SPECIFIC TRANSACTION. IF YOU DESIRE LEGAL OR TAX ADVICE, CONSULT AN APPROPRIATE PROFESSIONAL.
COPYRIGHT© UTAH ASSOCIATION OF REALTORS® - 1999 - REVISED 09.21.17 - ALL RIGHTS RESERVED

UAR FORM 18B

Page 1 of 1

 Utah Association of REALTORS®

**RESOLUTION OF DUE DILIGENCE ADDENDUM NO. ____
TO
REAL ESTATE PURCHASE CONTRACT**

 EQUAL HOUSING OPPORTUNITY

THIS IS AN [ ] ADDENDUM [ ] COUNTEROFFER to that REAL ESTATE PURCHASE CONTRACT (the "REPC") with an Offer Reference Date of _____, including all prior addenda and counteroffers, between _____, as Buyer, and _____ as Seller, regarding the Property located at _____. The terms of this Addendum are hereby incorporated as part of the REPC, and to the extent the terms of this Addendum modify or conflict with any provisions of the REPC, including all prior addenda and counteroffers, these terms shall control.

Seller and Buyer Agree as follows: (Check Applicable Boxes)
1. [ ] CLOSING COSTS. Seller and Buyer agree that Buyer accepts the Property as provided in Sections 10.2 and 10.3 of the REPC. Seller shall contribute at Settlement the amount of $_____ to be applied at Buyer's discretion toward any or all of the following: (a) a permanent reduction, or temporary reduction, in the mortgage loan interest rate; (b) mortgage financing costs; (c) closing costs; and (d) Prepaids/Escrows. Any unused portion of Seller's contribution may, at Buyer's option, be used to reduce the Purchase Price. If in a prior addendum to the REPC Seller has agreed to pay an amount toward Buyer's closing costs (the "Prior Contribution"), the amount shown in this Section 1 above, shall be in addition to the Prior Contribution.
2. [ ] PURCHASE PRICE REDUCTION. Seller and Buyer agree that Buyer accepts the Property as provided in Sections 10.2 and 10.3 of the REPC and that the Purchase Price shall be reduced and that the new Purchase Price is $_____.
3. [ ] REPAIRS TO BE MADE BY SELLER. Seller and Buyer agree that Seller will be responsible for completion of the repairs by the Settlement Deadline. Unless otherwise agreed to in writing, Seller shall, through contractors, complete the repairs to comply with applicable Law, including governmental permit, inspection and approval requirements. All repairs shall be performed in a workmanlike manner with materials of quality and appearance comparable to existing materials.
Agreed Upon Repairs (specify): _____
_____

3.1 Buyer Remedies for Unfinished Repairs. If, as of the Settlement Deadline, the repairs have not been completed, then Buyer may enter into an escrow agreement with the Seller, approved by the Lender, (if applicable) to finish the repairs after Closing ("the Escrow"). In the event Seller and Buyer cannot agree on the Escrow, or it is not approved by the Lender (if applicable), then Buyer may alternatively elect **one** of the following remedies in 3.1(A) or 3.1(B) below. If 3.1(A) or 3.1(B) is not checked, then the Escrow is the **sole remedy** for incomplete or unfinished repairs.
(Check Applicable Box):
A. [ ] Buyer may cancel the REPC and in addition to the return of the Earnest Money Deposit, or Deposits, if applicable, accept from Seller, as liquidated damages, a sum equal to the Earnest Money Deposit, or Deposits, if applicable. Seller agrees to pay the liquidated damages to Buyer upon demand.;
OR
B. [ ] Buyer may complete the purchase of the Property and then pursue any other remedies available at law after Closing. The terms of this Section 3 inclusive shall survive Closing.
4. Due Diligence Condition. Upon acceptance of this ADDENDUM, Buyer's objections to the Due Diligence shall be deemed resolved and the Due Diligence Condition **IS** waived by Buyer unless checked below.
A. [ ] Buyer's Due Diligence Condition **IS NOT** waived.

ALL OTHER TERMS of the REPC, including all prior addenda and counteroffers, not modified by this ADDENDUM shall remain the same. **[ ] Seller [ ] Buyer** shall have until __:__ [ ] AM [ ] PM Mountain Time on _____ (Date), to accept the terms of this ADDENDUM in accordance with the provisions of Section 23 of the REPC. Unless so accepted, the offer as set forth in this ADDENDUM shall lapse.

[ ] Buyer [ ] Seller Signature	(Date)	(Time)	[ ] Buyer [ ] Seller Signature	(Date)	(Time)

ACCEPTANCE/COUNTEROFFER/REJECTION

CHECK ONE:
[ ] ACCEPTANCE: [ ] Seller [ ] Buyer hereby accepts the terms of this ADDENDUM/COUNTER OFFER.
[ ] COUNTEROFFER: [ ] Seller [ ] Buyer presents as a counteroffer the terms of attached ADDENDUM/COUNTER OFFER NO. ___.
[ ] REJECTION: [ ] Seller [ ] Buyer rejects the foregoing ADDENDUM/COUNTER OFFER.

(Signature)	(Date)	(Time)	(Signature)	(Date)	(Time)

This form is COPYRIGHTED by the UTAH ASSOCIATION OF REALTORS® for use solely by its members. Any unauthorized use, modification, copying or distribution without written consent is prohibited. NO REPRESENTATION IS MADE AS TO THE LEGAL VALIDITY OR ADEQUACY OF ANY PROVISION OF THIS FORM IN ANY SPECIFIC TRANSACTION. IF YOU DESIRE SPECIFIC LEGAL OR TAX ADVICE, CONSULT AN APPROPRIATE PROFESSIONAL.
COPYRIGHT® UTAH ASSOCIATION OF REALTORS® - 7-1-17 REVISED 09.21.17 ALL RIGHTS RESERVED   UAR FORM 60

Page 1 of 1

Standard Supplementary Clauses

The "addendum / counter offer" form is largely blank allowing for custom language for each situation. The licensee must be very careful they do not cross over into the practice of law when filling out this form. Except for brief statements of terms such as "Sale Price shall be $150,000", the licensee should only use *Standard Supplemental Clauses* to convey the clients' wishes. Going beyond these clauses by creating custom language should be left for legal counsel to prepare.

Trade associations such as the Association of Realtors® have created forms for the use of their members. They have been prepared by competent legal counsel and may all be used by the licensee subject to copyright restrictions.

Standard Supplemental Clauses
A. 1031 Exchange
B. Acknowledgement of Third Party Approval
C. Seller's Contribution to Closing Costs
D. Contingent Cancellation
E. Credit Report Contingency
F. Disclosure of Interest
G. Flexible Settlement Date
H. Interest-Bearing Trust Account
I. Option to Keep House on Market
J. Reinstatement of REPC
K. Secondary (Backup) Contract
L. Subject to Seller Acquiring New Residence
M. Subordination Clause
N. Third Party Approval of the Property
O. Third Party Approval of the REPC
P. Undisclosed Purchaser

STANDARD SUPPLEMENTARY CLAUSES

A. 1031 EXCHANGE

☐ Seller - 1031 Exchange. Seller desires to enter into this transaction and to sell the Property as a "Relinquished Property" under Section 1031 of the Internal Revenue Code. Accordingly Buyer agrees to fully cooperate with the Seller in completing the 1031 Exchange, at no expense or liability to Buyer; or

☐ Buyer - 1031 Exchange. Buyer desires to enter into this transaction and to acquire the Property as a suitable "like-kind" exchange property under Section 1031 of the Internal Revenue Code. Accordingly Seller agrees to fully cooperate with the Buyer in completing the 1031 Exchange, at no expense or liability to Seller.

B. ACKNOWLEDGEMENT OF THIRD PARTY APPROVAL

1. Acknowledgement of Third Party Approval. In accordance with Section 2 inclusive of the Short Sale Addendum, Buyer and Seller agree as follows:

   (a) As referenced in Section 2.1 of the Short Sale Addendum, the Third Parties have provided written approval of a Short Sale of the Property as contained in a document issued by _____ (Third Party #1) and, if applicable, _____ (Third Party #2) attached to this Addendum as Exhibit "A".
   (b) Exhibit "A" contains any Third Party Modifications to the REPC and any Additional Third Party Requirements for approval of the Short Sale as those terms are defined in Sections 2.1 through 2.3 of the Short Sale Addendum.
   (c) Seller and Buyer agree to any Third Party Modifications to the REPC and any Additional Third Party Requirements for approval of the Short Sale as contained in Exhibit "A".
   (d) Based on the above, Seller and Buyer acknowledge and agree that Seller, Buyer, and the Third Parties have now reached Third Party Approval as that term is defined in Section 2 inclusive of the Short Sale Addendum.

2. CONTRACT DEADLINES. Based on the above, the Contract Deadlines referenced in Section 24 of the REPC, Section 8 of the Short Sale Addendum, and any other addenda/counteroffers, are now as follows:

Seller Disclosure Deadline	_____	(Date)
Due Diligence Deadline	_____	(Date)
Financing & Appraisal Deadline	_____	(Date)
Settlement Deadline	_____	(Date)

C. SELLER'S CONTRIBUTION TO CLOSING COSTS

Seller's Contribution to Closing Costs. Seller agrees to contribute at Settlement the amount of $_____ to be applied at Buyer's discretion toward any or all of the following: (a) a permanent reduction, or temporary reduction, in the mortgage loan interest rate; (b) mortgage financing costs; (c) closing costs; and (d) Prepaids/Escrows. Any unused portion of Seller's contribution may, at Buyer's option, be used to reduce the Purchase Price.

D. CONTINGENT CANCELLATION

1.   Extension of Deadlines. Seller and Buyer hereby agree to the following (check applicable boxes):
  ☐(a) Due Diligence Deadline is extended to   _____ (Date)
  ☐(b) Financing & Appraisal Deadline is extended to _____ (Date)

2.   Notice of Cancellation. If for any reason, Seller does not accept the terms of this Addendum in its entirety by the applicable deadline provided below, this Addendum shall act as Buyer's written notice of cancellation of the REPC pursuant to the (check applicable box):
  ☐(a) Due Diligence Condition – REPC Section 8.1(b)
  ☐(b) Financing Condition – REPC Section 8.3(a)

3.   Deadline to Accept this Addendum. Seller shall have until (check applicable box):
  ☐(a) the last mutually accepted Due Diligence Deadline prior to this Addendum;
  ☐(b) the last mutually accepted Financing & Appraisal Deadline prior to this Addendum;

to accept the terms of this Addendum in accordance with Section 23 of the REPC. Unless so accepted, the REPC shall be deemed cancelled as provided in Section 2 above whereupon any Earnest Money Deposit shall be released to Buyer without the requirement of further written authorization from Seller.

E. CREDIT REPORT CONTINGENCY

The Buyer authorizes the Seller to obtain at Seller's expense a credit report from a Consumer Credit Bureau and to use the report in evaluating the creditworthiness of the Buyer for a note to be taken back by the Seller from the Buyer in this transaction. If in the Seller's sole discretion the report is unsatisfactory, the Seller shall so notify the Buyer on or before the _____ at:

Street _____

City/State/Zip _____

The timely receipt of the notice will make this Agreement null and void, and the earnest money deposit will be returned to the Buyer. If this Agreement is not so made null and void, this contingency will automatically expire and this Agreement will remain in full force and effect.

F. DISCLOSURE OF INTEREST

The☐ Buyer☐ Seller is either:☐a relative of a real estate broker or sales agent participating in this transaction; or☐a real estate broker or sales agent licensed as such under the laws of the State of Utah, who may share in the brokerage fee paid for this transaction.

G. FLEXIBLE SETTLEMENT DATE

Settlement shall take place between the _____ and the _____. The exact date will be decided by ☐Buyer or ☐Seller who will provide at least_____ day(s) notice to the other party at:
Street _____
City/State/Zip _____
In the absence of such notice, settlement shall be on the last day stated above.

H. INTEREST-BEARING EARNEST MONEY DEPOSIT

Buyer and Seller authorize and direct that Buyer's Earnest Money Deposit shall be placed into an interest bearing trust account with: ☐ the Brokerage ☐ Other (specify)_____. All interest shall accrue to the benefit of: ☐ Buyer ☐Seller☐Other (specify)_____. Any processing fee required by the brokerage, and all costs of setting up, maintaining and closing the account shall be paid for by:
☐Buyer ☐Seller ☐ Shared Equally by Buyer and Seller. Social Security Number or Federal Identification Number of Seller is:_____; of Buyer is:_____. Buyer and Seller understand that such fees and costs may exceed the interest earned.

I. OPTION TO KEEP HOUSE ON MARKET (TIME CLAUSE)

1.1 Right to Accept Other Offers. Buyer and Seller agree that Seller may continue to offer the Property for sale and to accept other offers subject to the rights of Buyer as provided below. If Seller accepts any such offers, Seller will notify Buyer in writing within ____ calendar days after entering into such a contract.

1.2 Right to Remove Conditions. Buyer shall have ____ hours after receipt of Seller's written notice in which to either: (a) agree in writing to remove from the REPC the following condition(s) (check applicable boxes): ☐ Due Diligence Condition; ☐ Financing & Appraisal Condition; ☐ Subject to the Sale of Buyer's Residence; ☐ Other (explain): _____ or (b) by failing to respond in writing to Seller's notice, allow the REPC to automatically become canceled, in which instance, the Earnest Money Deposit, or Deposits, if applicable, shall be released to Buyer.

J. REINSTATEMENT OF REPC

1. Acknowledgement of Prior Cancellation. Buyer and Seller acknowledge that the REPC was previously cancelled by Buyer in accordance with the (check applicable box): ☐ Due Diligence Condition ☐ Appraisal Condition ☐ Financing Condition ☐ Other _____ .

2. Reinstatement of REPC. Notwithstanding the prior cancellation referenced above, Buyer and Seller wish to proceed forward with this transaction and reinstate the REPC. Accordingly, upon the mutual acceptance of this Addendum, Buyer and Seller agree that their respective rights and obligations under the REPC including all prior addenda and counteroffers are reinstated in their entirety and are in full force and effect. Buyer and Seller further agree that the contract deadlines referenced in Section 24 of the REPC and as modified by any prior addenda and counteroffers, are modified as follows (check applicable boxes):
☐ Due Diligence Deadline shall be   _____ (Date)
☐ Financing & Appraisal Deadline shall be   _____ (Date)
☐ Settlement Deadline shall be   _____ (Date)
☐ REPC Deadlines Remain Unchanged
3. Other Terms. Additional terms are as follows: _____
_____

K. SECONDARY (BACKUP) CONTRACT

1.1 Backup Contract. Buyer acknowledges that this REPC is a "Backup Contract", and that Seller has already contracted to sell the Property to another buyer based on a "Primary Contract". The Primary Contract was accepted on the _____.

    1.2 Seller's Right to Modify. Buyer agrees that Seller may, in Seller's sole discretion, amend or modify the Primary Contract.

    1.3 Buyer's Right to Cancel. At any time prior to the Backup Contract becoming the Primary Contract (as provided in Section 1.4 below) Buyer may cancel the Backup Contract by providing written notice to Seller.

    1.4 Termination of Primary Contract. If the Primary Contract is canceled or withdrawn (a "termination"), Seller will within four (4) days after such event, provide Buyer with written notice of such termination ("Seller's Notice"). Except as provided in Section 1.3, upon Buyer's receipt of the Seller's Notice, this Backup Contract shall become the "New Primary Contract".

2.   CONTRACT DEADLINES: In reference to the Contract Deadlines in Section 24 of the REPC, Buyer and Seller agree that the following deadlines shall apply to the REPC:

    2.1 Seller Disclosure Deadline _____ days after Buyer's receipt of Seller's Notice.

    2.2 Due Diligence Deadline _____ days after Buyer's receipt of Seller's Notice.

    2.3 Financing & Appraisal Deadline _____ days after Buyer's receipt of Seller's Notice.

    2.4 Settlement Deadline _____ days after Buyer's receipt of Seller's Notice.

2.5 If the Settlement Deadline referenced in Section 2.4 above falls on a Saturday, Sunday, State or Federal legal holiday, performance shall be required on the next succeeding business day.

 3.   EARNEST MONEY DEPOSIT: Buyer agrees to deliver to Buyer's Brokerage no later than seven (7) calendar days after Buyer's receipt of Seller's Notice, Buyer's Earnest Money in the form of: _____ .

L. SUBJECT TO SELLER ACQUIRING NEW RESIDENCE

1.1 Subject to Seller Acquiring New Residence. Seller's obligation to sell the Property is conditioned upon the Seller signing a contract to purchase another residence (the "Replacement Residence") by 5:00 P.M. (MST) on the _____; (the "Replacement Contract Deadline"). Seller agrees to diligently pursue such a purchase contract.

1.2 Right to Cancel. If Seller has not contracted for the purchase of a Replacement Residence by the Replacement Contract Deadline, Buyer or Seller may, within three calendar days after the Replacement Contract Deadline, cancel the REPC by providing written notice to the other party. In the event of such cancellation, the Earnest Money Deposit shall be released to Buyer. Seller may however, remove this condition at any time prior to the Replacement Contract Deadline by providing written notice to Buyer.

M. SUBORDINATION CLAUSE

The instrument securing the Buyer's note to the Seller or, if applicable, the Uniform Real Estate Contract between the Buyer and the Seller for the portion of the purchase price indicated in Paragraph 2 of the Real Estate Purchase Contract shall contain a provision permitting the subordination of the instrument securing the Buyer's obligation to pay the Seller. This subordination shall enable a recognized financial institution which lends money to the buyer within _____ days of this Agreement to take a position on the record prior to that of the Seller. The amount of this loan shall not exceed _____ dollars; it shall bear interest at a rate not in excess of _____ per cent per annum; monthly principal and interest payment shall not exceed dollars; and no principal payments other than those included in the monthly amount stated above shall be required before the _____. The proceeds of the loan to which the Seller's interest will be subordinated must be used only to finance improvements on the securing property. The proceeds may also be used to pay a reasonable fee for a loan which otherwise meets the requirements of this paragraph. This right of subordination may be exercised only _____ times.

N. THIRD PARTY APPROVAL OF THE PROPERTY

1.1 Third Party Approval of the Property. Buyer's obligation to purchase the Property is conditioned upon the approval of the Property by: _____ (the "Third Party"). The Third Party shall have until 5:00 P.M. (MST) on the _____ (the "Approval Deadline") in which to approve or disapprove of the Property. If the Third Party does not approve of the Property, Buyer may cancel this Contract by providing written notice to Seller no later than the Approval Deadline; whereupon the Earnest Money deposit shall be released to Buyer. If, by the Approval Deadline, the Contract is not canceled by Buyer, the Third Party shall be deemed to have approved the Property.

O. THIRD PARTY APPROVAL OF THE REPC

1.1 Third Party Approval of the REPC. Buyer's obligation to purchase the Property is conditioned upon the approval of the REPC by: _____ (the "Third Party"). The Third Party shall have until 5:00 P.M. (MST) on the _____ (the "Approval Deadline") in which to approve or disapprove of the terms and conditions of the REPC. If the Third Party does not approve of the terms and conditions of the REPC, Buyer may cancel this Contract by providing written notice to Seller no later than the Approval Deadline; whereupon the Earnest Money deposit shall be released to Buyer. If, by the Approval Deadline, the Contract is not canceled by Buyer, the Third Party shall be deemed to have approved the terms and conditions of the REPC.

P. UNDISCLOSED PURCHASER

The Buyer is acting on behalf of an undisclosed purchaser. The Buyer (does; does not) have written authorization from the undisclosed purchaser to make this offer to purchase on the terms and conditions stated. If the Buyer is acting without the written authorization of the undisclosed purchaser as represented above, the Buyer will be personally liable to the Seller under the terms of this Agreement.

Review Questions

1. A licensee may only use _____ forms in their practice of the real estate profession.

2. If no form approved by the Real Estate Commission is available to meet the need of your client you may use a form created by a licensed _____.

3. Only licensees who are _____ or associate _____ can fill out closing documents.

4. A sales agent (may/may not) fill in the blanks of any form created by the sales agent under the direction of the buyer or seller.

5. Name 5 approved forms:

    _____

    _____

    _____

    _____

    _____

6. It was a simple transaction, a cash sale for a small piece of land. The closing was set to take place in the brokerage conference room. The documents needed were a real estate purchase contract, a closing statement, and a warranty deed. Who of the following cannot fill out these documents legally.
    a. Title company officer
    b. Seller
    c. Associate Broker
    d. Sales Agent

7. As a licensed sales agent W can now fill out any of the following forms except:
    a. Documents associated with the closing of a real estate transaction.
    b. A listing contract created by the broker's attorney
    c. A lease form prepared by the sales agent's attorney
    d. A form lease prepared by an attorney and purchased at the bookstore

22. Closing Disclosure Instruction

General Instructions

The settlement agent shall complete the Closing Disclosure to itemize all charges imposed upon the Borrower and the Seller by the loan originator and all sales commissions, whether to be paid at settlement or outside of settlement, and any other charges which either the Borrower or the Seller will pay at settlement.

The Consumer Finance Protection Bureau (CFPB) was created in 2010 by the Dodd-Frank Act, with the purpose of enforcing the Real Estate Settlement Procedures Act (RESPA) and implementing new regulations. As of October 3, 2015, all federally regulated transactions must use the new disclosures, the Loan Estimate form and the Closing Disclosure.

The Closing Disclosure replaces the HUD-1 form, as well as the Truth-in-Lending (TIL) statement that were the standard closing forms in years past. It is intended to provide a clean, easy to read, and easy to understand summary and breakdown of the entire transaction between the buyer and seller. It includes any costs dealing with the lender, the title agent, the real estate agents, and any other parties that performed a service related to the transaction.

Closing Disclosure Overview

In this section, we will look at all the different parts of the Closing Disclosure in detail. You can see an example Closing Disclosure at the end of this chapter to reference as we cover each page of the document.

Page 1 - Closing Information

This section outlines the details about the closing and settlement.

Date issued – The date that the Closing Disclosure is issued. It must be sent to the borrower at least 3 days before the Closing Date.

Closing Date – The date that closing occurs. This is where the parties to the transaction sign the closing document, and the title to the property legally changes owners.

Disbursement Date – The date that the funds for the purchase of the property are disbursed from the lender to the seller, and any other parties that will receive monies from the buyer.

Settlement Agent – The agent that oversees the settlement of the transaction. This is frequently a title agent, but the broker can also perform this role.

File # - The file that the transaction will be recorded under with the settlement agent.

Property – The address of the property that will be exchanged at settlement.

Sale Price – The official sale price of the property. This may not equal the total amount the seller receives, after factoring in the other costs involved in selling the property.

Transaction Information

This section outlines the parties to the transaction. You should verify that this information is correct, because even a minor misspelling could cause an issue when the paperwork is processed.

Borrower – The buyer, the party that is purchasing the property, and creating a new mortgage on the property.

Seller – The owner who is selling the property.

Lender – The entity that is lending the money toward the mortgage.

Loan Information

This section lists the basic terms of the loan. These terms should match what was provided to the borrower in the Loan Estimate. If they don't, then you should contact the lender and resolve any discrepancy before proceeding with closing.

Loan Term – The term in years that the loan will be written for.

Purpose – The purpose that the loan funds will be used for.

Product – The type of loan that will be created, as offered by the lender.

Loan Type – The type of loan being issued. A Conventional loan is a standard agreement between the lender and the borrower. An FHA loan is a loan backed by the FHA. A VA loan is a loan insured by the VA.

Loan ID# – The identifier for the loan provided by the lender, from their files.

MIC# – The Mortgage Insurance Case number (MIC) identifying the policy provided by the Mortgage Insurance company.

Loan Terms

This section calls attention to these important terms of the loan. A typical mortgage loan includes many pages of legal clauses and terms. If can be difficult for a borrower to identify the terms that will have the biggest impact on their decision to finance the property. The Closing Disclosure has been designed to highlight these important terms, so that the borrower can easily understand them.

There is a column titled "Can this amount increase after closing?" Depending on the terms of the loan, each of these items may change. We expect that the loan amount will decrease, for example. However in an interest only loan, the loan amount will not decrease. In a negative amortization loan, the loan amount will actually increase. This form is designed to make sure the borrower is aware if any of these items can increase.

Loan Amount – The total amount that the borrower is receiving from the lender, and will owe. This is often different from the purchase price. In some loans, such as a negative amortization loan, this amount can increase over the life of the loan.

Interest Rate – The annual interest rate that will be applied to the principle at the beginning of the loan. In an adjustable rate mortgage, this could increase.

Monthly Principal and Interest – The principle and interest portion the monthly payment due at the beginning of the loan. This could increase if the interest rate changes, or if the principle due changed. The total monthly payment is usually higher, as outlined in the Projected Payments section below.

Prepayment penalty – This indicates if there is a penalty, such as a dollar amount due, if the loan principle is paid before the original duration of the loan transpires. This is important if the borrower intends to transfer the property again before the loan term is complete.

Balloon Payment – This indicates of there is a lump sum payment due at some point during the loan. This is important because it is a large expenditure, often tens of thousands of dollars or more, expected at a later date.

Projected Payment

This section shows the costs that go into the monthly payment on the loan. Here you can see the total monthly payment, and where that money is going.

Principle and Interest – This value should equal the amount shown in the Loan Terms section at the beginning of the loan, but here you would see if that will change over the course of the loan.

Mortgage Insurance – This shows the monthly mortgage insurance amount which is part of the monthly payment. Mortgage insurance is typically required for loans that have a loan-to-value ratio of more than 80%. Once the loan-to-value ratio drops below 80%, the mortgage insurance is typically removed, and that is reflected here.

Estimated Escrow – This includes all the items that will be charged monthly, and put into escrow to pay costs related to home ownership that are charged annually, such as homeowner's insurance and property taxes. These are itemized on page 2 of the Closing Disclosure.

Estimated Total Monthly Payment – This is the sum of the previous items, giving you the total monthly payment during the course of the loan.

Estimated Taxes, Insurance & Assessments – This includes items in escrow, and other items that may be owed monthly as part of home ownership.

Costs at Closing

Closing Costs – This is the total amount the borrower will be charged at the closing to complete the transaction and get the loan. Sometimes some of these costs will be financed with the loan.

Cash to Close – This is the total dollar amount that the borrower will have to pay on the date of closing to complete the transaction. Any items that are financed will not be included in this line.

Page 2 – Loan Costs

This page outlines in detail all the costs included in the closing, including costs that were paid previously in relation to the loan, and costs that will be paid at the date of closing. Here you can see each amount, and whom it will be paid to. The page is divided into columns that indicate who will pay each item, and whether it was paid before closing, or whether it will be paid at closing.

A. Origination Charges – This section lists the costs that are charged to the borrower in relation to the creation of the new loan. This includes items such as the application fee, underwriting fee, and any other charged from the lender directly, such as points paid to lower the interest rate on the loan.

B. Services Borrower Did Not Shop For – This section lists all the costs that were incurred in the creation of the loan from other providers, that the lender **DID NOT** allow the borrower to choose a provider for. These items might vary from what was disclosed on the Loan Estimate, but should be close. This includes items such as the appraisal fees, credit report, and other services the lender requires to evaluate the borrower and the property.

C. Services Borrower Did Shop For – This section lists the costs that were incurred in the creation of the loan from other providers, that the lender **ALLOWED** the borrower to choose a provider for. This usually includes title fees, survey fees, etc.

D. Total Loan Costs – This is the sum of the costs outlined in the Loan Costs section.

Other Costs

This section lists costs related to closing outside of the loan costs.

E. Taxes and Other Government Fees – This section lists any transfer taxes or recording fees charged by the government on the sale of real estate.

F. Prepaids – This section lists items that must be pre-paid, such as interest due from the closing date until the first regular monthly payment.

G. Initial Escrow Payment at Closing – This section lists the amount that must be paid into escrow at the beginning of the loan term, at closing.

H. Other – This section is a catch all for costs that must be paid at closing, which don't fall into any other category. Real estate agent commissions are listed here, as well as any HOA fees, home warranty, or owner's title insurance.

I. Total Other Costs – This is the sum of all costs in the Other Costs section, owed by the borrower.

J. Total Closing Costs – This is the sum of the Other Costs and the Loan Costs, giving us the Total Closing Costs. This value should match the total closing costs listed on page 1.

Calculating Cash to Close

This section outlines the difference between the Loan Estimate that was provided to the borrower previously, and the final costs. Here you can see which items changed, and by how much.

This section gives the detailed numbers that calculate how much cash the borrower will have to pay at closing to complete the transaction.

Summaries of Transactions

This section outlines the borrower's side of the transaction, and the seller's side of the transaction. Here you can see what each party is contributing.

K. Due from the borrower at Closing – Here we see what the borrower owes at closing. This includes the sale price of the property, as well as the closing costs. We can see any adjustments for items paid by the seller in advance.

M. Due to the Seller at Closing – Here we see how much is due the seller at closing, including the purchase price of the property, and any items the seller had paid already, that the borrower will benefit from.

L. Paid Already by or on Behalf of Borrower at Closing – This section lists all the items that have already been paid, or will be paid on behalf of the borrower, such as loan funds being paid toward the purchase price of the property. Included here are any adjustments necessary for items owed on the property that the seller has benefited from, but not yet paid, such as annual property taxes.

N. Due from the Seller at Closing – This section lists all the items that the seller owes at closing, such as paying off a previous mortgage loan, so that the property is free of encumbrances. This also includes and items unpaid by the seller, such as property taxes.

CALCULATIONS – At the bottom of the page we see the final calculations for the borrower and the seller, finalizing the transaction and outlining what monies are owed, and what monies will be received by either party.

Page 4 – Loan Disclosures

This section describes many common clauses of a loan, as well as the breakdown of funds that will go into the escrow account.

Assumption – This section advises the borrower if there is an option in their loan for another party to assume the loan. This would be desirable if they have an interest rate on the loan that is lower than the market rate at the time they decide to sell the home, because it gives them something of value to offer to the buyer, with a lower interest rate.

Demand Feature – This section outlines if the loan contains a Demand Feature. A Demand Feature means that there is a condition in the loan that would allow the lender to call the full amount of the loan due at some point before the full term of the loan has elapsed. This could have a large impact on a family with a budget if the full value of the loan were called unexpectedly, so this section makes it clear whether the loan contains that feature or not.

Late Payment – This section describes what time period is considered late for a payment, and what fees might be charged.

Negative Amortization – This section explains if the loan has possible Negative Amortization. That means that the payments do not cover all the interest due, and the interest that is not paid in the monthly payment will be added to the principle, meaning that the borrower will owe **more** money each month. This section makes that clear, before the loan begins.

Partial Payments – This section describes the lender's policy on accepting partial payments and how they will be handled, whether the payment will be applied immediately, or held in escrow until a full payment is received.

Security Interest – This section explains that the loan is being tied to collateral, generally the property that is being purchased with the loan amount. It reminds the borrower that if they do not pay the loan, that they may lose the property.

Escrow Account – This section gives the full details about the escrow account, including what monies are collected, and for what purpose.

If your loan does not have an escrow account, then you will be required to pay the annual property taxes and homeowners insurance. Sometimes the lender charges a fee to the borrower if they do not have an escrow account with the loan.

Page 5 – Loan Calculations

This section gives an overview of the total costs of the loan. This is a good high-level view of what the borrower is entering into when they close on the property.

Total of Payments – This is the sum total of all expected payments on the loan. This includes all principle and interest paid over the life of the loan, over 30 years or whatever the loan term is.

Finance Charge – This is the total amount of interest and other charges that the borrower will pay over the course of the loan. At a percentage rate of 5% or lower, this amount will be less than the amount borrowed. At a percentage rate of 5.5% or higher, this amount will be **more** than the amount borrowed.

Amount Financed – This is the total amount borrowed from the lender.

Annual Percentage Rate (APR) – This is the total Finance Charge for the loan, expressed as an annual percentage rate. This is different from the interest rate in the loan terms.

Total Interest Percentage (TIP) – This is the total Finance Charge for the loan, expressed as a percentage of the total loan amount.

Other Disclosures

This section discloses to the borrower other details related to the loan, and property ownership.

Appraisal – This section explains to the borrower that they have a right to view the appraisal, if any, done on the property before closing.

Contract Details – This section is a reminder to the borrower to be familiar with the terms of their loan, specifically issues that may cause additional expense, or early termination of the loan.

Liability after Foreclosure – This section makes the borrower aware of what their responsibilities might be if a foreclosure were to take place in the future.

Refinance – This section reminds the borrower that any refinance would be a new financial contract, and that it will be conditioned upon the market and the financial condition of the borrower at that time.

Tax Deductions – This section gives some basic information to the borrower about the ability to deduct interest payments on a mortgage loan from their federal income taxes.

Contact Information

This section lists the contact information to all parties of the transaction. This includes the buyer's broker, the seller's broker, the settlement agent, the lender, and the mortgage broker.

Confirm Receipt

This section confirms that the borrower and any co-applicant have received this Closing Disclosure by signature.

Closing Disclosure Example

There is a sample Closing Disclosure with an example transaction on the following pages. You can reference this example as you review this chapter.

Closing Disclosure

This form is a statement of final loan terms and closing costs. Compare this document with your Loan Estimate.

Closing Information		Transaction Information		Loan Information	
Date Issued	4/15/2013	Borrower	Michael Jones and Mary Stone	Loan Term	30 years
Closing Date	4/15/2013		123 Anywhere Street	Purpose	Purchase
Disbursement Date	4/15/2013		Anytown, ST 12345	Product	Fixed Rate
Settlement Agent	Epsilon Title Co.	Seller	Steve Cole and Amy Doe		
File #	12-3456		321 Somewhere Drive	Loan Type	☒ Conventional ☐ FHA
Property	456 Somewhere Ave		Anytown, ST 12345		☐ VA ☐ _____
	Anytown, ST 12345	Lender	Ficus Bank	Loan ID #	123456789
Sale Price	$180,000			MIC #	000654321

Loan Terms

		Can this amount increase after closing?
Loan Amount	$162,000	**NO**
Interest Rate	3.875%	**NO**
Monthly Principal & Interest *See Projected Payments below for your Estimated Total Monthly Payment*	$761.78	**NO**
		Does the loan have these features?
Prepayment Penalty	**YES**	• **As high as $3,240** if you pay off the loan during the first 2 years
Balloon Payment	**NO**	

Projected Payments

Payment Calculation		Years 1-7		Years 8-30
Principal & Interest		$761.78		$761.78
Mortgage Insurance	+	82.35	+	—
Estimated Escrow *Amount can increase over time*	+	206.13	+	206.13
Estimated Total Monthly Payment		**$1,050.26**		**$967.91**

Estimated Taxes, Insurance & Assessments *Amount can increase over time* *See page 4 for details*	$356.13 a month	This estimate includes	In escrow?
		☒ Property Taxes	YES
		☒ Homeowner's Insurance	YES
		☒ Other: Homeowner's Association Dues	NO
		See Escrow Account on page 4 for details. You must pay for other property costs separately.	

Costs at Closing

Closing Costs	$9,712.10	Includes $4,694.05 in Loan Costs + $5,018.05 in Other Costs – $0 in Lender Credits. *See page 2 for details.*
Cash to Close	$14,147.26	Includes Closing Costs. *See Calculating Cash to Close on page 3 for details.*

Closing Cost Details

Loan Costs	Borrower-Paid		Seller-Paid		Paid by Others
	At Closing	Before Closing	At Closing	Before Closing	
A. Origination Charges	**$1,802.00**				
01 0.25 % of Loan Amount (Points)	$405.00				
02 Application Fee	$300.00				
03 Underwriting Fee	$1,097.00				
04					
05					
06					
07					
08					
B. Services Borrower Did Not Shop For	**$236.55**				
01 Appraisal Fee to John Smith Appraisers Inc.					$405.00
02 Credit Report Fee to Information Inc.		$29.80			
03 Flood Determination Fee to Info Co.	$20.00				
04 Flood Monitoring Fee to Info Co.	$31.75				
05 Tax Monitoring Fee to Info Co.	$75.00				
06 Tax Status Research Fee to Info Co.	$80.00				
07					
08					
09					
10					
C. Services Borrower Did Shop For	**$2,655.50**				
01 Pest Inspection Fee to Pests Co.	$120.50				
02 Survey Fee to Surveys Co.	$85.00				
03 Title – Insurance Binder to Epsilon Title Co.	$650.00				
04 Title – Lender's Title Insurance to Epsilon Title Co.	$500.00				
05 Title – Settlement Agent Fee to Epsilon Title Co.	$500.00				
06 Title – Title Search to Epsilon Title Co.	$800.00				
07					
08					
D. TOTAL LOAN COSTS (Borrower-Paid)	**$4,694.05**				
Loan Costs Subtotals (A + B + C)	$4,664.25	$29.80			

Other Costs	Borrower-Paid		Seller-Paid		Paid by Others
	At Closing	Before Closing	At Closing	Before Closing	
E. Taxes and Other Government Fees	**$85.00**				
01 Recording Fees Deed: $40.00 Mortgage: $45.00	$85.00				
02 Transfer Tax to Any State			$950.00		
F. Prepaids	**$2,120.80**				
01 Homeowner's Insurance Premium (12 mo.) to Insurance Co.	$1,209.96				
02 Mortgage Insurance Premium (mo.)					
03 Prepaid Interest ($17.44 per day from 4/15/13 to 5/1/13)	$279.04				
04 Property Taxes (6 mo.) to Any County USA	$631.80				
05					
G. Initial Escrow Payment at Closing	**$412.25**				
01 Homeowner's Insurance $100.83 per month for 2 mo.	$201.66				
02 Mortgage Insurance per month for mo.					
03 Property Taxes $105.30 per month for 2 mo.	$210.60				
04					
05					
06					
07					
08 Aggregate Adjustment	– 0.01				
H. Other	**$2,400.00**				
01 HOA Capital Contribution to HOA Acre Inc.	$500.00				
02 HOA Processing Fee to HOA Acre Inc.	$150.00				
03 Home Inspection Fee to Engineers Inc.	$750.00			$750.00	
04 Home Warranty Fee to XYZ Warranty Inc.			$450.00		
05 Real Estate Commission to Alpha Real Estate Broker			$5,700.00		
06 Real Estate Commission to Omega Real Estate Broker			$5,700.00		
07 Title – Owner's Title Insurance (optional) to Epsilon Title Co.	$1,000.00				
08					
I. TOTAL OTHER COSTS (Borrower-Paid)	**$5,018.05**				
Other Costs Subtotals (E + F + G + H)	$5,018.05				
J. TOTAL CLOSING COSTS (Borrower-Paid)	**$9,712.10**				
Closing Costs Subtotals (D + I)	$9,682.30	$29.80	$12,800.00	$750.00	$405.00
Lender Credits					

Calculating Cash to Close

Use this table to see what has changed from your Loan Estimate.

	Loan Estimate	Final	Did this change?
Total Closing Costs (J)	$8,054.00	$9,712.10	YES · See **Total Loan Costs (D)** and **Total Other Costs (I)**
Closing Costs Paid Before Closing	$0	− $29.80	YES · You paid these Closing Costs **before closing**
Closing Costs Financed (Paid from your Loan Amount)	$0	$0	NO
Down Payment/Funds from Borrower	$18,000.00	$18,000.00	NO
Deposit	− $10,000.00	− $10,000.00	NO
Funds for Borrower	$0	$0	NO
Seller Credits	$0	− $2,500.00	YES · See Seller Credits in **Section L**
Adjustments and Other Credits	$0	− $1,035.04	YES · See details in **Sections K and L**
Cash to Close	$16,054.00	$14,147.26	

Summaries of Transactions

Use this table to see a summary of your transaction.

BORROWER'S TRANSACTION

K. Due from Borrower at Closing	$189,762.30
01 Sale Price of Property	$180,000.00
02 Sale Price of Any Personal Property Included in Sale	
03 Closing Costs Paid at Closing (J)	$9,682.30
04	
Adjustments	
05	
06	
07	
Adjustments for Items Paid by Seller in Advance	
08 City/Town Taxes to	
09 County Taxes to	
10 Assessments to	
11 HOA Dues 4/15/13 to 4/30/13	$80.00
12	
13	
14	
15	

L. Paid Already by or on Behalf of Borrower at Closing	$175,615.04
01 Deposit	$10,000.00
02 Loan Amount	$162,000.00
03 Existing Loan(s) Assumed or Taken Subject to	
04	
05 Seller Credit	$2,500.00
Other Credits	
06 Rebate from Epsilon Title Co.	$750.00
07	
Adjustments	
08	
09	
10	
11	
Adjustments for Items Unpaid by Seller	
12 City/Town Taxes 1/1/13 to 4/14/13	$365.04
13 County Taxes to	
14 Assessments to	
15	
16	
17	

SELLER'S TRANSACTION

M. Due to Seller at Closing	$180,080.00
01 Sale Price of Property	$180,000.00
02 Sale Price of Any Personal Property Included in Sale	
03	
04	
05	
06	
07	
08	
Adjustments for Items Paid by Seller in Advance	
09 City/Town Taxes to	
10 County Taxes to	
11 Assessments to	
12 HOA Dues 4/15/13 to 4/30/13	$80.00
13	
14	
15	
16	

N. Due from Seller at Closing	$115,665.04
01 Excess Deposit	
02 Closing Costs Paid at Closing (J)	$12,800.00
03 Existing Loan(s) Assumed or Taken Subject to	
04 Payoff of First Mortgage Loan	$100,000.00
05 Payoff of Second Mortgage Loan	
06	
07	
08 Seller Credit	$2,500.00
09	
10	
11	
12	
13	
Adjustments for Items Unpaid by Seller	
14 City/Town Taxes 1/1/13 to 4/14/13	$365.04
15 County Taxes to	
16 Assessments to	
17	
18	
19	

CALCULATION

Total Due from Borrower at Closing (K)	$189,762.30
Total Paid Already by or on Behalf of Borrower at Closing (L)	− $175,615.04
Cash to Close ☒ From ☐ To Borrower	**$14,147.26**

CALCULATION

Total Due to Seller at Closing (M)	$180,080.00
Total Due from Seller at Closing (N)	− $115,665.04
Cash ☐ From ☒ To Seller	**$64,414.96**

Additional Information About This Loan

Loan Disclosures

Assumption
If you sell or transfer this property to another person, your lender

☐ will allow, under certain conditions, this person to assume this loan on the original terms.

☒ will not allow assumption of this loan on the original terms.

Demand Feature
Your loan

☐ has a demand feature, which permits your lender to require early repayment of the loan. You should review your note for details.

☒ does not have a demand feature.

Late Payment
If your payment is more than 15 days late, your lender will charge a late fee of 5% of the monthly principal and interest payment.

Negative Amortization (Increase in Loan Amount)
Under your loan terms, you

☐ are scheduled to make monthly payments that do not pay all of the interest due that month. As a result, your loan amount will increase (negatively amortize), and your loan amount will likely become larger than your original loan amount. Increases in your loan amount lower the equity you have in this property.

☐ may have monthly payments that do not pay all of the interest due that month. If you do, your loan amount will increase (negatively amortize), and, as a result, your loan amount may become larger than your original loan amount. Increases in your loan amount lower the equity you have in this property.

☒ do not have a negative amortization feature.

Partial Payments
Your lender

☒ may accept payments that are less than the full amount due (partial payments) and apply them to your loan.

☐ may hold them in a separate account until you pay the rest of the payment, and then apply the full payment to your loan.

☐ does not accept any partial payments.

If this loan is sold, your new lender may have a different policy.

Security Interest
You are granting a security interest in
456 Somewhere Ave., Anytown, ST 12345

You may lose this property if you do not make your payments or satisfy other obligations for this loan.

Escrow Account
For now, your loan

☒ will have an escrow account (also called an "impound" or "trust" account) to pay the property costs listed below. Without an escrow account, you would pay them directly, possibly in one or two large payments a year. Your lender may be liable for penalties and interest for failing to make a payment.

Escrow		
Escrowed Property Costs over Year 1	$2,473.56	Estimated total amount over year 1 for your escrowed property costs: *Homeowner's Insurance Property Taxes*
Non-Escrowed Property Costs over Year 1	$1,800.00	Estimated total amount over year 1 for your non-escrowed property costs: *Homeowner's Association Dues* You may have other property costs.
Initial Escrow Payment	$412.25	A cushion for the escrow account you pay at closing. See Section G on page 2.
Monthly Escrow Payment	$206.13	The amount included in your total monthly payment.

☐ will not have an escrow account because ☐ you declined it ☐ your lender does not offer one. You must directly pay your property costs, such as taxes and homeowner's insurance. Contact your lender to ask if your loan can have an escrow account.

No Escrow		
Estimated Property Costs over Year 1		Estimated total amount over year 1. You must pay these costs directly, possibly in one or two large payments a year.
Escrow Waiver Fee		

In the future,
Your property costs may change and, as a result, your escrow payment may change. You may be able to cancel your escrow account, but if you do, you must pay your property costs directly. If you fail to pay your property taxes, your state or local government may (1) impose fines and penalties or (2) place a tax lien on this property. If you fail to pay any of your property costs, your lender may (1) add the amounts to your loan balance, (2) add an escrow account to your loan, or (3) require you to pay for property insurance that the lender buys on your behalf, which likely would cost more and provide fewer benefits than what you could buy on your own.

Loan Calculations

Total of Payments. Total you will have paid after you make all payments of principal, interest, mortgage insurance, and loan costs, as scheduled.	$285,803.36
Finance Charge. The dollar amount the loan will cost you.	$118,830.27
Amount Financed. The loan amount available after paying your upfront finance charge.	$162,000.00
Annual Percentage Rate (APR). Your costs over the loan term expressed as a rate. This is not your interest rate.	4.174%
Total Interest Percentage (TIP). The total amount of interest that you will pay over the loan term as a percentage of your loan amount.	69.46%

 Questions? If you have questions about the loan terms or costs on this form, use the contact information below. To get more information or make a complaint, contact the Consumer Financial Protection Bureau at **www.consumerfinance.gov/mortgage-closing**

Other Disclosures

Appraisal
If the property was appraised for your loan, your lender is required to give you a copy at no additional cost at least 3 days before closing. If you have not yet received it, please contact your lender at the information listed below.

Contract Details
See your note and security instrument for information about
- what happens if you fail to make your payments,
- what is a default on the loan,
- situations in which your lender can require early repayment of the loan, and
- the rules for making payments before they are due.

Liability after Foreclosure
If your lender forecloses on this property and the foreclosure does not cover the amount of unpaid balance on this loan,
- [X] state law may protect you from liability for the unpaid balance. If you refinance or take on any additional debt on this property, you may lose this protection and have to pay any debt remaining even after foreclosure. You may want to consult a lawyer for more information.
- [ ] state law does not protect you from liability for the unpaid balance.

Refinance
Refinancing this loan will depend on your future financial situation, the property value, and market conditions. You may not be able to refinance this loan.

Tax Deductions
If you borrow more than this property is worth, the interest on the loan amount above this property's fair market value is not deductible from your federal income taxes. You should consult a tax advisor for more information.

Contact Information

	Lender	Mortgage Broker	Real Estate Broker (B)	Real Estate Broker (S)	Settlement Agent
Name	Ficus Bank		Omega Real Estate Broker Inc.	Alpha Real Estate Broker Co.	Epsilon Title Co.
Address	4321 Random Blvd. Somecity, ST 12340		789 Local Lane Sometown, ST 12345	987 Suburb Ct. Someplace, ST 12340	123 Commerce Pl. Somecity, ST 12344
NMLS ID					
ST License ID			Z765416	Z61456	Z61616
Contact	Joe Smith		Samuel Green	Joseph Cain	Sarah Arnold
Contact NMLS ID	12345				
Contact ST License ID			P16415	P51461	PT1234
Email	joesmith@ ficusbank.com		sam@omegare.biz	joe@alphare.biz	sarah@ epsilontitle.com
Phone	123-456-7890		123-555-1717	321-555-7171	987-555-4321

Confirm Receipt

By signing, you are only confirming that you have received this form. You do not have to accept this loan because you have signed or received this form.

_____   _____   _____   _____
Applicant Signature   Date   Co-Applicant Signature   Date

Review Questions

1. On the Closing Disclosure, where can the borrower find the interest rate on their loan?
   a. Page 1 in the Loan Terms Section
   b. Page 1 in the Loan Information Section
   c. Page 2 under D. Total Loan Costs
   d. Page 2 under J. Total Closing Costs

2. On the Closing Disclosure, where can the borrower find cost of the transfer tax?
   a. Page 2 section F
   b. Page 2 section E
   c. Page 2 section H
   d. Page 2 section B

3. On the Closing Disclosure, where can the borrower find the monthly payment during the 11th year of the loan?
   a. Page 2 section D
   b. Page 1 under Loan Terms
   c. Page 2 section I
   d. Page 1 under Projected Payments

4. On the Closing Disclosure, where can the borrower find a comparison of costs between the Loan Estimate and the Closing Disclosure?
   a. Page 3 under Calculating Cash to Close
   b. Page 1 under Costs at Closing
   c. Page 2 under Other Costs
   d. Page 4 under Loan Disclosures

5. On the Closing Disclosure, where can the borrower find the total cash that they need to bring to closing?
   a. Page 1 under Loan Terms
   b. Page 2 under Total Loan Costs
   c. Page 1 under Costs at Closing
   d. Page 2 under Total Closing Costs

6. On the Closing Disclosure, where can the borrower find out if their loan has a demand feature?
   a. Page 1 under Loan Terms
   b. Page 2 under Other Costs
   c. Page 3 under Summaries of Transactions
   d. Page 4 under Loan Disclosures

7. On the Closing Disclosure, where can the borrower find the total cost of all payments under the terms of the loan?
   a. Page 3 under Summaries of Transactions
   b. Page 3 under Calculating Costs to Close
   c. Page 4 under Loan Calculations
   d. Page 4 under Other Disclosures

8. On the Closing Disclosure, where can the borrower find the contact information for the real estate agents involved in the transaction?
   a. Page 2
   b. Page 3
   c. Page 4
   d. Page 5

23.   Real Estate Purchase Contract

Approved Form

The Real Estate Purchase Contract (REPC) is a form that has been approved by the Real Estate Commission, working together with the Real Estate Division, the Attorney General and counsel, for use by real estate licensees in transactions involving residential real estate transactions.

The REPC has been updated over the years, with the most recent updates happening in 2008 and 2017, to address new market conditions, and new realities of the real estate market, in an attempt to protect consumers from the most common pitfalls and oversights in a real estate transaction.

The REPC favors the buyer in most respects, affording them the opportunity to evaluate a property, do inspections, secure financing, and get the property appraised before they are fully committed to the purchase. It does give the seller some assurances as well, such as earnest money to commit the buyer to the transaction. The sale of a residence is an involved process, many things need to be done before it can be realized, and the REPC addresses those items one by one.

The approved REPC and all other approved forms can be found on the Division of Real Estate website at https://realestate.utah.gov/.

A blank REPC is included in the Forms chapter, and a sample REPC from a completed transaction is included at the end of this chapter.

Practice of Contract Law

If a client has questions about the language in the REPC or any other contract, they should be referred to an attorney, who can give them professional legal advice on how the contract language may be interpreted in their transaction.

If a client wants to make a change to the REPC during a transaction, a real estate licensee is prohibited from crossing out language in the contract, or writing in the margins. This is considered practice of law, and a real estate licensee is not legally permitted to practice law. A real estate licensee is limited to filling in the blanks on the form, and if additions are needed, filling in the blank on an addendum form.

At the top of the form is this disclaimer:

> **This is a legally binding Real Estate Purchase Contract ("REPC"). Utah law requires real estate licensees to use this form. Buyer and Seller, however, may agree to alter or delete its provisions or to use a different form. If you desire legal or tax advice, consult your attorney or tax advisor.**

A buyer will fill out the REPC, and the real estate agent can assist them in filling out this approved form.

REPC Overview

In this section we will look at the different clauses of the Real Estate Purchase Contract in detail. There is a sample executed Real Estate Purchase Contract at the end of the chapter that you should reference as we review each clause. This contract will be used on nearly every residential transaction, and we recommend getting familiar with the real language of the contract.

Earnest Money Deposit

In the first section of the contract, the buyer and seller are named, and the date of the contract. Also it is specified what amount of earnest money will be deposited for the offer.

Earnest money on a purchase contract is an assurance from the buyer to the seller that they are serious about the transaction. Even before a sale is closed, there is a lot of work that is done in preparation for the sale. Earnest money assures the seller that the buyer will be following through on the purchase of the home, unless there is some extenuating circumstance, or they find new information that changes their desire to purchase the home.

The earnest money is deposited with the broker. State law says that earnest money must be deposited within 3 business days, or as determined by the contract. The approved REPC states that the earnest money should be deposited within 4 calendar days. This can also be changed by addendum.

1. The Property

Section 1 of the REPC describes the property that is named in the contract. There is a blank for the property description, such as a legal description or an address, including additional fields for city, county, and zip code. There is also a field for the Tax ID number that you can find on the county records.

1.1 lists all of the items that are included with the property. Fixtures are automatically included with a property by law, but having items names explicitly in the contract removes any confusion, and prevents disputes about the definition of a fixture. This section makes very clear what items are included with the property, including landscaping, and many other items such as security systems, solar panels, drapery, heating and air conditioning, etc.

In section 1.2 the offeror is given the opportunity to list any other items that they want to include that are not affixed to the property, such as refrigerators, washer and dryer, and there is a blank where they can fill in any other items that they want included.

If any items are included that are personal property, they cannot be transferred with the deed, and will need to have a separate bill written up in addition to the REPC to purchase them.

In section 1.3 there is a blank where the offeror can list any items that are to be excluded from the sale. This can include items that are fixtures, or attached to the property, if the offeror does not want them to be included.

Water service and water rights are generally included with residential property sales, as specified in section 1.4.

2. Purchase Price

The purchase price of the property is the total dollar amount that the buyer will transfer to the seller to consummate the transfer of the property. Some buyers have cash to purchase, but many buyers get money from a mortgage to purchase a property. The total purchase price is listed here, along with other sources of funds that will be used in the purchase.

  a. The **Earnest Money** listed at the beginning of the contract usually becomes part of the purchase price, like a down payment.
  b. There may be **Additional Earnest Money** that will be specified in section 8 of the REPC that will also be used.
  c. The most common source of funds for the residential purchase is a **New Loan** from a mortgage lender. The loan typically has not yet been granted when an offer is submitted, so the amount listed here is an estimate of what the buyer expects to get.
  d. Sometimes the seller finances the purchase directly with the buyer, and that amount would be listed here. If they do so, there will be a separate addendum defining the terms of **Seller Financing**.
  e. Finally, any remaining balance will be paid in **Cash at Settlement**.

The purchase price is then listed again here, which should be the total of items a through e.

Sometimes the buyer cannot purchase the home until they sell their current home. This is because most buyers cannot afford to finance two homes at the same time. If this is the case, they would indicate in 2.2 that the purchase of the home is conditioned on the sale of their current property.

3. Settlement and Closing

This section defines the terms of Settlement and Closing.

Settlement is where the sale of the property is completed, and title transferred from the seller to the buyer. The REPC specifies a deadline for settlement, which includes all documents required by the lender, by the title insurance or closing office, and by the REPC itself, as well as any money to be paid by buyer or seller as required.

Closing is when the settlement is complete, loan proceeds have been delivered, and all document have been recorded, which by the contract cannot be more than 4 days after settlement.

Section 3.3 determines when the buyer can take possession of the property. Since the buyer becomes responsible for the property as soon as recording is complete, possession is usually delivered on that day, or as close to that day as possible, but it can be anything that the buyer and seller agree on.

4. Prorations, Assessments and other Payment Obligations

There are many ongoing payments that are involved in home ownership, such as property taxes, rents paid in advance, special assessments, and homeowner's association (HOA) fees. This section specified how those items will be divided between the buyer and the seller. Prorated items will be determined by the settlement deadline.

Any pre-paid rents or rental deposits shall be credited to the buyer upon closing.

HOA's sometimes have fees that must be paid anytime a property in the association transfers owners. These transfer fees can be paid by either the buyer or the seller, as agreed upon in the contract.

Buyers agree to become responsible for all utilities that are connected to the property after the settlement deadline as well.

The escrow office is authorized to withhold any money necessary to pay off the seller's obligations on the property, such as their existing mortgage, and any judgements or liens against the property.

5. Confirmation of Agency Disclosure

This section serves to inform both parties to the transaction if there is any representation for either party. A real estate agent is required to have a signed agency agreement before they can submit any offer for a client. That must already be in place before the REPC is signed. This section only serves as a disclosure, or confirmation of the agency relationships that were already created. There is a blank for the agent and their brokerage, and the license number for each, for both the buyer's agent and the seller's agent.

6. Title & Title Insurance

In this section the seller commits that they have fee title, and they commit to transfer the property by general warranty deed to the buyer. The seller also commits to purchase title insurance in favor of the buyer.

The buyer agrees to accept all long-term and short-term leases and rental agreements that are currently in effect on the property. Long-term leases are any lease that is longer than 30 consecutive days.

7. Seller Disclosures

There is a list of disclosures that the seller must give to the buyer, to inform them of the current status of the properties physical condition, as well as any other agreements that might currently affect the property. These disclosures must be delivered to the buyer before the Seller Disclosure Deadline listed in section 24(a).

(a) Current condition of the property. This includes the physical condition of the structure, plumbing, heating and air conditioning, and any other physical elements, whether they are in working order, or in need of repair. This also includes any known issues about the land and the grounds surrounding the home.

(b) If the property was built prior to 1978, the seller must also disclose any knowledge of lead based paint on the property, using the approved Lead-Based Paint Disclosure & Acknowledgement.

(c) They must provide a Commitment for Title Insurance as described in 6.1.

(d) Any Covenants, Conditions & Restrictions (CC&Rs) that affect the property need to be disclosed.

(e) Current information about any HOA, recent meeting minutes, budget, and financial statements.

(f) Copies of long-term leases or rental agreements.

(g) Copies of short-term leases.

(h) Copies of existing property management agreements.

(i) Water rights and water shares, as well as any known conditions or claims relating to building and zoning code, or environmental problems.

(j) The seller must disclose if they are a "foreign person", which is any non-resident alien, foreign corporation, or other foreign business entity, so that the buyer can withhold any required taxes.

(k) This line is left blank to allow the buyer to require any additional disclosures that they believe are relevant to the current transaction.

8. Buyer's Conditions of Purchase

The REPC allows for several conditions on which the buyer can cancel the purchase contract, once additional information is discovered or made available. The buyer can select whether or not the contract is conditioned upon these clauses to purchase the property. They are all favorable to the buyer, but they could be negotiated to make an offer more attractive to the seller.

DUE DILIGENCE CONDITION

This section allows the buyer to review the condition of the property in detail. This includes not only the direct physical state of the roof, walls, foundation, plumbing, electrical and other systems, but also any other factors such as environmental issues, property line accuracy, regulatory use restrictions, HOAs, utilities and more. The Due Diligence condition is intended to cover all elements dealing directly with the property itself. Any material facts about the property or legal considerations would be covered under this condition. All inspections are at the buyer's cost, but will be facilitated by the seller.

The deadline for the Due Diligence Condition, if it is exercised, is listed in section 24(b).

If the buyer determines, based on information they found in their inspections related to the due diligence condition, that they would like to cancel the REPC, they can do so by notifying the seller in writing. If they do so before the Due Diligence Deadline, they will keep the earnest money.

If they do not cancel by the deadline, the earnest money becomes non-refundable. If they do nothing and the deadline passes, then that is the same as if they had waived that condition.

APPRAISAL CONDITION

This section allows the buyer to condition the sale of the property on a third party appraisal of the property value. The buyer can choose whether or not to make this a condition of the purchase.

If the buyer is planning to finance the purchase, such as getting a new mortgage on the property, the lender will usually require that the home be sufficient collateral for the mortgage loan, and they determine the value of the home by using a third party appraisal, so this condition will be very common in transactions that involve mortgage lending.

If the buyer determines, based on the appraisal, that they would like to cancel the REPC, they must notify the seller in writing. If they do so before the Appraisal Deadline, then they will keep the earnest money.

If they wait until after the Appraisal Deadline, they are effectively waiving the Appraisal Condition, and forfeit the earnest money.

FINANCING CONDITION

The buyer can also condition the property purchase on whether they are able to obtain financing, such as a mortgage loan, to purchase the property. They can select that financing is not required, or that financing is required. If the buyer selects that it is required, then they agree to work diligently to obtain that loan.

If the buyer is unable to obtain financing, or if they are not satisfied with the terms of the loan that is offered, then they can cancel the REPC. If they do so before the Financing Deadline, then they specify how much of the earnest money they are able to retain, either all of it, or some portion of it.

If a buyer does not cancel the REPC before the Financing Deadline, but they are ultimately unable to get the loan before closing, then they are not obligated to purchase the property. However, under this circumstance, the seller will receive the earnest money.

ADDITIONAL EARNEST MONEY

The buyer has the option to deposit additional earnest money toward the purchase of the property. Here they would indicate how much additional earnest money they will be depositing. Any additional earnest money must be deposited before the Due Diligence Deadline, or the Financing and Appraisal Deadline, whichever is later.

9. Addenda

If the real estate agent needs to make any changes to the REPC, or if there are other conditions or criteria that the client would like to add to the contract, they can do so by adding Addenda to the contract.

This section allows the buyer to indicate which addenda will be included, and enforceable with the REPC.

10. Home Warranty Plan / As-Is Condition of the Property

The buyer has the option to include a home warranty plan with the purchase of the property, and they can select who, buyer or seller, will order the warranty, who will select the company, and who will pay for the home warranty at settlement. They can also select what the maximum cost of the home warranty will be.

The buyer agrees that the home is purchased without any implied warranty, and that the purchase is "As-Is". Legally, As-Is means that a purchase is accepted in the status it is currently in, with all faults and current conditions included.

The seller agrees to disclose all known conditions of the property that would materially affect the property value, and could reasonably be discovered by a reasonable inspection. The property must be delivered in the same condition that it was at the time the offer was accepted.

11. Final Pre-Settlement Walkthrough Inspection

The buyer has the right to do a final visual inspection of the property within 7 days before closing, to ensure that everything is as promised in the REPC. However, even if they do not perform a final inspection, this does not waive their right to receive the property in the condition promised in the REPC.

12. Changes During Transaction

The seller agrees that no substantial changes will be made to the property from the date of acceptance, until the date of closing. This is to preserve the property in the same condition.

1. No improvements or alterations will be performed.
2. No new financial encumbrances or changes to title
3. No changes to property management agreements
4. No changes to long-term lease or rental agreements, no new agreements
5. No new short-term rental agreements

13. Authority of Signers	The person signing the REPC for both buyer and seller warrant that they are authorized to do so.
14. Complete Contract	The parties agree that the REPC is the complete contract, and that there are no other contracts that would take precedence. No verbal agreements are binding, and this contract along with all addenda, exhibits, and disclosures is the complete agreement.
15. Mediation	The buyer can select if any disputes should be first submitted to mediation. Legal battles typically take more time, and create a greater expense, and so mediation is often a desirable alternative. This option. They can choose if a dispute is first submitted to mediation, or if it will be at the option of the parties.
16. Default	This section details what happens if the buyer or seller default on the contract.
	If the buyer defaults, the seller can either cancel the REPC and retain the earnest money, or maintain the earnest money in trust and sue to enforce the REPC, or return the earnest money and pursue other legal remedies.
	If the seller defaults, the buyer can follow similar remedies, with the seller paying an equal amount to the earnest money deposit where applicable.
17. Attorney Fees and Costs/Governing Law	If any litigation arises from the transaction involving the REPC, the sections states that the winner of the suit will be entitled to repayment of attorney fees.
18. Notices	All communication required by the REPC must be in writing, and signed by the party giving notice, or their real estate agent or brokerage.
19. No Assignment	The buyer cannot assign the REPC to another buyer, without written consent from the seller. Some exceptions are allowed for entities in which the buyer holds legal interest.

20. Insurance & Risk of Loss

If there is any damage to the property by accident, or through any other source before closing, it is the responsibility of the seller. If the damages exceed 10% of the purchase price, then either party may cancel the REPC and return the earnest money to the buyer.

The buyer is responsible for insurance on the property after the closing date.

21. Time is of the Essence

Time is of the Essence is a legal term that means that the times and dates in the contract are enforceable. If either the buyer or the seller fail to adhere to the timelines described in the contract, they may be at fault, and could be in breach of contract.

22. Electronic Transmission and Counterparts

The REPC can be signed physically, or can be signed by electronic signatures, and either will be considered valid.

The contract can be executed in counterparts, meaning that separate parts of the contract can each sign separately, and the contract will still be valid, as long as the signed copies are delivered to the other party.

23. Acceptance

This section defines "Acceptance" as when both the buyer and seller have signed the REPC, marked acceptance, and the buyer and seller or their agents have communicated to the other party that the contract has been signed.

24. Contract Deadlines

All of the deadlines for the different conditions in the REPC are gathered in this section.

    (a) Seller Disclosure Deadline
    (b) Due Diligence Deadline
    (c) Financing & Appraisal Deadline
    (d) Settlement Deadline

25. Offer and Time for Acceptance

In this section, the buyer sets an expiration date and time for the offer. They sign the contract, with a signature date, to make the contract official.

The seller then has the option in this section to Accept the offer, to Reject the offer, or to make a Counteroffer. They can then sign and date the contract as well.

The buyer and seller must also initial and date each page of the contract.

Any modification to the contract by the seller, after the buyer has submitted the offer, is considered a counteroffer, and automatically rejects the original offer.

Addendum to the Real Estate Purchase Contract

Any changes that a real estate agent needs to make to the REPC, the can do by adding one or more Addenda to the contract. The state approved Addendum to the Real Estate Purchase Contract provides the framework for the agent to make these changes.

This form can also be used to create a counteroffer to a REPC that has already been prepared.

At the top of the addendum, an agent enters the information from the original REPC that the addendum will modify, including the date of the offer, the buyer and seller, and the property description and location.

Next there is simply a series of blank lines, where the agent can write in any changes to the REPC requested by their client.

CHANGE TO DEADLINES

There is a checkbox indicating whether the deadlines on the REPC will remain the same, or if they will be changed, with a blank where the new deadlines can be entered.

CONFIRMATION AND ACCEPTANCE

The addendum confirms that all other terms of the REPC not changed by the addendum are to remain the same, and it gives allows the offering party to set a deadline for acceptance. The offering party can then sign and date the addendum.

Finally, the receiving party has the option to Accept the addendum, reject it, or present another counteroffer. Any counteroffer automatically rejects the terms of the existing offer.

Real Estate Purchase Contract Example

There is a sample Real Estate Purchase Contract for a completed transaction on the following pages. You can reference this example as you review this chapter.

There is a blank copy of the Real Estate Purchase Contract in Chapter 21.

REAL ESTATE PURCHASE CONTRACT

This is a legally binding Real Estate Purchase Contract ("REPC"). Utah law requires real estate licensees to use this form. Buyer and Seller, however, may agree to alter or delete its provisions or to use a different form. If you desire legal or tax advice, consult your attorney or tax advisor.

EARNEST MONEY DEPOSIT

On this __16th__ day of __September__, 20 __17__ ("Offer Reference Date") ___Bill Buyer___ ("Buyer") offers to purchase from ___Sally Seller___ ("Seller") the Property described below and **agrees to deliver no later than four (4) calendar days after Acceptance (as defined in Section 23)**, an Earnest Money Deposit in the amount of $ __500__ in the form of___Cash___. After Acceptance of the REPC by Buyer and Seller, and receipt of the Earnest Money by the Brokerage, the Brokerage shall have four (4) calendar days in which to deposit the Earnest Money into the Brokerage Real Estate Trust Account.

OFFER TO PURCHASE

1.   PROPERTY: ___123 Pleasant Street___

City of ___Pleasantburg___, County of ___Glad___, State of Utah, Zip __84000__ Tax ID No. __12-345-6789__ (the "Property"). Any reference below to the term "Property" shall include the Property described above, together with the Included Items and water rights/water shares, if any, referenced in Sections 1.1, 1.2 and 1.4.

   1.1   **Included Items.** Unless excluded herein, this sale includes the following items if presently owned and in place on the Property: plumbing, heating, air conditioning fixtures and equipment; solar panels; ovens, ranges and hoods; cook tops; dishwashers; ceiling fans; water heaters; water softeners; light fixtures and bulbs; bathroom fixtures and bathroom mirrors; all window coverings including curtains, draperies, rods, window blinds and shutters; window and door screens; storm doors and windows; awnings; satellite dishes; all installed TV mounting brackets; all wall and ceiling mounted speakers; affixed carpets; automatic garage door openers and accompanying transmitters; security system; fencing and any landscaping.

   1.2   **Other Included Items.** The following items that are presently owned and in place on the Property have been left for the convenience of the parties and are also included in this sale (**check applicable box**): [ ] washers [ ] dryers [X] refrigerators [ ] microwave ovens [ ] other **(specify)** _____

The above checked items shall be conveyed to Buyer under separate bill of sale with warranties as to title. In addition to any boxes checked in this Section 1.2 above, there [ ] ARE [X] ARE NOT additional items of personal property Buyer intends to acquire from Seller at Closing by separate written agreement.

   1.3   **Excluded Items.** The following items are excluded from this sale: ___Satellite Dish___

   1.4   **Water Service.** The Purchase Price for the Property shall include all water rights/water shares, if any, that are the legal source for Seller's current culinary water service and irrigation water service, if any, to the Property. The water rights/water shares will be conveyed or otherwise transferred to Buyer at Closing by applicable deed or legal instruments. The following water rights/water shares, if applicable, are specifically excluded from this sale: _____

2.   PURCHASE PRICE.
   2.1   **Payment of Purchase Price.** The Purchase Price for the Property is $ __180,000__. Except as provided in this Section, the Purchase Price shall be paid as provided in Sections 2.1(a) through 2.1(e) below. Any amounts shown in Sections 2.1(c) and 2.1(e) may be adjusted as deemed necessary by Buyer and the Lender (the "Lender").

$__500__   (a) **Earnest Money Deposit.** Under certain conditions described in the REPC, this deposit may become totally non-refundable.

$__0__   (b) **Additional Earnest Money Deposit** (see Section 8.4 if applicable)

$__165,000__   (c) **New Loan.** Buyer may apply for mortgage loan financing (the "Loan") on terms acceptable to Buyer: If an FHA/VA loan applies, see attached FHA/VA Loan Addendum.

$__0__   (d) **Seller Financing** (see attached Seller Financing Addendum)

$__14,500__   (e) **Balance of Purchase Price in Cash at Settlement**

$__180,000__   **PURCHASE PRICE. Total of lines (a) through (e)**

   2.2   **Sale of Buyer's Property.** Buyer's ability to purchase the Property, to obtain the Loan referenced in Section 2.1(c) above, and/or any portion of the cash referenced in Section 2.1(e) above [ ] IS [X] IS NOT conditioned upon the sale of real estate owned by Buyer. If checked in the affirmative, the terms of the attached subject to sale of Buyer's property addendum apply.

3.   SETTLEMENT AND CLOSING.
   3.1   **Settlement.** Settlement shall take place no later than the Settlement Deadline referenced in Section 24(d), or as otherwise mutually agreed by Buyer and Seller in writing. "Settlement" shall occur only when all of the following have been completed: (a) Buyer and Seller have signed

Page 1 of 6 pages   Buyer's Initials____*BB*____ Date_9/16/2017_   Seller's Initials____*SS*____ Date_9/16/2017_

and delivered to each other or to the escrow/closing office all documents required by the REPC, by the Lender, by the title insurance and escrow/closing offices, by written escrow instructions (including any split closing instructions, if applicable), or by applicable law; (b) any monies required to be paid by Buyer or Seller under these documents (except for the proceeds of any Loan) have been delivered by Buyer or Seller to the other party, or to the escrow/closing office, in the form of cash, wire transfer, cashier's check, or other form acceptable to the escrow/closing office.

3.2 Closing. For purposes of the REPC, "Closing" means that: (a) Settlement has been completed; (b) the proceeds of any new Loan have been delivered by the Lender to Seller or to the escrow/closing office; and (c) the applicable Closing documents have been recorded in the office of the county recorder ("Recording"). The actions described in 3.2 (b) and (c) shall be completed no later than four calendar days after Settlement.

3.3 Possession. Except as provided in Section 6.1(a) and (b), Seller shall deliver physical possession of the Property to Buyer as follows: [ ] Upon Recording; [ ] ____Hours after Recording; [X] _1_ Calendar Days after Recording. Any contracted rental of the Property prior to or after Closing, between Buyer and Seller, shall be by separate written agreement. Seller and Buyer shall each be responsible for any insurance coverage each party deems necessary for the Property including any personal property and belongings. The provisions of this Section 3.3 shall survive Closing.

4. PRORATIONS / ASSESSMENTS / OTHER PAYMENT OBLIGATIONS.

4.1 Prorations. All prorations, including, but not limited to, homeowner's association dues, property taxes for the current year, rents, and interest on assumed obligations, if any, shall be made as of the Settlement Deadline referenced in Section 24(d), unless otherwise agreed to in writing by the parties. Such writing could include the settlement statement. The provisions of this Section 4.1 shall survive Closing.

4.2 Special Assessments. Any assessments for capital improvements as approved by the homeowner's association ("HOA") (pursuant to HOA governing documents) or as assessed by a municipality or special improvement district, prior to the Settlement Deadline shall be paid for by: [X] Seller [ ] Buyer [ ] Split Equally Between Buyer and Seller [ ] Other (explain) _____ . The provisions of this Section 4.2 shall survive Closing.

4.3 Fees/Costs/Payment Obligations.

(a) Escrow Fees. Unless otherwise agreed to in writing, Seller and Buyer shall each pay their respective fees charged by the escrow/closing office for its services in the settlement/closing process. The provisions of this Section 4.3(a) shall survive Closing.

(b) Rental Deposits/Prepaid Rents. Rental deposits (including, but not limited to, security deposits, cleaning deposits and prepaid rents) for long term lease or rental agreements, as defined in Section 6.1(a), and short-term rental bookings, as defined in Section 6.1(b), not expiring prior to Closing, shall be paid or credited by Seller to Buyer at Settlement. The provisions of this Section 4.3(b) shall survive Closing.

(c) HOA/Other Entity Fees Due Upon Change of Ownership. Some HOA's, special improvement districts and/or other specially planned areas, under their governing documents charge a fee that is due to such entity as a result of the transfer of title to the Property from Seller to Buyer. Such fees are sometimes referred to as transfer fees, community enhancement fees, HOA reinvestment fees, etc. (collectively referred to in this section as "change of ownership fees"). Regardless of how the change of ownership fee is titled in the applicable governing documents, if a change of ownership fee is due upon the transfer of title to the Property from Seller to Buyer, that change of ownership fee shall, at Settlement, be paid for by: [X] Seller [ ] Buyer [ ] Split Equally Between Buyer and Seller [ ] Other (explain) _____ . The provisions of this Section 4.3(c) shall survive Closing.

(d) Utility Services. Buyer agrees to be responsible for all utilities and other services provided to the Property after the Settlement Deadline. The provisions of this Section 4.3(d) shall survive Closing.

(e) Sales Proceeds Withholding. The escrow/closing office is authorized and directed to withhold from Seller's proceeds at Closing, sufficient funds to pay off on Seller's behalf all mortgages, trust deeds, judgments, mechanic's liens, tax liens and warrants. The provisions of this Section 4.3(e) shall survive Closing.

5. CONFIRMATION OF AGENCY DISCLOSURE. Buyer and Seller acknowledge prior written receipt of agency disclosure provided by their respective agent that has disclosed the agency relationships confirmed below. At the signing of the REPC:

Seller's Agent(s) __Affable Agent_____, represent(s) [X] Seller [ ] both Buyer and Seller as Limited Agent(s);

Seller's Agent(s) Utah Real Estate License Number(s):___1234567-SA00_____.

Seller's Brokerage __Friendly Brokerage_____, represents [X] Seller [ ] both Buyer and Seller as Limited Agent;

Seller's Brokerage Utah Real Estate License Number:____1234567-CN00_____.

Buyer's Agent(s) __Benny Broker_____, represent(s) [X] Buyer [ ] both Buyer and Seller as Limited Agent(s);

Buyer's Agent(s) Utah Real Estate License Number(s):___1234567-AB00_____.

Buyer's Brokerage___Quick Brokerage_____, represents [X] Buyer [ ] both Buyer and Seller as a Limited Agent.

Buyer's Brokerage Utah Real Estate License Number:____9876543-CN00_____.

6. TITLE & TITLE INSURANCE.

6.1 Title to Property. Seller represents that Seller has fee title to the Property and will convey marketable title to the Property to Buyer at Closing by general warranty deed. Buyer does agree to accept title to the Property subject to the contents of the Commitment for Title Insurance (the "Commitment") provided by Seller under Section 7, and as reviewed and approved by Buyer under Section 8.

(a) Long-Term Lease or Rental Agreements. Buyer agrees to accept title to the Property subject to any long-term tenant lease or rental agreements (meaning for periods of thirty (30) or more consecutive days) affecting the Property not expiring prior to Closing. Buyer also agrees to accept title to the Property subject to any existing rental and property management agreements affecting the Property not expiring prior to Closing.

Page 2 of 6 pages   Buyer's Initials____*BB*____ Date_9/16/2017_   Seller's Initials____*SS*____ Date_9/16/2017_

The provisions of this Section 6.1(a) shall survive Closing.

      (b) Short-Term Rental Bookings. Buyer agrees to accept title to the Property subject to any short-term rental bookings (meaning for periods of less than thirty (30) consecutive days) affecting the Property not expiring prior to Closing. The provisions of this Section 6.1(b) shall survive Closing.

      6.2 Title Insurance. At Settlement, Seller agrees to pay for and cause to be issued in favor of Buyer, through the title insurance agency that issued the Commitment (the "Issuing Agent"), the most current version of the *ALTA Homeowner's Policy of Title Insurance* (the "*Homeowner's Policy*"). If the *Homeowner's Policy* is not available through the Issuing Agent, Buyer and Seller further agree as follows: (a) Seller agrees to pay for the *Homeowner's Policy* if available through any other title insurance agency selected by Buyer; (b) if the *Homeowner's Policy* is not available either through the Issuing Agent or any other title insurance agency, then Seller agrees to pay for, and Buyer agrees to accept, the most current available version of an *ALTA Owner's Policy of Title Insurance* ("*Owner's Policy*") available through the Issuing Agent.

7. SELLER DISCLOSURES. No later than the Seller Disclosure Deadline referenced in Section 24(a), Seller shall provide to Buyer the following documents in hard copy or electronic format which are collectively referred to as the "Seller Disclosures":

(a) a written Seller property condition disclosure for the Property, completed, signed and dated by Seller as provided in Section 10.3;
(b) a *Lead-Based Paint Disclosure & Acknowledgement* for the Property, completed, signed and dated by Seller (only if the Property was built prior to 1978);
(c) a Commitment for Title Insurance as referenced in Section 6.1;
(d) a copy of any restrictive covenants (CC&R's), rules and regulations affecting the Property;
(e) a copy of the most recent minutes, budget and financial statement for the homeowners' association, if any;
(f) a copy of any long-term tenant lease or rental agreements affecting the Property not expiring prior to Closing;
(g) a copy of any short-term rental booking schedule (as of the Seller Disclosure Deadline) for guest use of the Property after Closing;
(h) a copy of any existing property management agreements affecting the Property;
(i) evidence of any water rights and/or water shares referenced in Section 1.4;
(j) written notice of any claims and/or conditions known to Seller relating to environmental problems and building or zoning code violations;
(k) In general, the sale or other disposition of a U.S. real property interest by a foreign person is subject to income tax withholding under the *Foreign Investment in Real Property Tax Act of 1980* (FIRPTA). A "foreign person" includes a non-resident alien individual, foreign corporation, partnership, trust or estate. If FIRPTA applies to Seller, Seller is advised that Buyer or other qualified substitute may be legally required to withhold this tax at Closing. In order to avoid closing delays, if Seller is a foreign person under FIRPTA, Seller shall advise Buyer in writing; and
(l) Other (specify) _____

8. BUYER'S CONDITIONS OF PURCHASE.
      8.1 DUE DILIGENCE CONDITION. Buyer's obligation to purchase the Property: [X] IS [ ] IS NOT conditioned upon Buyer's Due Diligence as defined in this Section 8.1(a) below. This condition is referred to as the "Due Diligence Condition." If checked in the affirmative, Sections 8.1(a) through 8.1(c) apply; otherwise they do not.
      (a) Due Diligence Items. Buyer's Due Diligence shall consist of Buyer's review and approval of the contents of the Seller Disclosures referenced in Section 7, and any other tests, evaluations and verifications of the Property deemed necessary or appropriate by Buyer, such as: the physical condition of the Property; the existence of any hazardous substances, environmental issues or geologic conditions; the square footage or acreage of the land and/or improvements; the condition of the roof, walls, and foundation; the condition of the plumbing, electrical, mechanical, heating and air conditioning systems and fixtures; the condition of all appliances; the costs and availability of homeowners' insurance and flood insurance, if applicable; water source, availability and quality; the location of property lines; regulatory use restrictions or violations; fees for services such as HOA dues, municipal services, and utility costs; convicted sex offenders residing in proximity to the Property; and any other matters deemed material to Buyer in making a decision to purchase the Property. Unless otherwise provided in the REPC, all of Buyer's Due Diligence shall be paid for by Buyer and shall be conducted by individuals or entities of Buyer's choice. Seller agrees to cooperate with Buyer's Due Diligence. Buyer agrees to pay for any damage to the Property resulting from any such inspections or tests during the Due Diligence.
      (b) Buyer's Right to Cancel or Resolve Objections. If Buyer determines, in Buyer's sole discretion, that the results of the Due Diligence are unacceptable, Buyer may either: (i) no later than the Due Diligence Deadline referenced in Section 24(b), cancel the REPC by providing written notice to Seller, whereupon the Earnest Money Deposit shall be released to Buyer without the requirement of further written authorization from Seller; or (ii) no later than the Due Diligence Deadline referenced in Section 24(b), resolve in writing with Seller any objections Buyer has arising from Buyer's Due Diligence.
      (c) Failure to Cancel or Resolve Objections. If Buyer fails to cancel the REPC or fails to resolve in writing with Seller any objections Buyer has arising from Buyer's Due Diligence, as provided in Section 8.1(b), Buyer shall be deemed to have waived the Due Diligence Condition, and except as provided in Sections 8.2(a) and 8.3(b)(i), the Earnest Money Deposit shall become non-refundable.

      8.2 APPRAISAL CONDITION. Buyer's obligation to purchase the Property: [X] IS [ ] IS NOT conditioned upon the Property appraising for not less than the Purchase Price. This condition is referred to as the "Appraisal Condition." If checked in the affirmative, Sections 8.2(a) and 8.2(b) apply; otherwise they do not.
      (a) Buyer's Right to Cancel. If after completion of an appraisal by a licensed appraiser, Buyer receives written notice from the Lender or the appraiser that the Property has appraised for less than the Purchase Price (a "Notice of Appraised Value"), Buyer may cancel the REPC by providing written notice to Seller (with a copy of the Notice of Appraised Value) no later than the Financing & Appraisal Deadline referenced in Section 24(c); whereupon the Earnest Money Deposit shall be released to Buyer without the requirement of further written authorization from Seller.
      (b) Failure to Cancel. If the REPC is not cancelled as provided in this section 8.2, Buyer shall be deemed to have waived the Appraisal

Condition, and except as provided in Sections 8.1(b) and 8.3(b)(i), the Earnest Money Deposit shall become non-refundable.

    8.3   FINANCING CONDITION. (Check Applicable Box)

        (a) [   ] No Financing Required. Buyer's obligation to purchase the Property **IS NOT** conditioned upon Buyer obtaining financing. If checked, Section 8.3(b) below does NOT apply.

        (b) [X] Financing Required. Buyer's obligation to purchase the Property **IS** conditioned upon Buyer obtaining the Loan referenced in Section 2.1(c). This Condition is referred to as the "Financing Condition." If checked, Sections 8.3(b)(i), (ii) and (iii) apply; otherwise they do not. If the REPC is not cancelled by Buyer as provided in Sections 8.1(b) or 8.2(a), then Buyer agrees to work diligently and in good faith to obtain the Loan.

        (i) Buyer's Right to Cancel Before the Financing & Appraisal Deadline. If Buyer, in Buyer's sole discretion, is not satisfied with the terms and conditions of the Loan, Buyer may, after the Due Diligence Deadline referenced in Section 24(b), if applicable, cancel the REPC by providing written notice to Seller no later than the Financing & Appraisal Deadline referenced in Section 24(c); whereupon $ 500   of Buyer's Earnest Money Deposit shall be released to Seller without the requirement of further written authorization from Buyer, and the remainder of Buyer's Earnest Money Deposit shall be released to Buyer without further written authorization from Seller.

        (ii) Buyer's Right to Cancel After the Financing & Appraisal Deadline. If after expiration of the Financing & Appraisal Deadline referenced in Section 24(c), Buyer fails to obtain the Loan, meaning that the proceeds of the Loan have not been delivered by the Lender to the escrow/closing office as required under Section 3.2, then Buyer shall not be obligated to purchase the Property and Buyer or Seller may cancel the REPC by providing written notice to the other party.

        (iii) Earnest Money Deposit(s) Released to Seller. If the REPC is cancelled as provided in Section 8.3(b)(ii), Buyer agrees that all of Buyer's Earnest Money Deposit, or Deposits, if applicable (see Section 8.4 below), shall be released to Seller without the requirement of further written authorization from Buyer. Seller agrees to accept, as Seller's exclusive remedy, the Earnest Money Deposit, or Deposits, if applicable, as liquidated damages. Buyer and Seller agree that liquidated damages would be difficult and impractical to calculate, and the Earnest Money Deposit, or Deposits, if applicable, is a fair and reasonable estimate of Seller's damages in the event Buyer fails to obtain the Loan.

    8.4   ADDITIONAL EARNEST MONEY DEPOSIT. If the REPC has not been previously canceled by Buyer as provided in Sections 8.1, 8.2 or 8.3, as applicable, then no later than the Due Diligence Deadline, or the Financing & Appraisal Deadline, whichever is later, Buyer: [   ] WILL [X] WILL NOT deliver to the Buyer's Brokerage, an Additional Earnest Money Deposit in the amount of $_____. The Earnest Money Deposit and the Additional Earnest Money Deposit, if applicable, are sometimes referred to herein as the "Deposits". The Earnest Money Deposit, or Deposits, if applicable, shall be credited toward the Purchase Price at Closing.

9. ADDENDA. There [   ] ARE [X] ARE NOT addenda to the REPC containing additional terms. If there are, the terms of the following addenda are incorporated into the REPC by this reference: [   ] Addendum No. _____ [   ] Seller Financing Addendum [   ] FHA/VA Loan Addendum [   ] Other (specify) _____.

10. HOME WARRANTY PLAN / AS-IS CONDITION OF PROPERTY.

    10.1   Home Warranty Plan. A one-year Home Warranty Plan [   ] WILL [X] WILL NOT be included in this transaction. If included, the Home Warranty Plan shall be ordered by [   ] Buyer [   ] Seller and shall be issued by a company selected by [   ] Buyer [   ] Seller. The cost of the Home Warranty Plan shall not exceed $ _____ and shall be paid for at Settlement by [   ] Buyer [   ] Seller.

    10.2   Condition of Property/Buyer Acknowledgements. Buyer acknowledges and agrees that in reference to the physical condition of the Property: (a) Buyer is purchasing the Property in its "As-Is" condition without expressed or implied warranties of any kind; (b) Buyer shall have, during Buyer's Due Diligence as referenced in Section 8.1, an opportunity to completely inspect and evaluate the condition of the Property; and (c) if based on the Buyer's Due Diligence, Buyer elects to proceed with the purchase of the Property, Buyer is relying wholly on Buyer's own judgment and that of any contractors or inspectors engaged by Buyer to review, evaluate and inspect the Property. The provisions of Section 10.2 shall survive Closing.

    10.3 Condition of Property/Seller Acknowledgements. Seller acknowledges and agrees that in reference to the physical condition of the Property, Seller agrees to: (a) disclose in writing to Buyer defects in the Property known to Seller that materially affect the value of the Property that cannot be discovered by a reasonable inspection by an ordinary prudent Buyer; (b) carefully review, complete, and provide to Buyer a written Seller property condition disclosure as stated in Section 7(a); (c) deliver the Property to Buyer in substantially the same general condition as it was on the date of Acceptance, as defined in Section 23, ordinary wear and tear excepted; (d) deliver the Property to Buyer in broom-clean condition and free of debris and personal belongings; and (e) repair any Seller or tenant moving-related damage to the Property at Seller's expense. The provisions of Section 10.3 shall survive Closing.

11. FINAL PRE-SETTLEMENT WALK-THROUGH INSPECTION. No earlier than seven (7) calendar days prior to Settlement, and upon reasonable notice and at a reasonable time, Buyer may conduct a final pre-Settlement walk-through inspection of the Property to determine only that the Property is "as represented," meaning that the items referenced in Sections 1.1, 1.2 and 8.1(b)(ii) ("the items") are respectively present, repaired or corrected as agreed. The failure to conduct a walk-through inspection or to claim that an item is not as represented shall not constitute a waiver by Buyer of the right to receive, on the date of possession, the items as represented.

12. CHANGES DURING TRANSACTION. Seller agrees that except as provided in Section 12.5 below, from the date of Acceptance until the date of Closing the following additional items apply:

    12.1   Alterations/Improvements to the Property. No substantial alterations or improvements to the Property shall be made or undertaken without prior written consent of Buyer.

    12.2   Financial Encumbrances/Changes to Legal Title. No further financial encumbrances to the Property shall be made, and no changes in

Page 4 of 6 pages   Buyer's Initials____*BB*____ Date_9/16/2017_   Seller's Initials____*SS*____ Date_9/16/2017_ the legal title to the Property shall be made without the prior written consent of Buyer.

    12.3   Property Management Agreements. No changes to any existing property management agreements shall be made and no new property management agreements may be entered into without the prior written consent of Buyer.

    12.4   Long-Term Lease or Rental Agreements. No changes to any existing tenant lease or rental agreements shall be made and no new long-term lease or rental agreements, as defined in Section 6.1(a), may be entered into without the prior written consent of Buyer.

    12.5   Short-Term Rental Bookings. If the Property is made available for short-term rental bookings as defined in Section 6.1(b), Seller **MAY NOT** after the Seller Disclosure Deadline continue to accept short-term rental bookings for guest use of the property without the prior written consent of Buyer.

13. AUTHORITY OF SIGNERS. If Buyer or Seller is a corporation, partnership, trust, estate, limited liability company or other entity, the person signing the REPC on its behalf warrants his or her authority to do so and to bind Buyer and Seller.

14. COMPLETE CONTRACT. The REPC together with its addenda, any attached exhibits, and Seller Disclosures (collectively referred to as the "REPC"), constitutes the entire contract between the parties and supersedes and replaces any and all prior negotiations, representations, warranties, understandings or contracts between the parties whether verbal or otherwise. The REPC cannot be changed except by written agreement of the parties.

15. MEDIATION. Any dispute relating to the REPC arising prior to or after Closing: [X] **SHALL** [ ] **MAY AT THE OPTION OF THE PARTIES** first be submitted to mediation. Mediation is a process in which the parties meet with an impartial person who helps to resolve the dispute informally and confidentially. Mediators cannot impose binding decisions. The parties to the dispute must agree before any settlement is binding. The parties will jointly appoint an acceptable mediator and share equally in the cost of such mediation. If mediation fails, the other procedures and remedies available under the REPC shall apply. Nothing in this Section 15 prohibits any party from seeking emergency legal or equitable relief, pending mediation. The provisions of this Section 15 shall survive Closing.

16. DEFAULT.

    16.1 Buyer Default. If Buyer defaults, Seller may elect one of the following remedies: (a) cancel the REPC and retain the Earnest Money Deposit, or Deposits, if applicable, as liquidated damages; (b) maintain the Earnest Money Deposit, or Deposits, if applicable, in trust and sue Buyer to specifically enforce the REPC; or (c) return the Earnest Money Deposit, or Deposits, if applicable, to Buyer and pursue any other remedies available at law.

    16.2 Seller Default. If Seller defaults, Buyer may elect one of the following remedies: (a) cancel the REPC, and in addition to the return of the Earnest Money Deposit, or Deposits, if applicable, Buyer may elect to accept from Seller, as liquidated damages, a sum equal to the Earnest Money Deposit, or Deposits, if applicable; or (b) maintain the Earnest Money Deposit, or Deposits, if applicable, in trust and sue Seller to specifically enforce the REPC; or (c) accept a return of the Earnest Money Deposit, or Deposits, if applicable, and pursue any other remedies available at law. If Buyer elects to accept liquidated damages, Seller agrees to pay the liquidated damages to Buyer upon demand.

17. ATTORNEY FEES AND COSTS/GOVERNING LAW. In the event of litigation or binding arbitration arising out of the transaction contemplated by the REPC, the prevailing party shall be entitled to costs and reasonable attorney fees. However, attorney fees shall not be awarded for participation in mediation under Section 15. This contract shall be governed by and construed in accordance with the laws of the State of Utah. The provisions of this Section 17 shall survive Closing.

18. NOTICES. Except as provided in Section 23, all notices required under the REPC must be: (a) in writing; (b) signed by the Buyer or Seller giving notice; and (c) received by the Buyer or the Seller, or their respective agent, or by the brokerage firm representing the Buyer or Seller, no later than the applicable date referenced in the REPC.

19. NO ASSIGNMENT. The REPC and the rights and obligations of Buyer hereunder, are personal to Buyer. The REPC may not be assigned by Buyer without the prior written consent of Seller. Provided, however, the transfer of Buyer's interest in the REPC to any business entity in which Buyer holds a legal interest, including, but not limited to, a family partnership, family trust, limited liability company, partnership, or corporation (collectively referred to as a "Permissible Transfer"), shall not be treated as an assignment by Buyer that requires Seller's prior written consent. Furthermore, the inclusion of "and/or assigns" or similar language on the line identifying Buyer on the first page of the REPC shall constitute Seller's written consent only to a Permissible Transfer.

20. INSURANCE & RISK OF LOSS.

    20.1 Insurance Coverage. As of Closing, Buyer shall be responsible to obtain casualty and liability insurance coverage on the Property in amounts acceptable to Buyer and Buyer's Lender, if applicable.

    20.2 Risk of Loss. If prior to Closing, any part of the Property is damaged or destroyed by fire, vandalism, flood, earthquake, or act of God, the risk of such loss or damage shall be borne by Seller; provided however, that if the cost of repairing such loss or damage would exceed ten percent (10%) of the Purchase Price referenced in Section 2, either Seller or Buyer may elect to cancel the REPC by providing written notice to the other party, in which instance the Earnest Money Deposit, or Deposits, if applicable, shall be returned to Buyer.

21. TIME IS OF THE ESSENCE. Time is of the essence regarding the dates set forth in the REPC. Extensions must be agreed to in writing by all parties. Unless otherwise explicitly stated in the REPC: (a) performance under each Section of the REPC which references a date shall absolutely be required by 5:00 PM Mountain Time on the stated date; and (b) the term "days" and "calendar days" shall mean calendar days and shall be counted beginning on the day following the event which triggers the timing requirement (e.g. Acceptance). Performance dates and times referenced herein shall not be binding upon title companies, lenders, appraisers and others not parties to the REPC, except as otherwise agreed to in writing by such non-party.

Page 5 of 6 pages   Buyer's Initials _____*BB*_____ **Date** 9/16/2017   **Seller's Initials**_____*SS*_____ **Date** 9/16/2017

22. ELECTRONIC TRANSMISSION AND COUNTERPARTS. The REPC may be executed in counterparts. Signatures on any of the Documents, whether executed physically or by use of electronic signatures, shall be deemed original signatures and shall have the same legal effect as original signatures.

23. ACCEPTANCE. "Acceptance" occurs only when all of the following have occurred: (a) Seller or Buyer has signed the offer or counteroffer where noted to indicate acceptance; and (b) Seller or Buyer or their agent has communicated to the other party or to the other party's agent that the offer or counteroffer has been signed as required.

24. CONTRACT DEADLINES. Buyer and Seller agree that the following deadlines shall apply to the REPC:

(a)	Seller Disclosure Deadline	9/22/2017	(Date)
(b)	Due Diligence Deadline	10/4/2017	(Date)
(c)	Financing & Appraisal Deadline	10/11/2017	(Date)
(d)	Settlement Deadline	10/18/2017	(Date)

25. OFFER AND TIME FOR ACCEPTANCE. Buyer offers to purchase the Property on the above terms and conditions. If Seller does not accept this offer by: __5:00__ [ ] AM [X] PM Mountain Time on __9/20/2017__ (Date), this offer shall lapse; and the Brokerage shall return any Earnest Money Deposit to Buyer.

Bill Buyer	9/16/2017		
(Buyer's Signature)	(Date)	(Buyer's Signature)	(Date)

ACCEPTANCE/COUNTEROFFER/REJECTION

CHECK ONE:
[X] ACCEPTANCE OF OFFER TO PURCHASE: Seller Accepts the foregoing offer on the terms and conditions specified above.
[ ] COUNTEROFFER: Seller presents for Buyer's Acceptance the terms of Buyer's offer subject to the exceptions or modifications as specified in the attached ADDENDUM NO. _____.
[ ] REJECTION: Seller rejects the foregoing offer.

Sally Seller	9/16/2017	4:30 PM			
(Seller's Signature)	(Date)	(Time)	(Seller's Signature)	(Date)	(Time)

THIS FORM APPROVED BY THE UTAH REAL ESTATE COMMISSION AND THE OFFICE OF THE UTAH ATTORNEY GENERAL, EFFECTIVE SEPTEMBER 1, 2017. AS OF JANUARY 1, 2018, IT WILL REPLACE AND SUPERSEDE THE PREVIOUSLY APPROVED VERSION OF THIS FORM.

Page 6 of 6 pages   Buyer's Initials __BB__   Date __9/16/2017__   Seller's Initials __SS__   Date __9/16/2017__

Review Questions

Refer to the Example REPC at the end of Chapter 23 to answer the following questions.

1. Which of the following is not included with this sale?
    a. Solar panels
    b. Dishwasher
    c. Water Heater
    d. Microwave Oven

2. How much is the estimated loan amount for the buyer in this purchase?
    a. $180,000
    b. $200,000
    c. $14,500
    d. $165,000

3. Who is responsible for any capital improvements to the property before prior to settlement?
    a. The Buyer
    b. The Seller
    c. Both Buyer and Seller
    d. The contract does not specify

4. In what section of the REPC is the agency between the buyer and his agent created?
    a. 5
    b. 7
    c. 23
    d. The REPC does not create agency agreements

5. According to the contract, after closing and the buyer owns the home, what happens to any rental agreements on the property?
    a. They automatically terminate
    b. They terminate at the buyer's option
    c. They remain in effect
    d. They follow the seller to their next property

6. The buyer is unable to obtain financing, and they cancel the REPC on 10/13/2017. Who gets the earnest money?
    a. The Buyer
    b. The Buyer's Agent
    c. The Seller
    d. The Seller's Agent

24.   Appendix - Answers to Chapter Questions

Answers to Review Questions

1 License Law

1.
   - a. N
   - b. N
   - c. Y
   - d. Y
   - e. N
   - f. N
   - g. N
   - h. N
   - i. N
   - j. Y
   - k. Y

2. C. Trustee selling property based on the duties as a trustee does not need a license. All others listed must be licensed

3. D. A salaried employee may assist his employer in selling property and does not necessarily need a license to do so. An agent selling for a commission always needs a license

4. C. Title insurance agents are licensed insurance agents and are therefore not required to also be licensed real estate agents.

5. A. Any real estate activity in exchange for a commission requires a real estate license.

6. D. Lawyers must be licensed if they represent others in the purchase, sale, leasing or management of real estate as a primary income producing activity. They are only exempt when the real estate activity is an incidental part of their low practice.

7. B. Managing property that is not owned by you or your employer requires a real estate license.

2 Licensing Requirements

1.
   - a. Sales Agent
   - b. Associate Broker
   - c. Broker
2. Principal Broker
3. 120
4. Qualifying, Criminal, States
5. 70, 75
6. Print, Background
7. Experience, 60
8. Three
9. Business
10. Table III

3 License Status Change

1. Inactive
2. Inactive, RELMS
3.
   - a. Hours, Education, Renewal
   - b. Continuing
4. 30
5. D
6. B
7. A
8. A
9. B   15 days
10. D
11. C. When a Broker's license expires all of the sales agents and associate brokers licensed with the broker automatically go on inactive status.
12. B. Evidence of points earned is only required in the initial application for a broker's license. It is not required at renewal
13. A. An agent notified by email of their termination is effectively terminated 10 days after the email is sent.

4 Office Procedures

1. 3, Brokerage
2. 30
3. Buyer, Seller
4. Broker
5. Broker
6. A
7. Inactive
8. Thursday
9. 21st 10 calendar days, plus 11th
10. ABC Real Estate Trust Account
11. Seller
12. Up to but not exceed $500
13. Buyer, Seller
14. Open, Trust Account
15. Agree, 5 Years, State Treasurer's Office
16. B
17. Associate broker
18. A. Three banking days would begin on Tuesday, Wednesday would be day two and Thursday would be day three.
19. A. A broker who collects rents for others only occasionally or who does so as a convenience for his clients and manages no more than six accounts may use the Brokerage trust account for this purpose. Having more than 6 property management accounts would require a second Trust Account.
20. C. The branch office must have a local person responsible for supervising agent activity. Utah requires that this person be a Associate Broker. The associate Broker (Branch Broker) must be designated in the application to register a branch office with the Division of Real Estate.

21. D. Commingling means mixing trust funds with personal or company funds in the same account.
22. D. Each Branch Broker can supervise up to 3 branch offices.

5 Property Management

1. A, B, D
2. Applying, Division of Real Estate
3. Does not
4. D. J could hold any of the positions listed and legally perform leasing and rent collection.
5. D. K is considered a resident apartment manager which is an exemption from real estate licensing requirements
6. D. A real estate license is required in order to prospect, or acquire new clients
7. B. A broker may choose to setup a separate property management company and act as broker for both the brokerage and the property management company or the broker may choose to manage property through the brokerage company.
8. B. An agent can be designated as a Property Management Sales Agent, which allows them to do property management through their broker's property management company, and real estate sales through their broker's primary brokerage.

6 Licensee Conduct

1. H
2. L
3. K
4. F
5. G
6. J
7. B
8. C
9. O
10. E
11. A
12. D
13. N
14. I
15. P
16. M
17. Q
18. C. All payments relating to real estate transactions must be paid directly to the agent by the Principal Broker.
19. D. T misrepresented the true facts. He should have been cautious when making a statement about something when he did not know for sure. A better answer would have been to say, "I am not sure, maybe we should arrange for a home inspector to inspect the property to put your mind at ease". T is probably financially responsible for his mistake.
20. B. Sales agents are obligated to use care (a Fiduciary Duty) Care would require that T be competent.
21. D. The only person a sales agent can look to for payment is their broker. It is the Broker who has the right to try to collect from the client.
22. C. The county recorder is not a signatory on the REPC and therefore is not guaranteed a copy of the documents by Utah Law. Sales agents must willingly furnish copies to all signatories to documents they are involved with in a transaction.. Recording is optional. The benefit of recording is that it fixes the date of public notice of the sale and sets the priority of encumbrances.

23. B. A licensee must have written permission to place a sign on a property. Installation errors would be the responsibility of the licensee to correct and prevent if possible because the Sign Company is an employee or contractor for and in behalf of the licensee.
24. C. A false device is a contract that does not represent the true nature of the agreement with the intent to deceive. This is also loan fraud.
25. D. Net listings are illegal because they tend to motivate the sales agent to not be forthright in coaching the seller as to the appropriate listing price for a property.
26. A. Real Estate Auctions are legal so long as they are held under the direction and supervision of a Licensed Principal Broker. The auctioneer need not be licensed. All advertising, forms and deposits must be in compliance with Utah Real Estate License Law.
27. C. The brokerage name must be included in all advertising or the advertising is considered a 'Blind Ad" and is illegal c Any act representing another in the purchase, sale or renting of property for a commission requires a real estate license.
28. C. Accepted payment for his services because one act for compensation qualifies a person as a broker or sales agent under Utah Law resulting in J acting as a sales agent without a license
29. A. An agent must disclose ownership inters in a transaction if his percentage of ownership is 10% or greater.
30. D. The statute of frauds requires all agency relationships must be in writing
31. D. The failure of the owner or the owner's agent to disclose that a property is stigmatized is not a material fact. Utah does not require disclosure of stigma.

7 Enforcement

1. Real Estate Commission
2. ~~(Sentence to Jail)~~
3. Executive Director
4. Not, Expenses
5. Division of Real Estate, Commission
6. Voluntary
7. 5
8. A, B
9. Director
10. Director, Real Estate Commission
11. Annual Report
12. will not

8 Pre-license Education

1. C
2. B
3. C
4. A
5. B

9 Continuing Education

1. C
2. D
3. A
4. C
5. B

10 Administrative Procedures

1. F. All of the answers are correct
2. True
3. False
4. A
5. False
6. B

11 Fractionalized Estates

1. B, C
2. A
3. A, B, D
4. A, B, C, D
5. A, C, D
6. A, B, D

12 Recovery Fund

1. A
2. D
3. A
4. B
5. C

13 Water Law

1. Engineer
2. Beneficial
3. Available
4. Abandoned
5. Prior-Appropriated

14 Land Sales Practices Act

1. Land, 10
2. A. Buildings
   B. 2
   C. First, Second, Third
   D. Industrial
   E. Cemetery
3. Public Offering
4. Public Offering Statement, 5 day Right to Rescind
5. Division of Real Estate
6. A.
7. B
8. D
9. D
10. A
11. C
12. C
13. B

15 Timeshare/ Camp Resort Act

1. Register
2. 5 Day Right to Rescind
3. B
4. D

16 Mechanic's lien

1.
    a. Yes
    b. No
    c. Yes
    d. No
    e. Yes
    f. Yes
    g. Yes
2. Labor, Material
3. Liens
4. 90
5. One Year, 180 Days
6. Lien Release
7. Lien
8. Class B Misdemeanor
9. Sue

17 Utah Homestead Act

1. Residential
2. a $30,000 per person on personal residence with a combined total of $60,000 per household if property is jointly owned.
3. Homestead Declaration
4. County Recorder's Office. Notice may be delivered directly to the Sheriff to prevent the Sheriff from conducting a Sheriffs sale under the direction of the court. The Declaration must still be filed with the county recorder's office as soon as possible.
5. The only item on the list that is exempt is the Judicial lien. Voluntary liens which include all other items on the list, are not exempt.

18 Marketable Record Tile Act

1. C
2. True
3. A
4. A
5. A

19 Utah Landlord/Tenant Law

1. C
2. B
3. A
4. C
5. A
6. B
7. D
8. A
9. D
10. B

20 Utah Statute of Frauds

1. F
2. F
3. A
4. T
5. F

21 Utah Approved Forms

1. Approved
2. Attorney
3. Brokers, Broker
4. may
5. • Real Estate Purchase Contract
   • Uniform Real Estate Contract;
   • All Inclusive Trust Deed;
   • All Inclusive Promissory Note Secured by All Inclusive Trust Deed;
   • Addendum/Counteroffer to Real Estate Purchase Contract;
   • Seller Financing Addendum to Real Estate Purchase Contract;
   • Buyer Financial Information Sheet;
   • FHA/VA Loan Addendum to Real Estate Purchase Contract;
   • Assumption Addendum to Real Estate Purchase Contract;
   • Lead-based Paint Addendum to Real Estate Purchase Contract;
   • Disclosure and Acknowledgment Regarding Lead-based Paint and/or Lead-based Paint Hazards.
6. D
7. A

22 Closing Disclosure

1. A
2. B
3. D
4. A
5. C
6. D
7. C
8. D

23 Real Estate Purchase

Contract

1. D. In section 1.1 and 1.2 you can see what is included with the sale. The microwave oven is not marked as included on this contract.
2. D. In section 2, Purchase Price, you can see the estimated Loan about for the buyer is $165,000.
3. B. In section 4.2 the contract says the seller is responsible for capital improvements before settlement.
4. D. The REPC does not create agency agreements, but section 5 does disclose who the agents are for each party. Their agency relationship is required to be created before the REPC is signed.
5. C. According to section 6.1 (a) and (b) all existing rental agreements remain in effect.
6. C. According to section 8.3(b)(iii) if the REPC is cancelled after the Financing Deadline indicated in section 24, the seller will receive the earnest money.

25.   Sample Final Exam

Exam
Select the single best answer

1. The Director of the Division of Real Estate was:
   a. Appointed by the governor
   b. Hired by the Real Estate Commission
   c. Appointed with the approval of the legislature
   d. Appointed by the Executive Director of the Department of Commerce

2. The Director of the Division of Real Estate will;
   a. Prosecute licensees in criminal court
   b. Overrule the Real Estate Commission in disciplinary matters if the accused is a licensee
   c. Prepare the Division of Real Estate budget
   d. Hold his position for a single 4-year term

3. The Real Estate Commission shall not;
   a. Make rules for the licensing of principal brokers
   b. Make rules for continuing education requirements for licensees
   c. Make rules concerning multiple listing service fees
   d. Make rules setting standards of practice for real estate licensees

4. To be a member of the Real Estate Commission you must meet all of the following requirements except;
   a. No more than one commissioner shall be appointed from any given county
   b. Be appointed by the Governor and confirmed by the senate
   c. Serve no more than one consecutive four-year term
   d. Be a principal broker, associate broker, sales agent or citizen at large

5. Administrative hearings held to ensure adherence to Division of Real Estate licensing rules are conducted or delegated by;
   a. The Executive Director
   b. The Director
   c. The Real Estate Commission
   d. The Governor

6. The Education, Research and Recovery Fund was created primarily to provide
   a. An additional source of revenue for the state
   b. A safety net for consumers harmed by real estate licensee's actions
   c. A benevolent fund for the education of real estate agent's children
   d. A fund to provide funding for legal counsel to real estate agents in matters of public interest.

7. The Utah pioneers established water rights using a different system than was prevalent in the east it is the system of;
    a. Riparian rights
    b. Alluvion rights
    c. Absolute rights
    d. Prior appropriation

8. An application for water must show
    a. A chain of ownership
    b. The usage of all adjacent neighbors
    c. A beneficial use
    d. The certificate of authority

9. B Account Services want to expand the services they provide. They only have a valid city license, what services may they legally perform for their existing clientele;
    a. Leasing vacant office space for their building owner client
    b. Collecting rent for their client who lives out of state and rents his home until he returns.
    c. Represent their Clothing Store client in selling his business including real estate and inventory
    d. Hiring and managing maintenance personnel for the building owner in the building where they occupy an office.

10. One act for compensation qualifies a person as a broker or sales agent if
    a. Acting as a licensed attorney
    b. Acting as a trustee in bankruptcy
    c. Representing a friend in a purchase
    d. Public utility employee buying property for the utility

11. The Director of the Division of Real Estate may
    a. Appoint the Real Estate Commission members
    b. Hire and direct division employees
    c. Establish "Rules" for the execution of the real estate code established by the legislature
    d. Review in an appellate posture the decisions of the Real Estate Commission

12. The Real Estate Commission shall not
    a. Advise the director on enforcement matters
    b. Establish licensing fees for real estate agents
    c. Appoint the director of the Division of Real Estate
    d. Consult with the Director on the Division of Real Estate budget

13. To be a member of the Real Estate Commission you must meet all of the following requirements except
    a. Four need have five years licensed real estate experience
    b. Reside in the same county as another commissioner
    c. Serve no more than one consecutive four-year term
    d. One may have no real estate experience

14. A Real Estate Principal Broker must have demonstrated bookkeeping skills sufficient to be licensed by
    a. Passing an exam
    b. Showing proof of employment as a bookkeeper
    c. Providing evidence of certain college courses completed
    d. Complete an apprenticeship program in office management

15. R was licensed last year, but never affiliated with a broker. R wants to represent a builder friend in selling new homes in a new development.
    a. R must show proof of financial stability to activate his license.
    b. R may sell the homes because the builder is licensed in Utah.
    c. R must start the licensing process all over.
    d. R must affiliate with a broker and show proof of completion of certain education requirements to change his license to "active" with the division

16. A Real Estate Principal Broker, to be licensed, must have demonstrated competency by
    1. Passing an exam
    2. Furnishing proof of adequate and appropriate experience
    3. Providing evidence of certain college courses completed
    4. Complete an apprenticeship program in office management

    a. 1&2 above
    b. 1&3 above
    c. 2&4 above
    d. 3&4 above

17. The Education, Research and Recovery Fund receives its funding from
    a. Taxes
    b. Fines and License Fees
    c. Awards of the court
    d. Charitable contributions from agents

18. In Utah water rights are managed by
    a. The Water Board
    b. The County
    c. The State Engineer
    d. The Water Master

19. Within 90 days after successful completion of the exam the applicant must provide the Division which of the following:
    a. Evidence of appropriate education completed within 90 days
    b. Evidence of appropriate education completed within 120 days
    c. Evidence of appropriate education completed within 6 months
    d. Evidence appropriate education completed within 1 year

20. All of the following have bearing on license acceptance except
    a. Civil judgments
    b. Misdemeanors
    c. Speeding tickets
    d. Suspended contractor's license

21. M a licensed sales agent has married and taken her husband's last name she must
    a. Notify the division of the change within 3 working days
    b. Notify the division of the change within 5 calendar days
    c. Notify the division of the change within 7 working days
    d. Notify the division of the change within 10 working days

22. When an active license expires
    a. The sales agent has a thirty-day grace period in which to complete the renewal process.
    b. The licensee's legal status changes to "unlicensed."
    c. The licensee may only put together transactions. He may not be paid until his license is renewed.
    d. The broker is fined for not supervising his agents,

23. All records relating to a transaction must be kept and made available to the Division on demand for a period of
    a. 5 years plus the transaction year
    b. 10 full calendar years
    c. 7 full calendar years
    d. 3 years plus transaction year

24. Q wrote an offer on behalf of her client, which was accepted. The closing is set for Friday.
    a. Q's broker is responsible for the accuracy of the closing documents and should be present or send a representative to the closing.
    b. Q's job is done. A sales agent's only responsibility is to get the offer signed.
    c. The buyer's mortgage company is responsible to properly prepare all forms needed at closing.
    d. The title officer is the only one who is legally concerned closing documents because the title company is furnishing title insurance.

25. T has taken a promissory note as earnest money for his client the seller. The promissory note should be made out to
    a. The Real Estate Trust Account of the brokerage
    b. The seller and held in the broker's file until closing.
    c. The brokerage and held in the brokerage file until closing.
    d. The sales agent and held in the agent's file until closing.

26. W, the offeror, has changed her mind and has asked the agent to return her earnest money deposit.
    a. The agent must return all moneys on demand
    b. Earnest moneys may only be disbursed by agreement of both parties to the transaction or by court order.
    c. Earnest moneys should not be refunded because that is the primary source of payment of real estate commissions to the brokerage.
    d. Earnest money deposits must remain in the trust account for at least 30 days so that they show on the bank statement in case of an audit.

27. Trust funds that are under dispute as to whom they may be paid must be held in the trust account until the dispute is resolved or
    a. Until five years has elapsed at which time the broker shall pay the funds over to the state treasury as abandoned property
    b. Until five years have passed at which time the broker shall pay the funds over to the Real Estate Recovery Fund
    c. Until five years have passed at which time the broker must force arbitration between the parties.
    d. Until five years have passed at which time the broker must force a lawsuit between the parties.

28. A branch office must be registered with the Division if
    a. The office is in a model home
    b. The office is in a project sales office less than a year
    c. The office is in a booth at the Utah State Fair
    d. The office will be used for only two years

29. E has managed the office building for his employer for 14 years as an unlicensed salaried employee. E has been asked to manage a 4-plex in exchange for a percentage of the rents collected by friend who is leaving the country for a couple of years. E is considering taking on this additional project.
    a. E may legally manage his friends' 4-plex without a real estate license so long as rents are sent directly to his friend.
    b. E must be a licensed real estate agent to manage the 4plex under these circumstances.
    c. E may show the property for lease but may not arrange repairs because he is not licensed.
    d. E may only manage an others property if he has notified the Division of his activities.

30. A licensee may not pay finder's fees or give any valuable consideration to an unlicensed person or entity for referring a prospect in a real estate transaction except token gifts:
    a. Of $25 or less
    b. Of $50 or less
    c. Of $100 or less
    d. Of $150 or less

31. T wants to create the impression that their brokerage is very friendly. T obtains a group photograph of all the agents and office staff and includes the photo in the weekly advertising layout in the newspaper.
    a. The photo must be a certain size or it may not be used.
    b. The broker must be in the Photo.
    c. Photos without company address are illegal.
    d. The brokerage name must be identified.

32. S has a property listed that is not selling. S needs to do something to stimulate interest. Her first idea is to advertise the property at a lower price than its current listing price.
    a. The best way to do this is to advertise that the owner will consider any offer.
    b. This is legal as long as the listing price is also included in the ad such as "newly reduced from".
    c. Prices lower than the listing price may not be advertised, only suggested in person.
    d. The listing price is the only price that may be advertised or quoted unless written consent of the owner is obtained.

33. P is running an ad to promote his own listings and is therefore including his own name and picture.
  a. The brokerage name must be shown clearly and easy to find
  b. The name of his team must be clearly visible
  c. P cannot legally display his picture in advertising
  d. All advertising must be approved by the Division

34. If the licensee advertises property in which he has an ownership interest and the property is not listed;
  a. The ad must include the brokerage name and the words "owner-agent" or "owner-broker."
  b. The ad need not include the brokerage name so long as the words "owner-agent" or "owner-broker" are included.
  c. Must contain the name of the agent and the words "owner-agent" or "owner-broker."
  d. The name of the brokerage must be at least one half the size of the agent's name.

35. An associate broker is;
  a. A broker contracted under the same multiple listing umbrella.
  b. A broker who has sales agents associated with her.
  c. Statutory employee of a broker.
  d. A person qualified by state license to be a principal broker except they lack their own trust account, registered business name and formal licensure as a broker by the Division.

36. J owns stock in Property Corporation. Property Corporation wants to purchase a new building. J represents Property Corporation as their agent. J must disclose to the seller that J is a stock holder if J owns:
  a. 5% of the company
  b. 9% of the company
  c. 15% of the company
  d. Any share of the company

37. Sales agent, associate brokers and brokers are required to complete how many hours to be eligible for their license exam?
  a. 80, 90, 90
  b. 90, 90, 90
  c. 90, 110, 120
  d. 120, 120, 120

38. If a brokerage closes the Broker must notify the Division of Real Estate and declare the location the brokerage records will be stared within:
  a. Immediately
  b. 5 Days
  c. 10 Days
  d. 30 Days

39. Broker candidates are required to have at least:
    a. 10 years licensed active experience
    b. 5 years licensed active experience
    c. 3 years licensed active experience
    d. 1 year licensed active experience

40. A sales agent has written an offer. The buyer and seller agree to change the closing date. The sales agent must:
    a. Ensure they shake hands
    b. Modify the contract by completing an addendum
    c. Send a letter to the Title Company notifying them of the changed date.
    d. Complete a change of date form.

41. W, after some very tough negotiation finally obtains a listing on a prime parcel. He and the Seller shake hands on the agreement. W dashes off to place a newspaper ad for his new listing. Before he can place an ad legally he must have:
    a. A complete legal description
    b. Approved ad layout
    c. A property disclosure form.
    d. Written Agency agreement and written permission to place advertising.

42. Closing documents may be prepared by:
    a. Only the Title Company
    b. Only the Mortgage Company
    c. Anyone can complete closing documents
    d. Associate Brokers, Brokers, and Title Companies

43. Your brother, a computer programmer, tells you about his neighbor who is looking for a house. You contact the neighbor and sell him a house. You want to show your brother you are grateful for his assistance. You may:
    a. Split your commission with him on this one deal only.
    b. Pay him up to $150 as a token gift.
    c. Pay him up to $500 as a token gift
    d. Not give him anything because payments to non-licensed persons are illegal

44. You believe you have earned a commission and your broker refuses to pay you. You may:
    a. File a complaint against your broker with the Real Estate Commission
    b. File a complaint against him with the Division of Real Estate
    c. File a lawsuit in the courts
    d. You have no recourse because you are a sub agent of the broker

45. J a licensee wants to buy a new house. He and his wife have located the perfect property. When making the offer J must:
    a. Forfeit the commission on the transaction
    b. Request a permit to purchase from the Division of Real Estate
    c. Notify the Division of Real Estate of the transaction
    d. Provide the seller written notice that J is a licensee

46. W a licensee has assisted the Wilson's in purchasing a manufactured home. The manufactured home dealer has mailed W a fee as an additional compensation for W's services in leading the buyer to the manufacturer's product.
    a. W may not accept the payment directly from the manufacturer, the fee must be paid through W's broker.
    b. W must provide notice to the Division that a fee will be paid to him by the manufacturer.
    c. No fees may be accepted from the manufacturer.
    d. W must disclose dual agency to accept the payment.

47. A double contract
    a. Is a contract designed to enforce a listing agreement
    b. Is a contract designed to hide the real agreement terms from the lender
    c. Would most likely be made between the broker and his agents
    d. Is used to renew a listing

48. An unlicensed assistant may perform all of the following tasks except:
    a. Obtain public records
    b. Deliver documents
    c. Call prospective clients for an appointment
    d. Make an appointment while performing receptionist duties

49. Licensed assistants may be paid:
    a. Only by salary
    b. Only by the sales agent they assist
    c. Only based on a standard commission split
    d. Only by the Broker

50. To receive payment from the Real Estate Recovery Fund the injured party must:
    a. File a notice of claim with the Real Estate Commission
    b. Win a law suit against the agent and obtain a judgment against the agent
    c. File a partition for payment with the Board of Realtors grievance committee
    d. Obtain a court order ordering the Fund to pay

51. You have received an earnest money payment in connection with an offer that has been accepted.
    a. The money must be deposited in the trust account in 3 calendar days
    b. The money must be deposited in the trust account in 3 business days
    c. The money must be deposited in the trust account in 4 calendar days
    d. The money must be deposited in the trust account on the day received

52. A promissory note received as earnest money must be made out to
    a. The sales agent receiving it
    b. The seller
    c. The Brokerage
    d. The Brokerage Trust Account

53. J has worked very hard to put the deal together. The Seller could see how hard J had worked. The seller gave J a $500 tip at closing.
    a. J earned it and may keep it
    b. The tip must be disclosed the buyer's agent
    c. Tips are illegal between sellers and their listing agent
    d. J must pass the money on to his Broker because only a broker may pay a sales agent

54. A broker deposits agent commissions and client trust money into the same account. This is an example of:
    a. Alluvion
    b. Commingling
    c. Segregation
    d. Harmony

55. The Marketable Record Title Act provides
    a. A sale price for a property over a certain age
    b. An opportunity to remove encumbrances that are 40 years old and inactive
    c. Documents for public sale.
    d. Transaction history for a given parcel

56. The Land Sales Practices act contains a provision that
    a. Provides a builder guidelines for the sale of land
    b. Controls the price a developer can charge for a lot
    c. Allows a 5 day right of rescission
    d. Limits the number of parcels an acre can be subdivided into

57. If you want water rights in Utah you need to apply with
    a. The Division of Real Estate
    b. The Utah Water Board
    c. The Division of Water Rights
    d. The Army Corps of Engineers

58. Filling a false mechanic's lien is a
    a. Third degree felony
    b. Class B misdemeanor
    c. Violation of license law
    d. Cause for cease and desist order

59. Sales agents selling timeshares must
    a. Pass a special exam
    b. Be associate brokers or brokers
    c. Register with the Division of Real Estate
    d. Only sell from onsite at the timeshare location

60. The Base line and prime meridian used for property descriptions in Utah are named:
    a. The Salt Lake Base Line and the Salt Lake Prime Meridian
    b. The Utah Base Line and the Utah Prime Meridian
    c. The Mountain States Base Line and the Mountain States Prime Meridian
    d. The Wasatch Base Line and the Wasatch Prime Meridian

Refer to the REPC Example at the end of Chapter 23 to answer the following questions.

61. How much earnest money is included with the offer?
    a. $500
    b. $1,000
    c. $1,500
    d. $5,000

62. Which of the following is included with this sale?
    a. Satellite dish
    b. Washer
    c. Refrigerator
    d. Dryer

63. When is the buyer contracted to take possession of the property?
    a. 1 day after Recording
    b. The same day as Closing
    c. 3 days after Closing
    d. 3 days after Recording

64. Who will hold rental deposits after settlement?
    a. Seller
    b. Seller's Agent
    c. Buyer
    d. Buyer's Agent

65. Which page must be initialed by the buyer?
    a. Page 1
    b. Page 2
    c. Page 6
    d. All of the pages

66. When is the last day the buyer can cancel the contract due to an appraisal coming in too low?
    a. 9/22/2017
    b. 10/11/2017
    c. 10/18/2017
    d. 10/4/2017

26. Final Exam Answers

1. d The Director is appointed by the Executive Director of the Department of Commerce.

2. c The director of the Division of Real Estate prepares the annual budget in consultation with the Real Estate Commission.

3. c Multiple listing services are private clubs. The Real Estate Commission has no power or authority over their fee structure.

4. b Real Estate Commissioners are appointed by the Governor and Confirmed by the Legislature

5. c The Real Estate Commission holds or delegates all disciplinary hearings. They may delegate the task to an administrative law judge who acts under their direction.

6. b The Education, Research and Recovery Fund was established to provide the public with a last resort means to recover losses caused by real estate licensees. The fund does allow use of excess moneys for Education and Research.

7. d Water in Utah is appropriated based on beneficial use. When an applicant applies for water the State Engineer checks to see if there is water that has not been PRIOR APPROPRIATED.

8. c Water may only be appropriated for Beneficial Use in Utah.

9. d Property maintenance management does not require a real estate license.

10. c Incidental real estate acts by an attorney, acts by a trustee under the direction of the bankruptcy court and public utility employees acting for their employer are all exempt form licensing.

11. b The Director of the Division of Real Estate is expected to hire and direct the employees of the Division as a part of his job.

12. c The Director of the Division of Real Estate is appointed by the Executive Director of the Department of Commerce.

13. b The members of the Real Estate Commission must all be from different counties.

14. a Real Estate Brokers are not required to be competent in book keeping skill except as it relates to the trust account. Their knowledge of the trust account bookkeeping requirements is determined by the licensing exam.

15. d We assume R placed his license on inactive status when it was obtained. Inactive status may be changed to active status by obtaining the required education and applying for an active license and paying the fee.

16. a College and apprenticeship are not required to become a licensed Broker. The Broker is required to take a licensing exam and prove that they have ad adequate and appropriate experience by submitting proof of eligibility for 60 experience points taken from table I, II, or III. The Exam may not be taken until the Broker candidate has complete the 120 hour Broker license course

17. b Licensee licensing fees and fines and interest earned on the fund are the only sources of money for the fund.

18. c The State Engineer is responsible for managing the appropriation of water because of his qualifications to determine what water is available and not prior-appropriated.

19. d The certificate of successful completion of the real estate licensing course is only valid for one year.

20. c   Minor traffic violations such as speeding tickets will not prevent licensure.

21. d   Changes of status such as name change and address change require notice to the division within 10 days.

22. b   There is no grace period for renewing the license late. If the license is not renewed on time the license is considered expired.

23. d   Record must be kept for three calendar years. A calendar year runs from January 1st to December 31st. Transactions occurring during the year must be kept a full three years starting January 1st after the transaction is complete.

24. a   The Broker is responsible for the accuracy and is required to attend the closing or send his representative. The sales agent is generally the representative sent to closing.

25. b   A promissory note should always be made out to the seller.

26. b   The earnest money may not be removed from the trust account except by written authorization of the party to the transaction not receiving the funds. If agreement cannot be reached between the parties to distribute the earnest money the money must remain in the account until agreement is reached, or by court order. After five years it may be paid over to the State as abandoned property.

27. a   Moneys still in the trust account after five years due to a dispute may be turned over to the State as abandoned property

28. d   Temporary sales offices are legal. An example of a temporary sales office is a model home. The time an office is considered temporary is limited to one year.

29. b   E needs a real estate license because he is paid a percentage which by definition is a commission.

30. d   Finders fees and thank you gifts are limited to $150 or less unless the person receiving the gift is the buyer or seller, landlord or tenant.

31. d   The brokerage name must be clearly and conspicuously identified in all advertisements.

32. d   In order to fulfill the requirement to be obedient to the principal in an agency (fiduciary) relationship the agent must only advertise prices that have been approved by the seller.

33. a   the brokerage name must be easily identified in the advertisement. Clearly and conspicuously.

34. b   If the property is not listed the advertisement need only identify the seller as an owner agent

35. d   An associate Broker holds the same license qualifications as a broker. The Broker only differs in that the Broker is required to register a business name, open a trust account and request Broker status from the Division of Real Estate. Because the Associate Broker has not been licensed as a broker they must be licensed under a broker.

36. d   Licensees are required to disclose their ownership interest if they own any percentage of a company

37. d   Sales agents need 120 hours, Associate brokers and brokers both need 120 hours

38. c   Notice of name change, brokerage change of address or change of location of records must be given within 10 days

39. c   Broker candidates need three years active experience out of the last five years

40. b   The contract must be modified with an addendum because the contract is binding. It has language in it that states that oral agreements are overruled by the contract, so get it in writing.

41. d   Listings must be in writing and written permission must be obtained before any advertising can legally occur.

42. d   Sales agents may not prepare closing documents only brokers and associate brokers may prepare closing documents. Title companies may also prepare the documents but the Principal Broker is responsible for closing document accuracy.

43. b   Token gifts to non-licensed persons are limited to $150 or less unless the person receiving the gift is the buyer or seller, in which case there are no limits to what may be given except that payments to the buyer or seller in a transaction must be disclosed to the other party.

44. c   The financial arrangements between sales agent and their broker are not regulated as to amount or timing. The governing document is the employment agreement. Your only recourse against a broker to enforce the agreement is in court or direct negotiation.

45. d   Licensees are required to notify everyone involved in a transaction that they are licensed. Normally that is apparent when the licensee represents one of the principals. When the licensees are acting for themselves they must disclose their licensee status and ownership interest in writing.

46. a   Licensees may only be paid by their broker. Payments of any kind must be disclosed to the parties of a transaction. Manufactured home dealers may pay commissions or fees to real estate professionals through their broker.

47. b   A double contract is usually a contract created after the sales agreement has been agreed to by both parties. The second contract is made with the intent to obtain a loan using false statements. The lender may not be aware of the actual agreement. The second contract presents a false picture of the transaction to the lender which might lead them to make a loan they would not make had they known the true facts.

48. c   Telephone soliciting may only be performed by licensed agents

49. d   Licensed assistants are by law sales agents and must be paid by their broker. The employment agreement outlines their duties. Their employment agreement may require them to assist a particular agent.

50. d   To obtain payment from the fund you must first notify the Division you are filling a law suit. You must win the suit. You must make every effort to collect from the agent then, when no other collection is possible, ask the court to order payment from the fund.

51. b   Earnest money must be deposited in three banking days from the date of receipt unless the contract provided for some other date such as after acceptance.

52. b   The note is required by law to be made out to the seller

53. d   Sales agents may only receive payments from their broker

54. b   Commingling means mixing broker money with client money in the trust account. The opposite of commingling is segregation.

55. b   The marketable Record Title Act is intended to remove old inactive encumbrances that would keep a title from being marketable (transferable). The statute states that inactive encumbrances over 40 years old are subject to the act.

56. c   The land Sales Practices Act provides for Disclosure of the actual condition of the property and provides the buyer a cooling off period in which they may change their mind. The cooling off period is known as the 5-day right to rescind the agreement. The buyer may cancel an agreement they have signed within 5 calendar days of signature.

57. c   The Division of Water Rights is a division of the State Engineers office.

58. b   Contractors who file a mechanic's lien for an amount more than the actual amount owed is punishable as a Class B misdemeanor

59. c   Time share sales people need not necessarily be licensed real estate sales people. If they sell on site they need not be licensed. Off site sales require a license. Both licensed and non-licensed sales people must register with the Division of Real Estate.

60. a   the Salt Lake Base line and the Salt Lake Prime Meridian intersect on the corner of South Temple and Main Street in Salt Lake City. The monument marking the intersection is located on the south east corner of Temple Square in the sidewalk.

61. a   In the first section titled Earnest Money Deposit, and in section 2 Purchase Price you can see that there is $500 in earnest money.

62. c   In section 1.1, 1.2 and 1.3 you can see what is included and what is excluded. The refrigerator is marked as included in this purchase.

63. a   In section 3.3 the contract says the buyer can take possession 1 day after Recording.

64. c   In section 4.3(b) it indicates that the buyer shall be paid or credited any rental deposits at settlement, and therefore will have them after settlement.

65. d   The buyer must initial and date all of the pages of the REPC.

66. b   The Appraisal Condition in 8.2 allows the buyer to cancel the contract on or before 10/11/2017, which is indicated in section 24 Contract Deadlines.

27. Index